Professionalism, Law, and the Ontario Educator

Professionalism, Law, and the Ontario Educator

SECOND EDITION

Julian Kitchen and Christine Bellini

Highland press

Published in 2016 by
Highland Press
Box 496, St. Davids, ON L0S 1P0
Telephone (905) 685 5568
Fax (905) 685 4327
E-mail hldpress@cogeco.ca

First published in 2010 by Highland Press

Library and Archives Canada Cataloguing in Publication

Kitchen, Julian D., 1960-, author
Professionalism, law, and the Ontario educator / Julian Kitchen B.A., B.Ed., Ph.D., Brock University, Christine Bellini, B.A., B.Ed., M.Ed. -- Second edition.

Includes bibliographical references and indexes.
ISBN 978-0-9865873-3-7 (paperback)

1. Teachers--Legal status, laws, etc.--Ontario. 2. Educational law and legislation--Ontario. I. Bellini, Christine, author II. Title.

KEO781.K58 2016   344.713'078   C2016-901579-3
KF4175.K58 2016

Cover design: Daniel Crack, KD Books, www.kdbooks.ca
Text design and typesetting: Casey Hooper Design
Editor and project coordinator: Donald G. Bastian,
Bastian Publishing Services Ltd. www.bastianpubserv.com

Printed and bound in Canada
1 2 3 4 5   14 13 12 11 10

CONTENTS

Preface

Effective classroom teachers act *in loco parentis* to ensure that students learn in safe and supportive school environments. A broad knowledge of education law helps new teachers understand their rights and responsibilities. The study of education law, however, should involve more than an understanding of "do's and don'ts" and correct procedures. It should address issues at the very heart of teaching as a profession grounded in an ethic of caring. Our aim is to capture the reader's interest by linking education law and professionalism to the central concerns of classroom teachers. It is also important that new and experienced teachers understand that the educational landscape has changed: educators are being held to a higher standard, and disciplinary procedures are becoming more and more transparent.

This second edition of *Professionalism, Law, and the Ontario Educator* has been significantly revised. The book includes up-to-date information on education legislation and more recent disciplinary cases involving teachers. It has also been reorganized into three sections. Part A introduces the topic of education law and delves into the legal and professional responsibilities of teachers. Part B weaves together themes on legal duties, negligence, and school safety. Part C looks at other important issues such as the rights and responsibilities of students, special education, and teachers in the workplace.

As in the first edition, each chapter is designed to stimulate thinking and generate discussion about topics of practical importance to teachers. Legal terminology is clearly defined and illustrated with examples. Concepts are broken into manageable chunks, with cases used to illustrate how education law relates to the teaching context. Summaries of significant legal cases are used to illustrate education law in action. These cases serve both as stories from the field and guideposts to help new teachers become prudent and effective practitioners. Some chapters feature controversial issues facing teachers or practical advice on working well with stakeholders in the education system.

Because education is primarily a provincial responsibility, much attention is given to the *Education Act* and other provincial legislation. Also, the role of the Ontario College of Teachers is considered in each chapter, often with examples of College rulings on cases of misconduct. There is also a greater focus on discipline processes at the school board level. Chapters end with a review of key information and a fictionalized case study.

Our perspective on the issues of this book is a reflection of our experiences as teachers and teacher educators.

Dr. Kitchen, currently Director of the Tecumseh Centre for Aboriginal Research and Education, has published extensively on teacher education and Indigenous education. An experienced classroom teacher, he has written on professionalism, diversity, Indigenous education, and teacher education. Christine Bellini has been a secondary school teacher since 2005 and is a sessional instructor for the faculties of education at Brock University and Lakehead University. She served for three years on the Discipline Committee of the Ontario College of Teachers, and is a doctoral candidate in the Department of Leadership, Adult, and Higher Education at the Ontario Institute for Studies in Education of the University of Toronto.

We thank the many people who provided us with input with regard to the second edition. These include the Ontario College of Teachers (which generously responded to our inquiries), Wendy Hershegger from Ontario Secondary School Teachers' Federation, readers of the first edition, and instructors who have used the book in their professionalism and law classes. All these people helped us create a more accessible and practical second edition to serve the needs of professional educators.

Finally, we acknowledge editor Don Bastian and Highland Press for enhancing the clarity of this book, and thank Christopher Dean for his contributions as co-author of the first edition.

We trust that our practical and theoretical backgrounds will serve to make the subject of professionalism and the law of interest and help to you.

Julian Kitchen & Christine Bellini

PART A

THE EDUCATION AND LEGAL SYSTEMS

CHAPTER 1

TEACHERS AS PROFESSIONALS

> *After reading this chapter, you will have a deeper understanding of teaching as a moral and ethical activity. You will also become aware of your legal duties as an educator and your professional rights and responsibilities as a member of the Ontario College of Teachers and the Ontario Teachers' Federation.*

Case Study: Professional Misconduct
Ontario College of Teachers v. SMV (2014)*

During a class trip in June 2010, teacher SMV slept in a cabin where she was supervising five female students. SMV allowed the students to leave the cabin unsupervised for a short period in the early morning hours to go on a trampoline, which was in an open field. After the trip, SMV posted photographs of her students from the trip on her personal Facebook page without parental permission.

The school board reviewed SMV's actions and suspended her five days without pay. A subsequent complaint with the Ontario College of Teachers led to a finding of professional misconduct against SMV—more specifically, that SMV:

- failed to maintain the standards of the profession;
- failed to supervise adequately;
- failed to comply with the Act or the regulations or the by-laws;
- failed to comply with the *Education Act* or regulations made under that Act;

- committed an act or omission that would reasonably be regarded as unprofessional; and
- committed acts unbecoming of a member.

The discipline panel noted, "Breaches in student supervision and student privacy will not be tolerated by the profession. The protection and safety of students, on or off school property, must be upheld at all times."

SMV pleaded guilty and appeared before a discipline panel to receive a reprimand for her lapses in professional judgment. Although SMV admitted to her lapses, she asked that her name not be published because the misconduct was minor, she worked in a small community, and she had worked without incident the following four years.

The panel, however, determined that the lapse in judgment was serious. Thus, she had no right to personal privacy, and publication of her name along with the finding of professional misconduct was necessary for purposes of general deterrence and public trust.

This case appears in *Professionally Speaking*, September 2014.

* In Ontario College of Teachers disciplinary cases featured in this book, only the initials of the educators involved are used. Full names can be found in the issue of *Professionally Speaking* in which the case appears.

---

(1) Why might it be inappropriate for an educator to permit students to use a trampoline unsupervised?

(2) Why might it be inappropriate for an educator to post photographs of students on social media?

(3) What are the expectations for supervision of students under education legislation?

(4) Do you think the punishment, including the publication of SMV's name, was appropriate?

Many new teachers, while committed to making a difference in the lives of students, may not have considered in systematic fashion the professional, ethical, and legal dimensions of teaching. Yet the events and interactions that unfold in classrooms and school contexts are imbued with ethical implications. This is evident in the case of SMV, who appears to have been a dedicated educator, as demonstrated by her willingness to supervise an overnight field trip. The social media post suggests that she was also genuinely interested in her students. Despite good intentions, she failed to meet the standards expected of educators by the profession and by society.

It would be easy to feel overwhelmed by the myriad laws, regulations, policies, and procedures that govern daily life in a society as complex as ours. Yet it would be virtually impossible for us to live and work without them. Given the importance of education, schools are bound by laws that regulate the behaviour and relationships of the various members of the school community. Without them, it would be difficult if not impossible for schools to function as safe and supportive environments where students and teachers work together to achieve common purposes.

Educators need to develop sound judgment in order to properly exercise their duty of care to students. The legal framework and professional standards that govern the school system reflect the values and beliefs of our society concerning the welfare of children. By developing an understanding of education law and professional expectations, teachers can be guided by the basic principles underlying the law rather than becoming intimidated by the minutiae of specific rules and regulations. Understanding cases such as the one above can help guide educators toward the ethical judgment necessary to meet professional and legal expectations.

The overview of law that follows in this chapter will give you a basic understanding of law, paving the way for you to understand all of the issues discussed in this book.

You may have become a teacher for many reasons, but chances are that you are motivated primarily by moral reasons. As David Hansen (2001) puts it:

> The idea that teaching is a moral endeavor is at least as old as recorded knowledge of the practice. Plato, Confucius, Lao Tzu, Aristotle, the Buddha, the Bhagavad Gita—to name only a few of the well-known sources—all provide arguments and testimonials about the moral significance of teaching. (p. 826)

Perhaps you have chosen to become a teacher because you care about children or are passionate about your subject area. You may be committed to making a difference in the lives of students or dedicated to teaching for social justice. Such reasons are moral in nature.

Teaching as a caring profession is infused with moral significance. In their mundane daily activities and in dilemmas of practice, teachers are guided by an ethic of caring for the students they are charged to supervise and teach.

Since education law is guided by moral and ethical thinking, these dimensions of teaching need to be considered thoughtfully. It is also important to understand that teaching is a caring profession guided by professional standards and regulated by the Ontario College of Teachers.

TEACHING AS A MORAL ACTIVITY

(1) Why did you decide to become a teacher?

(2) How do you view your main responsibilities as a teacher?

(3) What do you hope to achieve over the course of your career?

The moral dimension of teaching has been the subject of much profound discussion. Educational philosophers, in particular, have grappled with fundamental questions about the nature of teaching. In this section, the moral dimensions of teaching have been divided into three broad categories:

(1) the teacher as guardian

(2) the teacher as educator

(3) the teacher as moral educator.

THE TEACHER AS GUARDIAN

Primum non nocere, or "Above all, do no harm," is identified with the Hippocratic oath taken by medical doctors. It is useful advice for teachers, too, because it is essential for teachers to ensure that all students in their care are kept safe from physical and psychological harm, and that their basic intellectual and emotional needs are satisfied.

In common law, teachers are deemed to be acting *in loco parentis* (in the place of the parent); they are expected to act as a careful or prudent parent would. Ontario's *Education Act* also makes it clear that teachers owe a legal duty of care to their students similar to that of parents. Students, for example, are required to accept discipline as would be exercised by a "kind, firm, and judicious parent." The legal duties of teachers will be developed more fully in chapters 2 and 4, and their duty of care will be reinforced throughout this book.

As a result of these expectations, the courts have held that, depending on the circumstances, the relationship that exists between a teacher and a student could also be considered to involve the law of "fiduciary duty." This legal term based in common law describes the relationship of trust, power, and vulnerability that exists between two people; the party that has the power to affect the interests of the other has a fiduciary duty with respect to that party. The Supreme Court of Canada has defined it in the following way:

> Relationships in which a fiduciary obligation have [sic] been imposed seem to possess three general characteristics:
>
> (1) The fiduciary has scope for the exercise of some discretion or power.
> (2) The fiduciary can unilaterally exercise that power or discretion so as to affect the beneficiary's legal or practical interests.
> (3) The beneficiary is peculiarly vulnerable to or at the mercy of the fiduciary holding the discretion or power. (As quoted in Brown & Zuker, 2002, p. 166)

Generally, legal and professional bodies are most concerned with preventing careless behaviour or misconduct that puts students at risk.

THE TEACHER AS EDUCATOR

While safety is a baseline concern of students, parents, and society, the aim of the school system is to educate young people. Aristotle defines education as a systematic course of instruction designed to develop the character and mental powers of students.

Teaching, on one level, is an instrumental activity: a means to an end.

Teachers have a moral obligation to ensure that students learn the prescribed curriculum. In doing so, they are to be guided by provincial and local guidelines and expectations.

In *A Good Teacher in Every Classroom*, the National Academy of Education (2005, p. 5) identifies three general areas of knowledge as being necessary for effective teaching.

(1) Knowledge of *learners* and how they learn and develop within social contexts;

(2) Understanding of the *subject matter* and skills to be taught in light of the social purposes of education;

(3) Understanding of *teaching* in light of the content and learners to be taught, as informed by assessment and supported by a productive learning environment.

This elaboration of general areas of knowledge makes it clear that teachers must do more than simply cover the curriculum. They must also fulfill their professional and moral obligation to adapt that curriculum to the specific learning needs of their students and the communities in which they live.

As John Dewey (1938) writes, "Teachers discriminate between experiences that are worthwhile educationally and those that are not" (p. 33). They select "experiences that lead to growth" (p. 40) by taking into account both the student and context. The school system and the courts trust the professional expertise of teachers, giving them considerable latitude so long as they operate within the legal framework and act in a manner consistent with that trust.

THE TEACHER AS MORAL EDUCATOR

Aristotle cautions that excessive academic and vocational specialization can render citizens "unfit for the pursuit and practice of goodness." Many educators and members of the public share this concern. They see the aims of education "as political (e.g., promoting democratic life), as cultural (e.g., promoting cultural awareness), or as religious (e.g., advancing a particular set of religious values" (Hansen, 2001, p. 829). Aristotle and Dewey both argue that genuine intellectual development always implies moral development. As Hansen (2001) writes, "Learning encompasses the intellectual and the moral; it describes the emergence and formation of human being" (p. 833).

Alan Tom (1984) describes teaching as a "moral craft" involving "a subtle moral relationship between teacher and student" (p. 11). Teachers sensitively use their authority to bring important knowledge, skills, and ideas to the awareness of the student. "Teaching is moral," according to Tom, "in the sense that a curriculum plan selects certain objectives or pieces of content instead of others; this selective process either explicitly or implicitly reflects a conception of desirable ends" (p. 78). Furthermore, Tom continues, teaching should be regarded as moral because it requires the ability "to analyze situations and to use instruction skills appropriate to these situations" (p. 11).

Because of the vulnerability and potentiality of youth, society is concerned that teachers engage with students in a morally acceptable manner. This is why care, trust, respect, and integrity are emphasized in the Ethical Standards of the Teaching Profession section of the Ontario College of Teachers' (2006) *Foundations of Professional Practice*. These standards will be examined more closely later in this chapter. It is also why the College emphasizes the boundaries that must exist between the teacher and student. Like all professionals, teachers have an obligation to maintain a boundary between themselves and their students. This is not to say that teachers should not be friendly and welcoming, but that they must always remain professional. It has been well said that teachers may be friendly with their students but are not their friends. Students have their own friends. Most cases of professional misconduct reported to the Ontario College of Teachers begin when teachers step over the invisible line separating them from their students and place their own needs and interests above those of the students in their care. Maintaining boundaries will be discussed more fully in chapters 4 and 7.

The four qualities outlined in the Ethical Standards (care, trust, respect, and integrity) are essential to making moral judgments that are in the best interest of students. For example, according to philosopher Nel Noddings (2001), "a caring teacher is someone who has demonstrated that she can establish, more or less regularly, relations of care in a wider variety of situations" (pp. 100–01).

Noddings cautions that professionalism without caring can lead to aloofness in the teacher–student relationship. Instead, she argues, the means used by teachers must embody the ends of education, because the relationship between student and teacher is vital to learning and personal understanding.

Due to their special relationship with students, teachers are also regarded as role models. This has profound implications for the teaching profession, since, in addition to behaving appropriately in school, teachers are expected to embody moral qualities in their civic lives and even in their personal lives. Indeed, teachers should expect to be scrutinized more than ordinary citizens are. The degree to which the off-duty behaviour of teachers is judged by professional and legislative bodies will be explored later in this chapter and in subsequent chapters.

ETHICAL JUDGMENT IN TEACHING

- Should I direct my lesson to the majority of students who are keeping up with the curriculum or devote extra class time to assisting students who are struggling?
- Should I teach the history unit on immigration as laid out in the course of study or adapt it to the needs of the immigrant students in my inner-city school?
- If I smell marijuana on a student, should I report her to the vice-principal?
- If a student bolts from the classroom, should I follow him or remain with the rest of the class?
- If I suspect plagiarism, but cannot prove it, should I confront the student?

Teachers are continually faced with dilemmas of practice. Many of these have moral or ethical dimensions. Often there is no ideal solution.

Ethical judgment is the ability to make sound decisions when addressing dilemmas of practice. These dilemmas could be everyday situations or periodic crises. Effective teachers work through these dilemmas thoughtfully in order to enhance the knowledge and well-being of students. Effective novice teachers employ procedures and routines to guide their practice, whereas effective veteran teachers are more likely to have internalized these into their professional judgment (McBrien, 2015).

Whereas morality is essentially private, ethical judgments are inherently public. They lead to the actions through which our morality is made manifest to others. As Elizabeth Campbell (2003) writes:

> On the one hand, ethics seems easy and straightforward, especially in the most extreme situations; on the other hand, it is fraught with tensions and uncertainties that have challenged us for centuries to think deeply about the contextual realities of our lives as they influence our ethical knowledge. (pp. 16–17)

Campbell argues that teacher education would benefit from analyzing case studies that provide snapshots of teachers using ethical knowledge in their daily work. In this book, the legal cases embedded in each chapter act as snapshots of situations that occur in classrooms. The rulings of the courts offer guidance to teachers as they develop their practice. Similarly, cases from the Ontario College of Teachers offer guidance concerning the standards of the profession. The cases at the end of chapters in this book provide opportunities for teachers to apply ethical, professional, and legal judgments to authentic teaching situations.

Campbell states that "we must harness ethical knowledge as the new body of knowledge to define professionalism in teaching" (p. 114). While she values professional standards, she argues that

> ethical knowledge is fostered not by means of formalized codes and standards alone, but through a collective mission in which teachers become fully aware of their moral agency and of how their actions and beliefs have a profound ethical influence on students. (p. 114)

Teaching is a profession unique in its moral responsibilities. Reflecting on teaching as a profession, Strike & Ternansky (1993) argue:

> Teaching may seek the respect it deserves not by comparing itself to other

vocations but by focusing on the role and importance of teachers' moral and intellectual commitments to the lives of students and in society. (p. 220)

The Ontario College of Teachers seeks to promote respect for the teaching profession both by focusing on the ethical dimensions of teaching and by demonstrating the rigour of the self-regulatory bodies of other professions.

TEACHING AS A PROFESSION

Doctors and lawyers have long been recognized as professionals. One of the characteristics of a profession is "the ability to set its own standards of practice" (McIntyre & Bloom, 2002, p. 3). As a patient, if you have concerns about the competence of a physician, you may file a complaint with the College of Physicians and Surgeons of Ontario. Similarly, if you have concerns about the professional conduct of a lawyer, you may complain to the Law Society of Upper Canada. In both cases, the regulatory body involved will investigate your complaints and, as appropriate, conduct hearings into the conduct of the professional in question.

Until 1998, Ontario teachers governed themselves through the Ontario Teachers' Federation, the membership of which consists of the various federations (or unions) representing teachers in publicly funded schools.

One of the recommendations of the Ontario Royal Commission on Learning (1994) was the establishment of a college of teachers. The commissioners argued that "teaching should be a self-governing profession, with greater responsibility and greater autonomy for teachers" (p. 17).

As a result, in 1996 the government of Ontario passed the *Ontario College of Teachers Act*, which established the Ontario College of Teachers. Since 1998, the College has acted as the professional standards and regulatory body for the teaching profession. Ontario is only the second Canadian province to establish self-regulation for teachers. In 2011, the Ministry of Education in British Columbia disbanded the BC College of Teachers, replacing it with the Teacher Regulation Branch of the Ministry of Education (Glegg, 2012).

One of the reasons for this separation of tasks between OTF and OCT is the perception that professional standards need to be determined and maintained by an independent body. In medicine, for example, the Ontario Medical Association is the advocacy group for doctors, while the College of Physicians and Surgeons of Ontario remains at arm's-length. Another reason is that the profession can regulate itself more effectively than the government can. The government, however, does review the activities of various professional colleges, and the colleges must operate within the constraints imposed by the relevant acts and regulations.

DUTY OF CARE IN COMMON LAW

It is important to keep in mind that school boards, teachers, and principals have a special relationship with students and the parents who entrust their children to the school system. As a result of being held *in loco parentis* by the courts, those responsible for providing educational services have a legal obligation to conduct themselves in a manner consistent with this trust. The courts have also held that the relationship between teachers and students could involve the law of "fiduciary duty," the term used to describe the relationship of trust, power, and vulnerability existing, for example, between a parent and child.

In Ontario, the duties of principals and teachers are set out in legislation. This legislation reflects the high ethical, professional, and legal standards set by society for educators. Teaching in a manner consistent with these duties will ensure that students learn in safe classrooms and schools.

STATUTORY DUTIES UNDER THE EDUCATION ACT

The *Education Act* and its accompanying regulations provide the statutory basis for public education in Ontario. This comprehensive piece of legislation, which has been added to in an *ad hoc* manner for decades, covers, among other things, school board governance, provincial funding, curriculum, special education, discipline codes, and the duties of various education professionals.

Teachers employed by school boards assume statutory and regulatory duties as outlined in the *Education Act* and *Regulation 298*. These broad duties may be further defined—narrowed or expanded—in the collective agreement between a board and a teachers' federation. Teachers are charged with the duty of maintaining a safe and supportive learning environment within their classrooms. This responsibility also extends to their duties in other parts of school.

Section 264(1) of the *Education Act* states:

It is the duty of a teacher and a temporary teacher:

teach

(a) to teach diligently and faithfully the classes or subjects assigned to the teacher by the principal;

learning

(b) to encourage the pupils in the pursuit of learning;

religion and morals

(c) to inculcate by precept and example respect for religion and the principles of Judaeo-Christian morality and the highest regard for truth, justice, loyalty, love of country, humanity, benevolence, sobriety, industry, frugality, purity, temperance and all other virtues;

co-operation

(d) to assist in developing co-operation and co-ordination of effort among the members of the staff of the school;

discipline

(e) to maintain, under the direction of the principal, proper order and discipline in the teacher's classroom and while on duty in the school and on the school ground;

language of instruction

(f) in instruction and in all communications with the pupils in regard to discipline and the management of the school,

(i) to use the English language, except where it is impractical to do so by reason of the pupil not understanding English, and except in respect of instruction in a language other than English when such other language is being taught as one of the subjects in the course of study, or

(ii) to use the French language in schools or classes in which French is the language of instruction except where it is impractical to do so by reason of the pupil not understanding French, and except in respect of instruction in a language other than French when such other language is being taught as one of the subjects in the course of study;

timetable

(g) to conduct the teacher's class in accordance with a timetable which shall be accessible to pupils and to the principal and supervisory officers;

professional activity days

(h) to participate in professional activity days as designated by the board under the regulations;

absence from school

(i) to notify such person as is designated by the board if the teacher is to be absent from school and the reason therefore;

school property

(j) to deliver the register, the school key and other school property in the teacher's possession to the board on demand, or when the teacher's agreement with the board has expired, or when for any reason the teacher's employment has ceased; and

textbooks

(k) to use and permit to be used as a textbook in a class that he or she teaches in an elementary or a secondary school,

   (i) in a subject area for which textbooks are approved by the Minister, only textbooks that are approved by the Minister, and

   (ii) in all subject areas, only textbooks that are approved by the board;

duties assigned

(l) to perform all duties assigned in accordance with this Act and the regulations.

Section 20 of *Regulation 298* supplements the duties under the *Education Act* by indicating that teachers shall also:

(a) be responsible for effective instruction, training and evaluation of the progress of pupils in the subjects assigned to the teacher and for the management of the class or classes, and report to the principal on the progress of pupils on request;

(b) carry out the supervisory duties and instructional program assigned to the teacher by the principal and supply such information related thereto as the principal may require;

(c) where the board has appointed teachers under section 14 or 17, co-operate fully with such teachers and with the principal in all matters related to the instruction of pupils;

(d) unless otherwise assigned by the principal, be present in the classroom or teaching area and ensure that the classroom or teaching area is ready for the reception of pupils at least fifteen minutes before the commencement of classes in the school in the morning and, where applicable, five minutes before the commencement of classes in the school in the afternoon;

(e) assist the principal in maintaining close co-operation with the community;

(f) prepare for use in the teacher's class or classes such teaching plans and outlines as are required by the principal and the appropriate supervisory officer and submit the plans and outlines to the principal or the appropriate supervisory officer, as the case may be, on request;

(g) ensure that all reasonable safety procedures are carried out in courses and activities for which the teacher is responsible;

(h) co-operate with the principal and other teachers to establish and maintain consistent disciplinary practices in the school;

(i) ensure that report cards are fully and properly completed and processed in accordance with the guides known in English as Guide to the Provincial Report Card, Grades 1-8 and Guide to the Provincial Report Card, Grades 9-12, and in French …

(j) co-operate and assist in the administration of tests under the Education Quality and Accountability Office Act, 1996;

(k) participate in regular meetings with pupils' parents or guardians;

(l) perform duties as assigned by the principal in relation to co-operative placements of pupils; and

(m) perform duties normally associated with the graduation of pupils.

The *Education Act, Regulation 298,* and other legislation make it clear that teachers and principals owe a duty of care to their students due to their special relationship of trust. Since parents are required to send their children to school, they are entitled to expect that their children will receive excellent teaching in orderly and welcoming classrooms, in a safe and supportive school environment.

TEACHING PROFESSION ACT

Teachers have been considered professionals in Ontario since the *Teaching Profession Act, 1944,* which established the Ontario Teachers' Federation as the umbrella organization for the various bodies representing teachers in publicly funded schools. OTF now consists of four affiliate member organizations: the Elementary Teachers' Federation of Ontario (ETFO); the Ontario English Catholic Teachers' Association (OECTA); the Ontario Secondary School Teachers' Federation (OSSTF); and l'Association des enseignantes et des enseignants franco-ontariens (AEFO). Everyone employed by a board as a teacher is a member of the federation. This includes teacher librarians, guidance teachers, consultants, and teachers on special assignment. It does not include vice-principals, principals, supervisory officers, or instructors in a teacher training institution.

Before the creation of the College of Teachers, OTF had two related but somewhat conflicting goals. On the one hand, it was dedicated to maintaining standards of excellence for the teaching profession across the province; on the other, it was dedicated to protecting its members. Now that the College has assumed responsibility for licensing and discipline, OTF's major purpose, in practical terms, is protective. Nevertheless, as can be seen below, OTF still expects its members to maintain a high level of professionalism.

One of OTF's objectives, according to section 3(a), was to "promote and advance the cause of education." The legislation allowed the organization's board of governors to make regulations outlining a code of ethics for teachers. This code of ethics, in the Regulation Made Under the *Teaching Profession Act*, contains provisions with respect to the general duties of members, as well as duties of members to the public, educational authorities, their federation within OTF, and fellow members.

Regulation Made Under the *Teaching Profession Act*
General Duties of Members

13. A member shall strive at all times to achieve and maintain the highest degree of professional competence and to uphold the honour, dignity, and ethical standards of the teaching profession.

Duties of a Member to His or Her Pupils

14. A member shall,
    (a) regard as his first duty the effective education of his pupils and the maintenance of a high degree of professional competence in his teaching;
    (b) endeavour to develop in his pupils an appreciation of standards of excellence;
    (c) endeavour to inculcate in his pupils an appreciation of the principles of democracy;
    (d) show consistent justice and consideration in all his relations with pupils;
    (e) refuse to divulge beyond his proper duty confidential information about a pupil; and
    (f) concern himself with the welfare of his pupils while they are under his care.

Duties of a Member to Educational Authorities

15. (1) A member shall,
    (a) comply with the Acts and regulations administered by the Minister;

(b) co-operate with his educational authorities to improve public education;

(c) respect the legal authority of the board of trustees in the management of the school and in the employment of teachers;

(d) make in the proper manner such reports concerning teachers under his authority as may be required by the board of trustees; and

(e) present in the proper manner to the proper authorities the consequences to be expected from policies or practices which in his professional opinion are seriously detrimental to the interests of pupils.

(2) A member shall not,

(a) break a contract of employment with a board of trustees;

(b) violate a written or oral agreement to enter into a contract of employment with a board of trustees; or

(c) while holding a contract of employment with a board of trustees, make application for another position the acceptance of which would necessitate his seeking the termination of his contract by mutual consent of the teacher and the board of trustees, unless and until he has arranged with his board of trustees for such termination of contract if he obtains the other position.

Duties of a Member to the Public

16. A member shall,

(a) endeavour at all times to extend the public knowledge of his profession and discourage untrue, unfair or exaggerated statements with respect to teaching; and

(b) recognize a responsibility to promote respect for human rights.

Duties of a Member to the Federation

17. A member shall co-operate with the Federation to promote the welfare of the profession.

Duties of a Member to Fellow Members

18. (1) A member shall,

  (a) avoid interfering in an unwarranted manner between other teachers and pupils;

  (b) on making an adverse report on another member, furnish him with a written statement of the report at the earliest possible time and not later than three days after making the report;

  (c) notwithstanding section 18(1)(b), a member who makes an adverse report about another member respecting suspected sexual abuse of a student by that other member need not provide him or her with a copy of the report or with any information about the report. (WB02)

  (d) refuse to accept employment with a board of trustees whose relations with the Federation are unsatisfactory; and

  (e) where he is in an administrative or supervisory position, make an honest and determined effort to help and counsel a teacher before subscribing to the dismissal of that teacher.

  (2) Under clause (c) of subsection (1), the onus shall be on the member to ascertain personally from the Federation whether an unsatisfactory relationship exists.

  (3) A member shall not attempt to gain an advantage over other members by knowingly underbidding another member, or knowingly applying for a position not properly declared vacant, or by negotiating for salary independently of his local group of fellow-members.

The duties outlined in this regulation clearly convey the higher standards of conduct expected of teachers as professionals. Although, as noted above, OTF is no longer responsible for disciplining professional misconduct, this regulation remains in force and serves as a guide to teachers. In becoming a teacher, one commits to working within these ethical and professional standards.

THE ONTARIO COLLEGE OF TEACHERS' FOUNDATIONS OF PROFESSIONAL PRACTICE

Teachers in Ontario are guided by the profession's standards of practice. These standards, initially approved in 1999, outline in broad terms the knowledge, skills, and values inherent in the teaching profession. The standards were revised in 2006 following an extensive consultation with teachers and members of the public. Now formally known as the *Foundations of Professional Practice* (2006), they outline the principles of ethical behaviour, professional practice, and ongoing learning for the teaching profession in Ontario. The entire document may be found at the Ontario College of Teachers' website www.oct.on.ca.

According to the introduction of this document:

> The standards describe what it means to be a member of the teaching profession in Ontario and reflect widely shared beliefs within the profession. They articulate the goals and aspirations of a teaching profession dedicated to fostering student learning and preparing Ontario students to participate in a democratic society. College members use the standards to reflect on their own development as teaching professionals and inform their practice and ongoing learning choices. (p. 4)

The foundations of professional practice do not have the force of law. Rather, they are intended to act as guidelines for teachers in their classroom practice and ongoing professional development. Nonetheless, according to some experts, "it is reasonable to expect that they will be considered and applied" (McIntyre & Bloom, 2002, p. 74) in professional misconduct cases. Moreover, the five standards of practice described below are reflected in the sixteen competency statements used by principals and other school board officials to evaluate teachers. (The performance appraisal of new and experienced teachers is examined in more detail in chapter 10.)

The Ethical Standards for the Teaching Profession

The Ethical Standards for the Teaching Profession convey the professional beliefs and values that should guide all teachers in their professional practice and decision making. The four ethical standards—care, respect, trust, and integrity—establish the core ethics that inform all parts of the *Foundations of Professional Practice.*

The introduction to this section of the document states that the four standards "represent a vision of professional practice" centred on "a commitment to students and their learning" and responsibility to "students, parents, guardians, colleagues, educational partners, other professionals, the environment and the public" (p. 7).

The four ethical standards for the teaching profession are:

Care
The ethical standard of *Care* includes compassion, acceptance, interest and insight for developing students' potential. Members express their commitment to students' well-being and learning through positive influence, professional judgment and empathy in practice.

Trust
The ethical standard of *Trust* embodies fairness, openness and honesty. Members' professional relationships with students, colleagues, parents, guardians and the public are based on trust.

Respect
Intrinsic to the ethical standard of *Respect* is trust and fair-mindedness. Members honour human dignity, emotional wellness and cognitive development. In their professional practice, they model respect for spiritual and cultural values, social justice, confidentiality, freedom, democracy and the environment.

Integrity
Honesty, reliability and moral action are embodied in the ethical standard of *Integrity.* Continual reflection assists members in exercising integrity in their professional commitments and responsibilities.

The Standards of Practice for the Teaching Profession
These standards:

> provide a framework of principles that describes the knowledge, skills, and values inherent in Ontario's teaching profession. These standards articulate the goals and aspirations of the profession. These standards convey a collective vision of professionalism that guides the daily practices of members of the Ontario College of Teachers. (Introduction, p. 11)

The standards are intended to guide "professional judgment" and "promote a common language that fosters an understanding of what it means to be a member of the teaching profession" (p. 12).

The five standards are:

Commitment to Students and Student Learning
Members are dedicated in their care and commitment to students. They treat students equitably and with respect and are sensitive to factors that influence individual student learning. Members facilitate the development of students as contributing citizens of Canadian society.

Leadership in Learning Communities
Members promote and participate in the creation of collaborative, safe and supportive learning communities. They recognize their shared responsibilities and their leadership roles in order to facilitate student success. Members maintain and uphold the principles of the ethical standards in these learning communities.

Ongoing Professional Learning
Members recognize that a commitment to ongoing professional learning is integral to effective practice and to student learning. Professional practice and self-directed learning are informed by experience, research, collaboration and knowledge.

Professional Knowledge

Members strive to be current in their professional knowledge and recognize its relationship to practice. They understand and reflect on student development, learning theory, pedagogy, curriculum, ethics, educational research and related policies and legislation to inform professional judgment in practice.

Professional Practice

Members apply professional knowledge and experience to promote student learning. They use appropriate pedagogy, assessment and evaluation, resources and technology in planning for and responding to the needs of individual students and learning communities. Members refine their professional practice through ongoing inquiry, dialogue and reflection.

The Professional Learning Framework for the Teaching Profession

The final section of the document is the Professional Learning Framework for the Teaching Profession. This is designed to encourage ongoing professional learning. It identifies ways in which teachers can continuously develop their practice, through formal professional development and other learning opportunities.

Formal professional development includes additional qualification courses listed in *Regulation 184/97: Teachers' Qualifications.* The completion of such courses, taken through accredited providers such as universities, expands the formal qualifications of teachers and is recorded by the College on a teacher's Certificate of Qualification.

One of the most significant aspects of the revised standards is that the framework now recognizes that school-based professional development, mentoring, professional networks, teacher research, and even independent professional reading are valuable forms of professional development.

The framework identifies "the goal of professional learning as the ongoing improvement of practice" (p. 23):

Teacher learning is directly correlated to student learning.

The professional learning framework encourages learning activities based on provincial legislation and policy, system needs, personal growth needs and student learning needs. The framework also encourages members of the College to identify and pursue their strengths and personal interests to further their professional learning.

Standards-based professional learning provides for an integrated approach to teacher education.
All programs and professional learning activities accredited by the College must be designed to support The Standards of Practice for the Teaching Profession and The Ethical Standards for the Teaching Profession.

Exemplary professional learning opportunities are based on the principles of effective learning.
The framework takes into account individual career and personal priorities. It outlines professional learning activities that are varied, flexible and accessible to members of the College.

Teachers plan for and reflect on their professional learning.
Responsible lifelong learning is continuous learning that is initiated by members of the College and directed and reviewed by them on an ongoing basis.

Learning communities enhance professional learning.
The professional learning framework encourages collaboration. It supports ongoing commitment to the improvement and currency of teaching practice as an individual and collective responsibility.

In response to concerns expressed by teachers' federations, the College insists that the Professional Learning Framework and the standards as a whole are not guidelines for the evaluation of teachers. *Foundations of Professional Practice* states:

The standards are not intended to be the criteria for the ongoing performance appraisal of individual College members. Performance appraisal remains the responsibility of employers, who apply the criteria by which teaching performance is assessed. In publicly funded systems, this responsibility is outlined in the *Education Act* and *Regulation 99/02, Teacher Performance Appraisal* under this Act.

Nevertheless, as noted above, the five standards of practice do form the basis of the sixteen competency statements that together are one of the key components of teacher performance appraisal.

PROFESSIONAL JUDGMENT

The essence of professionalism is judgment. This begins with knowledge of and respect for the law and professional standards, but expert professionals develop sophisticated ethical decision-making skills. Justice Paul S. Rouleau (2006) assures educators that their duties need not be onerous and that their professionalism is respected by the courts. He writes:

> The law has imposed many rules and regulations on the education system. Educators have to follow them, but if their objective is to simply comply with all the rules, the art of expression, the beauty, is lost. Compliance with the laws is necessary but should not be the educator's primary objective. It is possible to work within the rules and still to be fully expressive, to be an artist that is a true educator.

Rouleau argues that "the courts show respect for decisions made by educators. Turning back to my example of sonnets, rules can be either a hindrance or helpful. Don't lose your focus on educating. Be mindful of the rules but don't let them consume you. Compliance alone does not ensure excellence."

The manner in which judges weigh ethical and legal issues can be instructive to us as educators. The *Canadian Charter of Rights and Freedoms*, which lists the civil rights and freedoms of all Canadians, is a living document that is interpreted in response to important issues that arise in a diverse and changing society. The courts are often called on to resolve complex cases in which fundamental rights are in conflict. Over the years, Supreme Court justices have had to rule on controversial issues such as abortion, corporal punishment of children, censorship of pornography, and same-sex marriage.

Since our education system is such an important public institution, events occurring in schools often lead to court cases, some of which have resulted in significant changes to our understanding of rights and freedoms in our society.

What happens when two rights or freedoms collide? The case below illustrates how the Supreme Court works through such complex issues.

Case Study: Exploring Religious Accommodation
Multani v. Commission Scolaire Marguerite-Bourgeoys (2006)

In 2001, twelve-year-old Gurbaj Singh Multani was playing in the school playground in Quebec when his kirpan fell to the ground. This playground incident led to a major constitutional case that will define human rights in Canada for decades to come.

The kirpan is a dagger worn by many devout Sikh men and boys. Although it once functioned as a dagger, it has become an important symbol of morality, justice, and faith.

The school administration, which permitted Sikh students to wear kirpans, regarded this as a safety issue. The parents were asked to safely secure the kirpan inside Gurbaj's clothing so it could not fall out again. The parents accepted this as a reasonable way to balance religious freedom and school safety.

When the school board learned of this incident, it revoked the agreement and determined that kirpans in schools constituted a potential threat to student safety and violated the school's code of conduct, which prohibited weapons. Since Gurbaj was forbidden to wear a kirpan, his parents withdrew him from the public school system and filed a lawsuit against the school board.

In May 2002, the Superior Court of Quebec rejected the board's ban on the wearing of kirpans. It did, however, stipulate that Gurbaj was to be required to secure his kirpan by placing it in a wooden case, wrapped in fabric, and sewn into his clothes.

The Quebec Court of Appeal overturned this judgment in March 2004. It ruled that kirpans constituted a potential safety threat. The school board's duty to ensure safety for all students was deemed to outweigh protecting one student's religious rights.

This controversial case, which raised many important ethical and legal issues, was then appealed to the Supreme Court of Canada. In March 2006, the Supreme Court ruled that a complete ban on kirpans violated section 2(a) of the *Canadian Charter of Rights and Freedoms*, which protects freedom of religion. The court did not regard the curtailing of this right as reasonable or justifiable under section 1 of the *Charter*. While the court acknowledged limits to freedom of religion, it did not find a total ban to be proportional to the threat posed by the kirpan. As a result, it affirmed the set of conditions designed by the Superior Court to address the safety concerns of the board.

---

(1) Why was Gurbaj wearing a kirpan?
(2) Why did the school board decide to ban kirpans?
(3) Do you think the Supreme Court ruling was fair? Why or why not?

The key concept guiding the court's decision in this and in similar cases was *reasonable accommodation*. Rather than decide that one right trumped another, the court attempted to maximize the exercise of both rights, so that Canadians would be able to feel both safe in schools and free to exercise freedom of religion. The justices of the Supreme Court reasoned that mutual respect and tolerance are essential to living in a multicultural society. Students could learn to distinguish between a weapon and a religious artifact important to one group. Also, the withdrawal of Gurbaj from the school underlined the importance of kirpans to the Sikh community. Whether or not one agrees with this legal decision, *reasonable accommodation* is a useful concept for grappling with the many ethical dilemmas that arise in education.

CHECKING YOUR UNDERSTANDING

- As a caring profession, teaching is infused with moral significance; teachers may be thought of as guardians, educators, and moral educators.
- As *guardians*, teachers are expected by the courts to act *in loco parentis* (in place of the parent) and as such are considered to owe their students a fiduciary duty.
- As *educators*, teachers not only should cover the curriculum but also should adapt it to the needs of their students and the communities in which they live.

- As *moral educators*, teachers must engage with students in a morally acceptable manner and embody the qualities of care, trust, respect, and integrity identified in the College's Ethical Standards for the Teaching Profession.
- As a result of being *in loco parentis*, educators are considered under common law to owe their students a *fiduciary duty*.
- The *Education Act* and its attendant regulations provide the statutory basis for public education in Ontario.
- The principal is responsible for the organization and management of the school and the instruction and discipline of students.
- The principal is also the person charged with ensuring that the school is a safe and healthy learning environment.
- Teachers have a number of duties outlined in the *Education Act* and *Regulation 298*. These duties may be further defined in collective agreements.
- Teachers have been considered professionals in Ontario since 1944, with the passage of the *Teaching Profession Act*, which established the Ontario Teachers' Federation. OTF now consists of four affiliates: AEFO, ETFO, OECTA, and OSSTF.
- The regulation made under the *Teaching Profession Act* outlines a code of ethics for teachers. Included in the code is a requirement that a member making an adverse report about a fellow member provide that member with a written copy of the report within three days, except in cases of suspected sexual abuse of a student.
- Although OTF still has a strong professional emphasis, its major purpose now is to protect and promote the interests of teachers. Only persons employed by a board as teachers are members of OTF. Principals and vice-principals, for example, are not members.
- Since the *Education Act* defines *teacher* as a member of the Ontario College of Teachers, only persons who hold a certificate of qualification in some form from the College are permitted to teach in a publicly funded school in Ontario.

- In Ontario, the teaching profession is grounded in a legal framework based on an ethic of caring and is regulated by the professional standards established by the Ontario College of Teachers.
- In 1998, teachers in Ontario became fully self-regulating with the creation of the Ontario College of Teachers, which has the power to issue, suspend, and revoke certificates.
- The College's mandate is to serve and protect the public interest.

APPLYING YOUR UNDERSTANDING

The *Foundations of Professional Practice* (OCT, 2006) states:

> College members use the ethical standards and the standards of practice to reflect on their own development as teaching professionals and inform their practice and ongoing learning choices. (p. 30)

The scenarios below, developed by the Ontario College of Teachers, are examples of dilemmas experienced by educators. They provide authentic experiences for integrating ethical knowledge and understanding through engagement in professional inquiry processes. Educators encounter such ethical dilemmas on a daily basis when grappling with curriculum planning, assessment, policy development, and relationships with others.

Scenario 1

You are newly appointed to your professional position. At a meeting with an educational leader, your supervisor makes what you perceive to be a biased comment. What do you do?

Scenario 2

You and your colleagues from the intermediate division have agreed that the consequence for not completing assigned homework is an after-school detention the following day. All parents have been notified of this policy. A student informs you that his homework is not completed because he went to a hockey game with his father, whom he rarely sees. What do you do?

Scenario 3

The past practice in your school has allowed the students to elect the president of their student council. You and a colleague are the staff advisers. During the tabulation of the results, a student whom both you and your colleague perceive as inappropriate for student council president wins the election by three votes. The second-place candidate is perceived by both of you as a better choice for student council president. Your colleague destroys four of the ballots, giving the student council presidency to the runner-up. What do you do?

---

(1) Which ethical standards apply to this case?
(2) Which standards of practice apply to this case?
(3) What course of action would you take as a member of the teaching profession?

CHAPTER 2

THE LEGAL SYSTEM IN CANADA AND EDUCATION SYSTEM IN ONTARIO

After reading this chapter, you will understand the purpose of law, its sources and categories, and where education law fits within the Canadian constitutional framework. In addition, you will understand the relationship between law, education, and what the stakeholders are in the Ontario education system. Stakeholders— parents, the community, school trustees, school boards, teachers, and students—have responsibilities to one another, making the education system highly complex.

Case Study: Should Police Sniffer Dogs Be Allowed in Schools?
R. v. A.M. (2008)

On November 7, 2002, three Sarnia police officers visited St. Patrick's High School with a sniffer dog. They were responding to an "open invitation" from the principal, who was enforcing a zero tolerance policy for possession of illegal drugs and alcohol. The principal gave them permission to conduct a search of the school premises even though there were no reports that drugs were present at the school that day.

After the principal informed students and teachers that they had to remain in their classrooms, the police and sniffer dog began their search of the premises. In the gym, the sniffer dog led police to a backpack containing ten bags of marijuana and ten magic mushrooms (psilocybin). The student identified by its contents as the owner of the bag was charged with possession for the purpose of trafficking marijuana and possession of psilocybin.

A lower court ruled that the search was unreasonable and violated the student's constitutional rights under the *Canadian Charter of Rights and Freedoms*. The police's actions were criticized as being unreasonable under criminal law and the *Education Act* since the "entire student body" was "held in detention" for a "warrantless random search."

The Crown appealed the lower court decision to the Supreme Court of Canada, where it was upheld by a majority of justices. They found that the police did not have the authority to conduct sniffer dog searches without an adequate basis. As for what constitutes an adequate basis, four justices set the bar high at "reasonable and probable grounds," while three were satisfied with "reasonable suspicion."

(1) What are the facts of the case?

(2) What important issues does this case raise?

(3) Why did the court rule in favour of the student?

(4) What are your thoughts on this case and the final court decision?

On the surface, *R. v. A.M.* seems like a clear and simple case in which someone was caught with illegal drugs and charged by the authorities. Yet the police, who were serving and protecting the public, were deemed to have acted unreasonably. The student possessing drugs shifted from being a criminal to being a victim of unreasonable police actions. How could this happen? Very simply, legal precedent and the *Canadian Charter of Rights and Freedoms* protect Canadians from both criminal acts by citizens and arbitrary and unfair actions by representatives of the state, including the police and educators.

Most Canadians are largely unfamiliar with the law, legal processes, and the education system. The purpose of this chapter is to provide an overview of how these operate conceptually and in practice.

THE LEGAL SYSTEM IN CANADA

THE PURPOSE OF LAW

What would happen if there were no rules guiding human behaviour? How would you manage to drive safely from your home to the downtown core? How would we protect our homes and families? How would schools be run? How much learning would take place? Who would pay the teachers?

Whenever people form into groups, whether formally or informally, they soon develop rules. Why? To maintain order. Without clear rules that apply to everyone in the group, there would be chaos or rule by the strongest. Canada is a highly complex society in which our individual actions are bound by laws intended to guide our conduct, protect everyone's rights and freedoms, and keep us safe from crime.

In democratic societies such as ours, the actions of both citizens and governments are guided by the rule of law. This fundamental principle of justice affirms that laws are necessary to regulate society, apply equally to everyone, and cannot arbitrarily be changed or interpreted by those in authority.

LAW AND MORALITY

Although we often focus on the practical purpose of particular laws, it is important to keep in mind that the law is essentially the enactment of a moral code for guiding the behaviour of citizens. Individual laws are generally derived from larger moral principles that are widely accepted as collective community standards. In Canada, many of these standards are based on the Judeo-Christian values of our forebears. This is reflected in the *Canadian Charter of Rights and Freedoms*, which states that "Canada is founded upon principles that recognize the supremacy of God and the rule of law."

Today not everyone accepts the collective community standards that have guided lawmakers in the past. Traditional social norms that remain deeply held by many have been successfully challenged by others who regard them as no longer relevant or meaningful. Recently, the issue of same-sex marriage has proven very divisive. In our multicultural and multi-faith society, new communities of belief sometimes clash with both traditional norms and contemporary standards. Requests for the application of sharia law by some Islamic groups is one example of this moral debate. Schools, as important social institutions, sometimes become battlegrounds for these issues. Prayer in schools and sex education are two examples of moral issues that have caused considerable debate among people with widely differing viewpoints.

It may be useful to distinguish between the moral domain and social norms (Nucci, 2001). The moral domain is centred on foundational principles or virtues such as honesty, justice, integrity, respect, kindness, and trustworthiness. These are universally accepted and can act as guides for the behaviour of all citizens. Social norms are non-principle-based conventions or personal preferences of particular religious, cultural, and social groups. As will be shown later, the courts are often guided by foundational principles as they rule on controversial court cases.

CANADA'S LEGAL TRADITION

Canada's law originates from three distinct yet interconnected sources: common law, statute law, and constitutional law. Understanding these general sources will help you make sense of the specific laws that relate to education in Ontario.

Common Law

Most people in medieval Europe worked as serfs on the feudal estates of nobles and lords. Under feudalism, which was brought to England by William the Conqueror in 1066, serfs obtained the right to work farmland by swearing fealty (loyalty and service) to their lords. Lords, in turn, swore fealty to the monarch, who owned all of the land in the kingdom. Among the duties of lords was acting as a judge in disputes taking place on their land.

As England grew in size and complexity, monarchs appointed travelling judges to rule on controversial cases. These judges met regularly to establish consistent laws and punishments in criminal and civil cases. From these legal decisions emerged the English tradition of common law. *Common law*, which applied across England, was based on the principle of precedent. A *precedent* is a previous legal decision that serves as a rule or example. The rulings in some cases became known by members of the legal community as particularly significant, leading judges to make similar decisions in cases with similar facts. Over time, these decisions were written down, and later all cases were systematically documented.

When English colonists settled in North America, they brought the English common law tradition with them. Today it remains a critical part of the Canadian and American legal systems.

Common law is also known as case law because, as mentioned, significant past cases serve as precedents for present legal rulings. In this book, key cases are cited to explain how the law applies to the work of educators in schools. Studying legal cases may seem daunting to many readers because of the legal nomenclature and language used. Yet very often they are interesting stories that pose dilemmas for jurists and society. Understanding these cases, and the lessons offered in the legal judgments associated with them, can improve our under-standing and practice as teachers. The case of *R. v. A.M.* is a good example.

Studying Cases

Each legal case has a formal case *citation*, or reference heading, designed as an aid to locating legal cases. The citation begins with the name of the case, such as *R. v. A.M.* The letter "R" for Rex (King) or Regina (Queen) denotes that this is a criminal case in which the Crown or government is charging a member of the public. The other name is that of the defendant; in this case, the defendant was a minor (under the age of eighteen), so his name does not appear in full. In civil cases where one person or organization sues another, two names appear. In *Chamberlain v. Surrey School District*, for example, the first name indicates that Chamberlain is the plaintiff suing the local school district, which is the defendant.

The year of the case appears next, followed by a reference to one of the case-law reporters. In general, when cases are cited in this book they will be identified simply by name and year of case.

Statute Law

While common law is an important part of our legal system, most of our laws are now made by democratically elected representatives. *Statute law* consists of all the laws or acts passed by the Parliament of Canada and the provincial and territorial legislatures.

In order to make or change a law, the elected government must work through a stringent process that ensures careful consideration of the law and its effects. When, for example, the Ontario government decided that teachers should be regulated through a professional body, it introduced a bill in the Ontario Provincial Parliament. This *bill*, or draft of proposed legislation, was prepared by the Ministry of Education and introduced to the legislature for *first reading* by the Minister of Education.

Once the bill passed first reading, which meant that approval was given to consider the bill, it was introduced again in *second reading*, during which it was debated in general terms before a second vote was taken. The bill was then sent to a *committee* of the legislature for careful consideration. At the committee stage, experts were called as witnesses, and interest groups and members of the public were invited to make deputations. Committee members studied the bill in detail and proposed changes to it. Each section of the bill was voted on separately.

Once the bill passed through the committee stage, it was re-introduced to the legislature for *third reading*. After a brief debate, a third vote was taken and the bill was approved by the legislature. Later it was signed by the Lieutenant Governor of Ontario and proclaimed into law. The *Ontario College of Teachers Act* became law in 1996, and a year later the Ontario College of Teachers (OCT) came into being.

Federal legislation follows a similar process, with bills passing through the same stages in both the elected House of Commons and the appointed Senate before being signed by the Governor General of Canada.

In addition to passing new laws, legislatures also amend existing laws through the same stringent process to meet perceived new needs. One law that has been amended often is the *Criminal Code*, which is a federal statute containing the majority of criminal laws passed by Parliament. It consists of both criminal offences, sentences for crimes, and procedures to be followed in criminal court cases. This act was first passed in 1892 as a codification of rules that had emerged from common law. Since then, the code has been amended almost every year to respond to changing needs and beliefs. Not all crimes are listed in the *Criminal Code*, because criminal law has become more complex over the years. Laws such as the *Youth Criminal Justice Act* and *Controlled Drug and Substances Act* also outline criminal offences.

Studying Statutes

Legislation can sometimes look imposing and even confusing to anyone lacking a legal background, but statutes and regulations essentially contain rules and procedures written out in precise and detailed legal language. Teachers need to be able to read and understand the statutes and regulations that guide the education system and their work as educators.

Statutes are divided into parts so they can be easily referenced and found by lawyers and citizens. The name of the act is written in italics and then divided into sections, subsections, paragraphs, etc. For example, *Ontario College of Teachers Act*, section 26(1) refers to section 26 of the act, which, in paragraph 1 states that any member of the public can launch a complaint against a member. Some acts, such as the *Criminal Code*, are divided into chapters before being divided into sections.

Statutes are revised periodically and bound into volumes. The most common abbreviation for these volumes is "R.S.", as in the Revised Statutes of Canada (R.S.C.) and the Revised Statutes of Ontario (R.S.O.). The *Ontario College of Teachers Act* is found in Statutes of Ontario, 1996. Generally, when common education legislation is cited in this book, no reference will be made to the revised statute volume in which the statute or regulations can be found.

Statutes are often supplemented by regulations, which typically elaborate on sections of the act under which they were created. *Regulations* are orders in council approved by the government without further legislation. No further legislation is needed since the statute under which the regulation is issued already gives the government the power to make regulations on a variety of topics. So, for example, section 11 of the *Education Act* gives the Minister the authority to make regulations on a wide range of issues, including the qualifications and duties of principals and teachers. In turn, *Regulation 298: Operation of Schools—General* adds considerable procedural detail about these two issues as well as other matters relating to the operation of schools that are not included in the *Education Act.* The advantage of a regulation is that, since it does not have to go through the same stringent process in the legislature as a statute, it can be amended much more easily.

Principals and other school administrators have books in their offices that contain most of the laws related to education. Two common volumes are the *Education Statutes and Regulations of Ontario* and *Consolidated Ontario Education Statutes and Regulations.* These are useful reference tools for teachers and school administrators when they need to check on particular legal points.

Constitutional Law

A third source of Canadian law is the Constitution. A constitution is a body of law dealing with the division of powers between levels of government, and the relationship between a government and its people.

Canada's first constitution is actually a statute of the British Parliament. The *British North America Act* (*BNA Act*), which took effect on July 1, 1867, created the Dominion of Canada, which originally consisted of Ontario, Quebec, New Brunswick, and Nova Scotia. Other provinces would later join the federation. Canada was not a fully independent country at the time; Britain controlled our foreign policy, and the Judicial Committee of the Privy Council in the U.K. was our highest court. Also, Canada could not change its constitution without requesting amendments by the British Parliament.

In 1931, the British Parliament passed the *Statute of Westminster,* which gave Canada control over its foreign affairs, and in 1949 the Supreme Court of Canada became the highest court of appeal for Canadian legal cases.

In 1982, after the majority of provinces (Quebec being the sole exception) agreed on a formula to amend the constitution, the *Constitution Act* was signed into law by Queen Elizabeth II. This new constitution guides the governments and courts of Canada on a wide range of important issues.

Constitution Act, 1867. The *BNA Act,* now renamed the *Constitution Act, 1867,* remains the main part of the new Constitution. The most significant sections of the 1867 act are the sections that outline the jurisdictions of the various levels of government. Section 91 outlines the powers of the federal government, while section 92 outlines the powers of provincial governments. Section 93 grants control over education to provincial governments.

DIVISION OF POWERS: CONSTITUTION ACT, 1867

Federal Powers (Section 91) include:	Provincial Powers (Sections 92 and 93) include:
• Peace, order, and good government • Criminal law • Banking and currency • Marriage and divorce • Aboriginal peoples and lands • Postal service • International trade	• Property rights • Civil rights • Police • Highways • Hospitals • Public schools • Separate schools

While the education of Canadian citizens may be of national interest, under the Constitution it lies (with the exception of First Nations education) within the exclusive jurisdiction of provincial governments. In Ontario, education is overseen by the Minister of Education, who through the *Education Act* has overarching control over nearly every aspect of the school system. The provincial government, if it so chose, could administer the whole system centrally, including, for example, hiring and firing teachers and paying their salaries. Traditionally, however, the government has delegated the day-to-day running of the system to locally elected school boards. It is important to remember that school boards, like municipal governments, are "creatures of the province," exercising powers and duties delegated to them by the provincial government. As such, their existence is not protected by the Constitution.

A major reason for designating education as a provincial area of jurisdiction in the *BNA Act* was the desire to protect religious and language rights. At the time of confederation, French-Canadian Roman Catholics believed that their educational interests could be served best if public education was administered by the government of Quebec rather than by a federal government dominated by English-speaking Protestants. They also believed that separate schools in Ontario would protect their religion and culture beyond the borders of Quebec. In return, they accepted constitutional guarantees for Protestant schools in Quebec.

Although section 93 of the *BNA Act* gave each province the exclusive right to make laws in relation to education, it went further to protect denominational rights in Canadian schools. It stated that no law "can prejudicially affect any Right or Privilege with respect to Denominational Schools which any Class of Persons have by Law in the Province at the Union" (the time of Confederation).

As a result, Roman Catholics in Ontario have a constitutional right that is not extended to members of other religious groups. The *Constitution Act, 1982* is explicit in guaranteeing that the *Charter of Rights and Freedoms* is not to abrogate these rights (Medway, 2014).

It is doubtful whether Confederation would have occurred if language and denominational concerns had not been addressed in the *BNA Act*, which had to be ratified by all the founding provinces. The implications for education in Ontario are outlined later in this chapter.

The Canadian Charter of Rights and Freedoms. The *Charter of Rights and Freedoms* is regarded by many as the most important part of the *Constitution Act, 1982*. The *Charter* also plays a critical role in education law. The *Charter* lists the civil rights and freedoms of all Canadians. These include:

- freedom of conscience and religion,
- freedom of thought and belief,
- the right to be secure from unreasonable search and seizure, and
- the right to equality without discrimination based on race, national or ethnic origin, colour, religion, sex, age or mental or physical disability.

Notwithstanding the various general rights and freedoms listed above, section 29 of the document makes clear that nothing in the *Charter* may interfere with the denominational rights of separate schools guaranteed under the original *Constitution Act, 1867*. In addition, section 23 establishes minority language educational rights for speakers of Canada's two national languages. In general terms, these rights guarantee citizens whose first language is that of the English or French linguistic minority population of the province in which they live the right to have their children educated in that language, numbers permitting.

The rights in the *Charter* are far more significant than any identified in common law or statute law, because not only the courts but all levels of government are required to abide by its guarantees. Furthermore, those who believe that their rights have been infringed may apply to the courts for a remedy. As a result, many groups have applied to the courts to protest laws or government policies that they perceive to be unconstitutional. The lawyers for the accused in *R. v. A.M.*, for example, argued that their client's constitutional right to be secure from unreasonable search and seizure had been violated. Other parties, as you will discover in subsequent chapters, have successfully appealed for remedies to perceived human and equality rights violations by teachers and school boards.

The *Charter*, like other common law and statute law, is subject to the interpretation of judges. Over the years, Supreme Court justices have had to rule on controversial issues such as abortion, corporal punishment of children, censorship of pornography, and same-sex marriage.

Since our education system is such an important public institution, events occurring in schools often lead to court cases, some of which have resulted in significant changes to our understanding of rights and freedoms in our society.

What happens when two rights or freedoms collide? The case of *Multani v. Commission Scolaire Marguerite-Bourgeoys* (see chapter 1) is a good illustration of how the court works through such complex issues. Other cases in this book involve similar contests between important rights and freedoms.

Studying Constitutional Cases

Constitutional challenges move through the courts in the same fashion as common law cases. Judges at various levels make rulings based on both the merits of the cases and their interpretation of existing laws. Judges are expected to defer to the rulings of higher-level courts in cases with similar facts. Major constitutional cases, such as *Multani v. Commission Scolaire Marguerite-Bourgeoys* and

R. v. A.M., often introduce new issues for the courts to consider. As these cases wind their way through the court system, individual judges—and later, panels of judges—weigh in on the constitutional and other issues at hand. By the time the Supreme Court hears the case, a significant body of legal thought already exists on the issues of the case.

The ruling of the Supreme Court is the final word on these issues, which makes it both an interpreter of the law and, in practical terms, a maker of the law. Courts often defer to the legislatures to make decisions. For example, the Supreme Court initially refused to make decisions on abortion cases until Parliament had debated the issue. The failure of Parliament to resolve the issue led the court to rule that women had the right to abortions, although the government could regulate conditions.

Constitutional cases can be difficult to understand because they are very complex and tightly argued. Making them all the more confusing is the fact that the Supreme Court ruling often involves detailed analyses of the decisions of various lower courts, many of which may have ruled on different sides of the issue. Nonetheless, studying these cases is worth the effort, because they define the society in which we live and the schools in which we work.

CATEGORIES OF LAW

There are many categories of law. Understanding these in broad terms helps us make sense of the laws that affect our practice as teachers. Unfortunately, they are not easily distinguished from one another. In many cases, several different categories of law apply to a single situation.

. The first broad distinction is between international law and domestic law. *International law* includes treaty law and laws written by international bodies such as the United Nations. These international laws do not apply directly to education in Canada. *Domestic law* refers to the laws that govern life within a nation's borders. In Canada, these laws include ones deriving from case, statute, and constitutional sources.

Domestic law is further divided into procedural law and substantive law. *Procedural law* outlines the legal processes that must be followed in order to protect an individual's rights given under substantive law. For the most part, this book will not examine procedural law, except for the

Statutory Powers Procedures Act, which outlines the processes that tribunals must follow in order to ensure that individuals are treated fairly under Ontario administrative law. (See the Disciplinary Investigations in Schools section in chapter 5).

Domestic substantive law comprises two broad categories: public law and private law. *Public law* addresses the relationship between the government and the people of a society. It is divided into constitutional law (discussed earlier), criminal law, and administrative law. *Criminal law* defines crimes and sets penalties for those crimes. Although criminal acts may be directed at individual citizens, the law regards these acts as violations of the public interest; thus, charges are laid by a Crown Attorney. In criminal cases, guilt must be proved beyond a reasonable doubt. *Administrative law* deals with the relationships between citizens and government agencies. The decisions of the Ministry of Education, school boards, and the Ontario College of Teachers, all based on principles of administrative law, have a profound impact on the lives of students and teachers.

Figure 1-1

DOMESTIC LAW IN CANADA

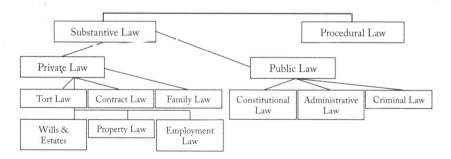

Private law, more generally known as *civil law*, deals with the relationships between individuals and/or organizations (e.g., companies and school boards). Its primary purpose is to manage the behaviour of people and organizations in conflict and award damages to those who have been wronged. There are no Crown Attorneys involved in civil cases. The filer of the lawsuit is known as the *plaintiff*, while the person who is being sued is the *defendant*. In civil cases, the standard of proof is "a balance of probabilities," rather than "beyond a reasonable doubt."

Branches of civil law are tort law, contract law, family law, wills and estates, property law, and employment law. The most significant of these for educators are tort law and employment law. *Tort law*, which will be covered in depth in later chapters, permits someone to sue an individual or organization for a wrong committed, whether intentional or unintentional. An example of tort law would be a former student's suit against a teacher and the school because s/he may have been sexually assaulted. A lawsuit could also be launched by someone who alleges s/he was been injured due to negligence (carelessness) on the part of a teacher. *Employment law* governs the relationship between employees and employers. In education, the *collective agreements* between teachers' federations and school districts govern issues such as salaries, working conditions, and dismissal and grievance procedures.

As you will discover, more than one category of law can apply to a particular situation. For example, a teacher who is alleged to have assaulted a student could be charged with assault or child abuse (criminal law), professionally disciplined by the Ontario College of Teachers (administrative law), suspended or dismissed (employment law), and/or sued for damages (tort law).

By acquiring the knowledge and skills of an ethical and professional practitioner who acts with care and prudence, you can avoid getting caught up in the complex machinery of the law.

EDUCATION LAW

Education law, or school law, is a term that refers broadly to the wide range of laws that apply to students, teachers, schools, and school boards. Some of these laws (e.g., the *Education Act*, the *Ontario College of Teachers Act*, and the *Teaching Profession Act*) relate specifically to schools. Other laws that apply to all Canadians (e.g., the *Criminal Code*) or to all Ontario citizens (e.g., the *Child and Family Services Act*) may have particular force within the educational context. For example, since teachers are responsible for the care of children, they are held to a higher standard of care than ordinary citizens.

In addition, teachers as professionals are expected to adhere to standards of practice befitting professionals. School boards constantly require legal advice to ensure that they are complying with the specific and specialized statutes, regulations, and policies that apply to education. The collective agreements between school boards and teachers' federations also require specialized understandings. Furthermore, as custodians of children, educators need to have some awareness of privacy law, family law, and criminal law.

Teachers who understand ethics, professionalism, and education law are better able to make sound educational decisions. Here's how Justice Paul S. Rouleau (2006) of the Court of Appeal for Ontario put it in his speech "Education in Transition: A Delicate Balance":

> Taken independently or as a whole, these cases show a consistent approach by the courts in recognizing the professionalism, rights and, importantly, the judgment of educators … I hope that the educators among you are able to take up my challenge and operate within the legal framework in a way that respects your ultimate professional goal or purpose: to be an effective educator. Know that courts show respect for decisions made by educators.

THE EDUCATION SYSTEM IN ONTARIO

Case Study: Are Parents Responsible for the Actions of Students?
Nanaimo-Ladysmith School No. 68 v. Dean (2015)

Carson Dean, a student in British Columbia, played a prank by locking a padlock to the ceiling sprinkler in his high school. This inadvertently disturbed the sprinkler's filament, causing the entire sprinkler system to activate. This action resulted in $48,630.47 in water damage to the school.

The school district argued that Carson Dean and his parents were responsible. It sued for financial compensation from the Deans due to Carson's negligence. In addition to case law, the school district focused on Section 10 of the *BC School Act*, which states that a student and his parents are jointly and severally liable for an intentional or negligent act causing damage to property. While the law was enacted in the 1950s, this interpretation of intentional act under Section 10 had never been considered by a court.

The school district argued that Carson reasonably could have foreseen that his inappropriate actions could cause damage to the school, which would make him negligent before the law as he owed a duty of care to others. The defendants denied liability, arguing that Carson did not intend to activate the sprinkler system or cause damage. They also minimized responsibility by suggesting that impulsive behaviour is to be expected from boys of that age, wear and tear on school hallways is expected, and parents reasonably expect the school board to ensure that buildings are resistant to damage by such pranks.

The court ruled in favour of the school district, holding that Carson reasonably should have foreseen that interference with the sprinkler head could cause it to activate. In owing the school a duty of care, Carson was found liable for the full amount of the school district's losses. As he was a ward of his parents, they were required to pay the legal penalty irrespective of any fault on their part.

The decision, while related to a specific B.C. law, is significant for applying the duty of care to students, parents, and other stakeholders in the education system.

---

(1) What are the facts of the case?

(2) What important issues does this case raise?

(3) Why did the court rule in favour of the school district?

(4) What are your thoughts on the court decision and the implications for educational stakeholders?

The Canadian education system began with one-room schoolhouses that included one teacher and a group of students ranging from approximately six to sixteen. As the country became more populated, the education system developed and became increasingly more complex. Grades were established based on age, schools eventually separated into elementary and secondary, and clusters of schools developed into school boards.

The education system includes many stakeholder groups that influence educational decision-making. The stakeholder model, developed by Edward Freeman (1984), has proven a useful framework for describing and analyzing the dynamic relationships and interconnectedness among groups both inside and outside educational and other organizations. Students, teachers, and parents all have important roles to play, individually and through student councils, school councils (see chapter 8), and teachers' federations (see chapter 3). Other stakeholders are also active in the education system. The most common additional stakeholders and their roles are identified and described below.

ONTARIO MINISTRY OF EDUCATION

The government of Ontario, through the Ministry of Education, provides the statutory basis for education in Ontario's publicly funded schools. The *Education Act*, along with its attendant regulations, guidelines, and policies, establishes rules for how school boards and schools are administered. For example, it sets policies and guidelines for school trustees, directors of education, principals, and other school board officials.

The Minister of Education, who is an elected member of the Ontario Provincial Parliament and an appointed member of the provincial cabinet, is responsible for public policy and political direction. The Deputy Minister, an appointed official, is responsible for the day-to-day operations of the Ministry.

The Ministry of Education administers the system of publicly funded elementary and secondary school education in Ontario, in accordance with the directions set by the provincial government. Provincial curriculum documents determine the subjects that are covered in classrooms. Diploma and graduation requirements are also determined at the provincial level, as are the textbooks that may be used in Ontario schools.

Other legislation and policy documents outline both codes of conduct for students and discipline procedures that teachers and principals may apply. Finally, much of the funding for education is either provided or controlled by the provincial government.

Increasingly, the Ministry of Education has been demanding greater accountability from schools and school boards. The Education Quality and Accountability Office (EQAO) was established by the Ontario government in 1996 to evaluate the quality and effectiveness of elementary and secondary school education. EQAO is responsible for:

- developing and administering tests to evaluate the achievement of Ontario elementary and secondary school students;

- reporting test results to the Minister and to the public; and
- providing recommendations to improve test results.

This increased scrutiny, combined with strict financial constraints, has been a source of considerable tension in recent years.

SCHOOL BOARDS

While educational policy is set at the provincial level, the running of schools at the local level is the responsibility of publicly funded and locally elected school boards. They work, within the administrative constraints set by the provincial government, to meet the specific educational needs of students within their jurisdictions.

Ontario's schools are administered by seventy-two district school boards and eleven school authorities. There are thirty-one English-language public school boards, which are non-denominational and open to all school-age students in the province. There are twenty-nine English-language Roman Catholic school boards. These are operated according to Roman Catholic principles but are also accessible to all students. In addition, there are four French-language public school boards and eight French-language Catholic school boards. In all cases, the boards are overseen by locally elected school trustees. School authorities consist of geographically isolated boards and hospital school boards.

School boards are responsible for all of the details of running a local school board and individual schools. These responsibilities can lead to heated debate in the community. Parents often attend meetings in large numbers to influence decisions concerning transportation to schools and the provision of special programs (e.g., French immersion). Opening new schools also tends to generate heated discussions about new school boundaries. Proposals to close existing schools usually face profound resistance.

School boards, in order to meet these demands, are very large and complex organizations. The school board must appoint a supervisory officer as Director of Education. The director runs the day-to-day operations of the school board, including implementing provincial and board policies and submitting an annual report (*Education Act*, section 283). Given the size of some school boards, the director is assisted by an Associate Director, eleven superintendents, and various departmental managers. According to the *Education Act*, a school board may employ "such other supervisory officers as it considers necessary to supervise all aspects of the programs under its jurisdiction" (section 279). The superintendents, according to regulation, must have successfully completed courses granting them Supervisory Officer papers; in the case of superintendents of education, these papers can be earned only after they have also completed principals' qualifications. A complex bureaucracy serves under them to keep the entire system running effectively. At the individual school level, the principal is the person with the authority and responsibility for the management and organization of the school.

Ontario school boards are funded through a funding formula developed by the provincial government. Initial funding is from local property taxes raised from businesses and residents in the local municipality. These funds are topped up by the province to the level allocated in the Foundation Grant. The Foundation Grant allocates money on a per pupil basis to cover salaries and benefits for educators, textbooks and materials, equipment, supplies, and local initiatives. Additional funding is provided for the repair, maintenance, and building of schools.

Further funds are provided for boards with unique needs such as special education classes, English as Second Language, and remote schools.

If a school board does not follow the rules imposed by the province, the Minister of Education may take it over. This could occur, for example, if a board fails to follow prescribed courses of study and minimum teaching time, or applies funds contrary to the Legislative Grant Regulations (*Education Act*, section 230). In addition, the Minister has the authority to scrutinize the financial affairs of a board. This includes the power to direct the board to comply with Ministry policies, such as the requirement that boards maintain a balanced operating budget. Failure to comply could lead to the appointment by the Minister of a supervisor to run the board in place of the elected trustees. This occurred in 2007 when the Dufferin-Peel Catholic District School Board refused to balance its budget by raising taxes or reducing costs.

In 2010, the government increased its oversight authority by granting the Minister of Education the authority to review a board's performance and recommend measures for improvement. Under *Regulation 43/10: Provincial Interest in Education,* the Minister may provide for a review of a board's performance if the Minister has concerns about any of the following:

- the academic achievement of students;
- the health and safety of students;
- board governance;
- the performance of the board or director of education in carrying out statutory duties;
- the level of involvement by parents.

The Minister may then make recommendations based on the findings of the reviewer, and require the board to report back on its implementation of the recommendations.

SCHOOL TRUSTEES

School trustees are representatives of the public who are responsible for educational policy and governance. They are elected every four years by the public and collectively establish policies for the board within the scope of their powers under the *Education Act.* Individually, they have no operational authority over the school system, as the day-to-day running of the system is guided by the director, with principals as managers of individual schools.

Some of the responsibilities of school board trustees under the *Education Act* include:

- determining the number, size, and location of schools;
- prudent management of the funds allocated by the province to support all board activities, including education programs for elementary and secondary school students, and the building and maintaining of schools;
- preparing an annual budget;
- developing policy for safe arrival programs for elementary schools;

- ensuring that schools abide by the *Education Act* and its regulations.

Meetings of the board and its standing committees are open to the public, though the board may hold parts of a meeting *in camera* (behind closed doors) if it is dealing with sensitive matters such as the security of board property; acquisition or disposal of a school site; intimate personal or financial information; salary negotiations; or litigation affecting the board (section 207).

STUDENT TRUSTEES

The role of student trustees was created to provide students with a voice in the political discussions at the school board level. Legislation now requires boards to arrange for the election of at least one but no more than three student trustees as representatives of all of the students in the jurisdiction (*Regulation 7/07*). Student trustees are elected by other students in a board. Hamilton District School Board, for example, has two student trustees, who may speak and vote on issues. They are neither members of the board (their votes are recorded but do not count as part of the official tally) nor entitled to attend *in camera* meetings.

SCHOOL ADMINISTRATORS

"Administrator" refers to principals and vice-principals who are responsible for the daily supervision and operations of a school. This involves maintaining school property and setting a school budget, ensuring the safety of both children and staff, and supervising staff. Administrators also hire teachers and administer Teacher Performance Appraisals (TPAs) on a regular basis.

The Ontario government removed administrators from the Ontario Teachers' Federation and its affiliates in 1996. This led to the formation of the Ontario Principals' Council and the Catholic Principals' Council of Ontario as professional bodies for administrators. Administrators must also maintain membership with the Ontario College of Teachers, which certifies and disciplines all educators.

COMMUNITY

The community refers to a wide variety of stakeholders such as parents, neighbours, community agencies, and businesses that surround a school. These may participate individually and informally, or they may form larger organizations to exert their influence. Community issues relate to student safety such as speed limits, bus drop-off zones, and well-lit schoolyards. The community is responsible for their property while the school board is responsible for board property. The community may also rent school buildings on the weekend to various sports or clubs. If a community centre or daycare is attached to the school, agreements are signed between the stakeholders.

The community also sets the moral standards, which directly affects schools and the educators who work in their proximity. This will be discussed further in chapter 7.

INDIGENOUS EDUCATION IN ONTARIO

While education is under provincial jurisdiction according to the *Constitution Act, 1867*, responsibility for Indigenous education is shared by the federal government and First Nations groups.

The Government of Canada, through the Ministry of Aboriginal Affairs and Northern Development, funds elementary and secondary education for First Nations students ordinarily residing on reserve and provides financial support for First Nation and Inuit post-secondary students.

While the federal government provides the funds, First Nations are generally responsible for providing education on reserve. For example, in Sioux Lookout District, Bearskin Lake's First Nations Local Education Authority manages and delivers elementary education in local schools. It builds the schools, hires principals and teachers, and coordinates all aspects of education. This is done through a tripartite education framework agreement between Canada, Ontario, and the Nishnawbe-Aski Nation (which represents forty-five First Nations encompassing almost 8,000 students). It then bands together with other First Nations to manage secondary education through the Northern Nishnawbe Education Council, which administers high schools and student residents in Pelican Falls and Thunder Bay. The Northern Nishnawbe Education Council also coordinates post-secondary student funding for Bearskin Lake and twenty-three other First Nations in Northwestern Ontario. Similar agreements exist in other parts of the country.

Aboriginal Affairs and Northern Development invests close to $2 billion per year in kindergarten to grade 12 education in support of 115,000 First Nations students. This includes funds to support First Nations students in provincial schools and seven federally operated schools. It also funds over 22,000 post-secondary students. While this is a large amount of money, it has fallen significantly below inflation and First Nations population growth. Particularly problematic, in the view of First Nations, is the large per-capita gap between funding on reserve and in provincial schools. First Nations students on reserve are funded $2,000 to $3,000 less than provincial school students, with no dedicated funds for special education and little funding for other supports. This funding shortfall has contributed to overcrowding in dilapidated, unhealthy buildings. When First Nations students are educated in public schools, however, those schools receive a funding level equivalent to that for provincial students.

This has led the Assembly of First Nations to promote increased funding and more local autonomy. In 2014, years of bilateral consultation led to the announcement of a *First Nations Education Act* with significantly more funding and accountability. First Nations across Canada vigorously opposed this federal legislation, alleging that it left the government with the power to set and apply standards for schools on reserves. First Nations, however, insist that they should control their children's education and ensure that First Nations languages and education are supported.

The Ontario government has also signalled a commitment to Indigenous education. This is outlined in the *Ontario First Nation, Métis, and Inuit Education Policy Framework* (Ontario Ministry of Education, 2005). The document identifies two key priorities: close the gap between Indigenous and non-Indigenous students in literacy and numeracy and increase rates of retention, graduation, and advancement to postsecondary studies for the 50,000 Indigenous students who attend provincially funded elementary and secondary schools in Ontario. The framework also clarifies the roles and relationships of the ministry, school boards, and schools in their efforts to help Indigenous students achieve their educational goals. Further, it identifies ways to engage First Nation, Métis, and Inuit students and the communities from which they come.

CHECKING YOUR UNDERSTANDING

- The law is a set of rules a society develops to protect the rights and freedoms of its citizens.

- Much of our law is derived from common law developed by judges in England.

- A precedent is a legal decision that applies to future cases with similar circumstances.

- Case citations are a nomenclature designed to assist in finding court decisions in legal books.

- A provincial statute is an act passed by the legislature and proclaimed as law by the Lieutenant Governor.

- A regulation is an order in council that supplements laws enacted through statute.

- Education is a provincial responsibility under the *Constitution Act, 1867*.

- Denominational rights of Roman Catholics in Ontario are protected under the *Constitution Act, 1867*.

- The *Canadian Charter of Rights and Freedoms* is the part of the Constitution that protects human and equality rights for all Canadians.

- The *Charter* also grants minority language educational rights to the English and French linguistic minority population of a province.

- Public law is divided into the categories of constitutional, criminal, and administrative law.

- Tort law and employment law are types of civil law.

- Education law is a term that refers to a range of laws that apply directly or indirectly to students, teachers, schools, and school boards.

- Under the *Education Act*, the Minister of Education has broad statutory authority over education in Ontario.

- Education at the local level is delegated to school boards consisting of elected trustees who develop policies in accordance with the duties and powers listed in the *Education Act*.

- Each board must appoint a director of education as chief executive officer; this person is responsible for running the system in accordance with board policy.

Applying Your Understanding

The administration of education in Ontario is shared between the Ministry of Education and local school boards.

With the help of Internet research, answer the following questions:

(1) Who is the Minister of Education?
(2) Who is the Deputy Minister of Education?
(3) Who is the Chair of the school board in your community?
(4) Who is the Director of Education in your local school board?

Also, consider attending a formal school board meeting to see your public school trustees in action. The dates and times of meetings can be found on the school board website.

CHAPTER 3

THE ONTARIO COLLEGE OF TEACHERS AND TEACHER FEDERATIONS

After reading this chapter, you will understand the development of the Ontario College of Teachers and the history of teacher federations. You will gain knowledge of the legislation that guides the College and examine disciplinary decisions.

Case Study: Maintaining Professionalism
Ontario College of Teachers v. JCKF (2013)

JCKF was employed as a secondary school teacher. On or about 2006, JCKF began to swear and throw chairs around the classroom in front of students. The outbursts continued, and JCKF began to yell and belittle support staff and demand services from them that were personal and inappropriate. Further problems arose when JCKF demanded that no one park in a particular parking spot at the school, to the point that teachers felt bullied and threatened. In a final incident, JCKF refused to teach because a chair was removed from the classroom. JCKF sent letters to board officials that were offensive and contained abusive language.

During a disciplinary hearing conducted by a discipline panel of the Ontario College of Teachers, testimony was given that JCKF was often difficult to get along with, had a history of being late, and had negative interactions with other teachers.

The discipline panel found JCKF guilty of professional misconduct and, more specifically, that:

- he failed to maintain the standards of the profession;
- he failed to comply with the *Education Act*;
- he committed acts that having regard to all of the circumstances would reasonably be regarded by members as disgraceful, dishonourable, or unprofessional;
- he engaged in conduct unbecoming a member.

Even though JCKF did retire from the profession, and chose not to attend his hearing, the discipline panel ordered that he receive a reprimand, complete a course on anger management, and undergo a psychiatric assessment, complying with any treatment plans suggested, before being allowed to return to the classroom.

In their decision, the discipline panel wrote that JCKF created a "culture of fear" in the school and that teachers are part of a team to create a "healthy, safe and secure environment."

This case appears in *Professionally Speaking*, June 2014.

---

(1) Do you think it is acceptable that the discipline panel ordered a psychiatric assessment?

(2) If a member of the profession retires, do they still have a disciplinary hearing?

(3) What impact did JCKF's actions have on students and teachers?

(4) What do you believe were the concerns of the discipline panel?

The case study above depicts behaviour that most would find unacceptable by a teacher. However, until 1997, there was no uniform code of conduct for teachers in Ontario. School boards and their local federations were responsible for monitoring teacher conduct and misconduct, and there was a great deal of variance throughout the province from one board to the next.

The need for more vigilance and a code of conduct was highlighted by the case of Ken Deluca, a teacher in Sault Ste. Marie, Ontario. Deluca was an elementary school teacher accused of sexual assault by thirteen female students from 1972 to 1993 (pre-Ontario College of Teachers). These actions ranged from forced kissing and groping, masturbating on top of girls, and sexual intercourse. Each student complained to their principal, who told them they were lying or exaggerating. The principals did not document the incidents or report them to the police or Children's Aid Society. Deluca was simply moved to another school where the abuse would start all over again (Robbins, 2000).

What brought Deluca's reign of terror to an end were parents who confronted the school board on three fronts beginning in 1993. First, they presented a petition with 10,000 signatures to the Ministry of Education, demanding an inquiry into the practices of the Sault Ste. Marie Roman Catholic District School Board regarding the conduct of Ken Deluca. Second, they had Deluca charged with forty-one offences of sexual assault dating as far back as the 1970s. Third, the parents also launched a class action against the Sault Ste. Marie Roman Catholic District School Board for neg-ligence and failing to protect the students, who had ranged from ages ten to eighteen (Zuker, Redmond & Gannon, 2013).

In April 1996, Deluca pleaded guilty and served forty months in prison. As well, the Sault Ste. Marie Roman Catholic District School Board settled the class-action lawsuit in 1998 by paying the thirteen families compensa-tion for their trauma and grief.

Considering the scope of public outcry, the Ministry of Education decided to launch a provincial investigation in 1999. Justice Sydney Robbins (2000) was hired to investigate the matter, and the Robbins Report revealed a complete lack of accountability by many school boards, administrators, teachers, and federations. Robbins also exposed a lack of consistency across the province regarding reporting procedures, documentation, accountabil-ity, and disciplining of teachers. The Deluca case occurred at a point when Ontario education was already undergoing drastic reform and the Ontario College of Teachers was in its first years of implementation.

THE DEVELOPMENT OF THE ONTARIO COLLEGE OF TEACHERS

Until 1998, Ontario teachers governed themselves through the Ontario Teachers' Federation (OTF), the membership of which consists of the various federations (or unions) representing teachers in publicly funded schools.

One of the recommendations of the Ontario's Royal Commission on Learning (1994) was the establishment of a college of teachers. The commissioners argued that "teaching should be a self-governing profession, with greater responsibility and greater autonomy for teachers" (p. 17).

As a result, in 1996 the government of Ontario passed the *Ontario College of Teachers Act,* which established the Ontario College of Teachers. Since 1998, the College has acted as the professional standards and regulatory body for the teaching profession. Ontario is only the second Canadian province to establish self-regulation for teachers. This is part of a broader trend in the 1990s that has resulted in provincial government legislation establishing self-regulatory colleges or councils for professions such as nurses, social workers, social service workers, and real estate agents.

One of the reasons for this separation of tasks between OTF and the College was the perception that professional standards needed to be determined and maintained by an independent body. In medicine, for example, the Ontario Medical Association is the advocacy group for doctors, while the College of Physicians and Surgeons of Ontario remains at arm's-length. Another reason is that the profession can regulate itself more effectively than the government can. The government, however, does review the activities of various professional colleges, and the colleges must operate within the constraints imposed by the relevant acts and regulations.

According to its website (http://www.the College.ca/about/), the College:

- ensures Ontario students are taught by skilled teachers who adhere to clear standards of practice and conduct;
- establishes standards of practice and conduct;
- issues teaching certificates and may suspend or revoke them;
- accredits teacher education programs and courses;
- provides for ongoing professional learning opportunities for members;
- investigates complaints of misconduct or incompetence made against members. Disciplinary hearings are open to the public

and a summary of each hearing and the outcome is published in *Professionally Speaking*, the College magazine, and online under Disciplinary Decisions;

- investigates complaints that members are unfit to practice due to medical or other reasons. This process is not public due to the nature of the complaints.

The specific objectives (or "objects") of the College are listed in section 3(1) of the act:

1. To regulate the profession of teaching and to govern its members.

2. To develop, establish and maintain qualifications for membership in the College.

3. To accredit professional teacher education programs offered by post-secondary educational institutions.

4. To accredit ongoing education programs for teachers offered by post-secondary educational institutions and other bodies.

5. To issue, renew, amend, suspend, cancel, revoke and reinstate certificates of qualification and registration.

6. To provide for the ongoing education of members of the College.

7. To establish and enforce professional standards and ethical standards applicable to members of the College.

8. To receive and investigate complaints against members of the College and to deal with discipline and fitness to practice issues.

9. To develop, provide and accredit educational programs leading to certificates of qualification additional to the certificate required for membership, including but not limited to certificates of qualification as a supervisory officer, and to issue, renew, amend, suspend, cancel, revoke and reinstate such additional certificates.

10. To communicate with the public on behalf of the members of the College.

11. To perform such additional functions as are prescribed by the regulations.

According to section 3(2), "in carrying out its objects, the College has a duty to serve and protect the public interest."

ORGANIZATION OF THE COLLEGE OF TEACHERS

The Ontario College of Teachers, like other self-regulatory professional bodies, has a board of directors and an administrative branch.

A Governing Council functions as the board of directors of the College. It has thirty-seven members, twenty-three of whom are elected by Ontario teachers and fourteen who are appointed by the Ontario government (and appointed by the Lieutenant Governor in Council). The teacher positions include representatives of principals' organizations, private schools, and faculties of education. The council, which has an elected chair, develops and approves policies that regulate the teaching profession. Members of the council are active on a wide range of College committees, including Accreditation, Human Resources, Editorial Board, Fitness to Practise, and Discipline.

The Registrar, the chief executive officer of the College, is directly accountable to the council. The Registrar is responsible for the College's operational duties and, with the assistance of a management team, directly supervises the staff to ensure that they are fulfilling their duties with respect to the College's functions. With over 239,000 members, the College is a large, complex, and sophisticated operation. Its staff is divided into four administrative departments:

1. Corporate and Council Services is responsible for administration, communication, policy and research, and information technology.
2. Membership Services maintains membership records, evaluates credentials, and provides client services.
3. Investigation and Hearings is responsible for the intake, investigation, and hearings of complaints of professional misconduct, incompetence, and incapacity.

4. Standards of Practice and Accreditation supports the development and implementation of professional standards, as well as ongoing professional development related to the standards.

MEMBERSHIP

The *Ontario College of Teachers Act* (1996) states that anyone holding a certificate of qualification and registration is a member of the College, and, since the *Education Act* defines "teacher" as a member of the College of Teachers, only persons who hold a certificate of qualification in some form from the College are legally permitted to teach in a publicly funded school in Ontario. Private schools are not bound by the *Education Act*, though many of them do prefer their teachers to be members of the College.

In order to remain in good standing, members must pay an annual membership fee. Members under investigation remain in good standing unless there is a finding of professional misconduct. Teachers in publicly funded schools pay their fees automatically through payroll deduction. Other members of the College not working in publicly funded schools may be billed annually. Administrative fees are charged to lapsed members who seek to reactivate their memberships.

The College maintains a registry of all past and present members (deceased members are removed from the public register). All teachers, including those whose membership has lapsed, can be found by going to Find a Teacher on the College website (www.oct.ca). This registry contains the names of members, as well as their professional qualifications. If there is a finding of professional misconduct against a member, this, too, is listed.

As teachers take further qualifications (e.g., through another degree or an additional qualification course), they provide documentation to the College so that the registry can be updated. These additional qualifications may also be considered by school boards for determining suitability to teach particular subjects or grade levels and, in some cases, for advances in levels of pay.

REGISTRATION

A teacher who graduates from an Ontario teacher education program may apply for a Certificate of Qualification and Registration. This certificate lists their academic and professional qualifications. Out-of-province and international applicants who are accepted for College membership receive an Interim Certificate of Qualification (ICQ). The more complicated application process for teachers educated outside of Canada is outlined online under "Internationally Educated Teachers." (Go to http://theCollege.ca.)

In 2007, an Iranian refugee won a thirteen-year battle to become qualified by the College of Teachers. Fatima Siadat had been unable to fulfill the requirement that her qualification papers must come directly from the issuing authorities, because she was a refugee from Iran. The College did not have an alternative method of evaluating her teaching qualifications and experience. In *Siadat v. Ontario College of Teachers* (2007), Justice John Brockenshire of the Ontario Superior Court of Justice wrote that the College had failed to meet the obligation to properly interpret and apply the relevant law and the obligation to provide adequate reasons for its decision, that its decision must be rescinded, and that the application of Ms. Siadat must be referred back to the committee for re-hearing.

After the ruling, the College agreed to work with Siadat to develop an innovative way to assess her teaching credentials.

Foundations of Professional Practice

Teachers in Ontario are guided by the profession's standards of practice. These standards, initially approved in 1999, outline in broad terms the knowledge, skills, and values inherent in the teaching profession. The standards were revised in 2006 following an extensive consultation with teachers and members of the public. Now formally known as the *Foundations of Professional Practice* (OCT, 2006), they outline the principles of ethical behaviour, professional practice, and ongoing learning for the teaching profession in Ontario. *Foundations of Professional Practice* is summarized in chapter 1.

According to the introduction of this document:

> The standards describe what it means to be a member of the teaching profession in Ontario and reflect widely shared beliefs within the profession. They articulate the goals and aspirations of a teaching profession dedicated to fostering student learning and preparing Ontario students

to participate in a democratic society. College members use the standards to reflect on their own development as teaching professionals and inform their practice and ongoing learning choices. (p. 4)

The foundations of professional practice do not have the force of law. Rather, they are intended to act as guidelines for teachers in their classroom practice and ongoing professional development. Nonetheless, according to some experts, "it is reasonable to expect that they will be considered and applied" (McIntyre & Bloom, 2002, p. 74) in professional misconduct cases. Moreover, the five standards of practice described below are reflected in the sixteen competency statements used by principals and other school board officials to evaluate teachers. (The performance appraisal of new and experienced teachers is examined in more detail in chapter 10.)

Case Study: Following the Standards of the Profession
Ontario College of Teachers v. MI (2014)

MI was employed as an elementary teacher. Believing the classroom to be too cold for students, MI brought a portable heater to the school, which subsequently fell and burned a student's hand. In one incident, MI grabbed a student's wrist and left a red mark. As a form of discipline, MI made students kneel on the ground and put tape across their mouth. The board investigated these allegations and determined that MI needed to take a course on classroom management and anger management. As well, MI was moved to another school.

A second incident occurred in which MI pushed a student into a closet. MI was suspended for ten days and reported to the Ontario College of Teachers.

MI attended the disciplinary hearing and pleaded guilty in front of a discipline panel. Legal counsel for both the College and the member presented an agreed statement of facts and joint submission on penalty. The discipline panel found MI guilty of professional misconduct, and ordered that she receive a reprimand and a one-month suspension and complete a second course on classroom management. As well, MI's name was published in *Professionally Speaking*, the College magazine, and online under Disciplinary Decisions on the College's website.

This case appears in *Professionally Speaking*, December 2014.

(1) What is the purpose of a suspension?

(2) What information do you think would be covered in a course on classroom management?

(3) What is the duty of care expected of a teacher?

PROFESSIONAL MISCONDUCT AND THE DISCIPLINARY PROCESS

The College, under a mandate set out in the *Ontario College of Teachers Act* (1997), investigates complaints against its members made by any member of the public or the profession, including colleagues, administrators, or parents. The discipline process is regulated by *Ontario Regulation 437/97: Professional Misconduct*, and all members of the Ontario College of Teachers, including teachers, administrators, superintendents, and directors, are bound by it. It is wise for all educators to make the details of this legislation known and the consequences for not adhering to it. Following are the items listed in *Regulation 437/97*.

REGULATION 437/97: PROFESSIONAL MISCONDUCT

1. The following acts are defined as professional misconduct for the purposes of subsection 30 (2) of the Act:

    1. Providing false information or documents to the College or any other person with respect to the member's professional qualifications.

    2. Inappropriately using a term, title or designation indicating a specialization in the profession which is not specified on the member's certificate of qualification and registration.

    3. Permitting, counselling or assisting any person who is not a member to represent himself or herself as a member of the College.

    4. Using a name other than the member's name, as set out in the register, in the course of his or her professional duties.

5. Failing to maintain the standards of the profession.

6. Releasing or disclosing information about a student to a person other than the student or, if the student is a minor, the student's parent or guardian. The release or disclosure of information is not an act of professional misconduct if,

    i.   the student (or if the student is a minor, the student's parent or guardian) consents to the release or disclosure, or

    ii. if the release or disclosure is required or allowed by law.

7. Abusing a student verbally.

7.1 Abusing a student physically.

7.2 Abusing a student psychologically or emotionally.

7.3 Abusing a student sexually.

8. Practising or purporting to practise the profession while under the influence of any substance or while adversely affected by any dysfunction,

    i.   which the member knows or ought to know impairs the member's ability to practise, and

    ii. in respect of which treatment has previously been recommended, ordered or prescribed but the member has failed to follow the treatment.

9. Contravening a term, condition or limitation imposed on the member's certificate of qualification and registration.

10. Failing to keep records as required by his or her professional duties.

11. Failing to supervise adequately a person who is under the professional supervision of the member.

12. Signing or issuing, in the member's professional capacity, a document that the member knows or ought to know contains a false, improper or misleading statement.

13. Falsifying a record relating to the member's professional responsibilities.

14. Failing to comply with the Act or the regulations or the by-laws.

15. Failing to comply with the *Education Act* or the regulations

made under that Act, if the member is subject to that Act.

16. Contravening a law if the contravention is relevant to the member's suitability to hold a certificate of qualification and registration.

17. Contravening a law if the contravention has caused or may cause a student who is under the member's professional supervision to be put at or to remain at risk.

18. An act or omission that, having regard to all the circumstances, would reasonably be regarded by members as disgraceful, dishonourable or unprofessional.

19. Conduct unbecoming a member.

20. Failing to appear before a panel of the Investigation Committee to be cautioned or admonished, if the Investigation Committee has required the member to appear under clause 26 (5) (c) of the Act:

21. Failing to comply with an order of a panel of the Discipline Committee or an order of a panel of the Fitness to Practise Committee.

22. Failing to co-operate in a College investigation.

23. Failing to take reasonable steps to ensure that the requested information is provided in a complete and accurate manner if the member is required to provide information to the College under the Act and the regulations.

24. Failing to abide by a written undertaking given by the member to the College or by an agreement entered into by the member with the College.

25. Failing to respond adequately or within a reasonable time to a written inquiry from the College.

26. Practising the profession while the member is in a conflict of interest.

27. Failing to comply with the member's duties under the *Child and Family Services Act*.

2. A finding of incompetence, professional misconduct or a similar

finding against a member by a governing authority of the teaching profession in a jurisdiction other than Ontario that is based on facts that would, in the opinion of the Discipline Committee, constitute professional misconduct as defined in section 1, is defined as professional misconduct for the purposes of subsection 30 (2) of the Act. O. Reg. 437/97, s. 2.

The Investigation Committee of the Ontario College of Teachers

The Investigation Committee, which includes members of College Council, meets on a regular basis to consider complaints made against a member. These meetings are not open to the public and a variety of outcomes may occur:

- The Committee may refuse to proceed further with a complaint if it finds the complaint to be frivolous, vexatious or otherwise an abuse of process, or that it is outside the jurisdiction of the College.
- The Committee may dismiss a complaint or suggest voluntary complaint resolution.
- The Committee may ratify an agreement reached through the College's Complaint Resolution Program.
- The Committee may caution or admonish the member in writing or in person, if issues need to be addressed but do not warrant discipline.
- The Committee may refer the matter in whole or in part to the Discipline Committee for a hearing if the information alleges professional misconduct or incompetence.
- The Committee may refer the matter to the Fitness to Practise Committee for a hearing if the information suggests that there may be health-related issues affecting the member's ability to teach such as a diagnosis of a physical or mental condition. (OCT)

Educator Support During the Investigative and Disciplinary Process

Educators may be protected and supported by a number of different associations and federations. The chart below outlines the various organizations that step in to support educators if an investigation, discipline measures, or a disciplinary hearing occur.

Title	Representative
Teacher	Teacher Federations (ETFO, OSSTF, OECTA, and AEFO)
Administrator	Ontario Principals' Council (OPC), Catholic Principals' Council of Ontario (CPCO) Association des directions et directions adjointes des écoles franco-ontariennes (ADFO)
Superintendent	Ontario Public Supervisory Officers Association (OPSOA)
Director	Council of Ontario Directors (CODE)

Several exceptions must be noted. Educators fired from a school board may not receive legal representation by their federation or association at a disciplinary hearing. The same is true for members found guilty of a criminal charge and incarcerated. In these cases, the educator has the option of hiring an independent lawyer or self-representing in a hearing.

Figure 3-1

THE INVESTIGATIVE AND DISCIPLINARY PROCESS FOR ONTARIO EDUCATORS

Canada's legal system is quite complex and involves a number of disciplinary pathways, as noted in chapter 2. An educator—a term that encompasses teachers, administrators, superintendents, and directors—can be disciplined by the school board, court system, and/or the Ontario College of Teachers. All of these systems can result in multiple investigations, hearings, and consequences.

This section focuses on the disciplinary process for educators set out in *Regulation 437/97: Professional Misconduct.* The prospect of professional discipline and sanctions is frightening. It is also a confusing process that most educators know very little about. The following diagrams take you through different scenarios and the steps that can occur if a teacher has been accused of wrongdoing.

Scenario 1: Accusation of Physical Abuse
Criminal Investigation

Figure 3-2

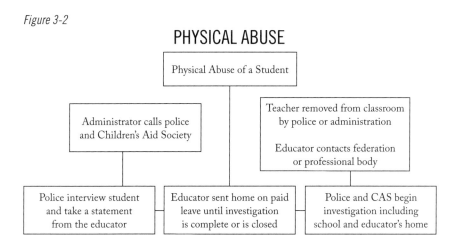

PHYSICAL ABUSE

Physical Abuse of a Student

Administrator calls police and Children's Aid Society

Teacher removed from classroom by police or administration

Educator contacts federation or professional body

Police interview student and take a statement from the educator

Educator sent home on paid leave until investigation is complete or is closed

Police and CAS begin investigation including school and educator's home

In scenario 1, a serious accusation of physical or sexual abuse involving a student has been made. In this case, it is the administrator's duty to inform both the police and Children's Aid Society (if the student is under sixteen years of age) immediately. School board, CAS, and criminal investigations may take place simultaneously, but they are very different in scope. A criminal investigation by the police and a CAS investigation can involve interviewing students, teachers, and family members, and the police can seize computers and cell phones, both at school and at an educator's home. A board investigation is limited to the school and involves interviewing students and teachers. As well, school boards have the right to seize any information that is part of board property including school computers, laptops, and information in school emails. Often, schools will cooperate with the police and hand over any information they have found.

The timeframe for board and police investigations can vary depending on the severity of the accusations. If the Crown Attorney believes it has enough evidence to convict an educator, a court date is set. If not, charges are dropped and the educator can return to work. However, if the board determines there was *professional misconduct*, with or without evidence of *criminal conduct*, it must refer the case to the Ontario College of Teachers to investigate. In this last instance, a third investigation by the College occurs and may result in a disciplinary hearing.

Case Study: Violating Student, Colleague, and Parent Trust
Ontario College of Teachers v. SM (2013)

Beginning in 2009, SM, a male teacher in an elementary school, pretended on social media to be a female student and befriended male students in the same school. SM asked the male students to expose their genitals via a webcam. A colleague found that her son had posted a sexually explicit video of himself on Facebook and contacted the police. The mother was concerned because her son and this young girl were both under the age of sixteen, and she wanted the police to contact the girl's parents. The mother and the police were unaware that the "female student" was actually her son's classroom teacher and the mother's friend and colleague.

A search warrant of SM's home revealed 18 external hard drives and a total of 3,374 images of child pornography and 582 movies of child pornography. SM was found guilty of 10 charges of luring a child via a computer for sexual exploitation and one account of making child pornography under the *Criminal Code of Canada*.

SM was fired from the school board. After serving three years in jail, he chose not to appear at his disciplinary hearing. However, he submitted a document and pleaded guilty to professional misconduct including sexually abusing students.

The discipline panel found SM guilty of professional misconduct—more specifically, that he failed to maintain the standards of the profession; he abused students verbally, psychologically, and sexually; he failed to comply with the *Education Act*; he contravened the law; and he committed acts that would be seen as dishonourable, disgraceful, and unprofessional.

In their reasons for revocation, the discipline panel stated, "Targeting and luring children and perpetuating a market for child pornography that thrives on the exploitation and abuse of children is a crime that is most heinous." SM's membership was immediately revoked.

This case appears in *Professionally Speaking*, December 2013.

(1) Do you know if there are guidelines for teachers regarding social media?

(2) Should teachers address, in the classroom, safety and social media?

(3) If you found a teacher in your school was friends with students on Facebook, what would you do?

(4) Do you think it is acceptable that personal computers can be seized from a teacher's home?

Scenario 2: Accusation of Professional Misconduct
Board Investigation

Figure 3-3

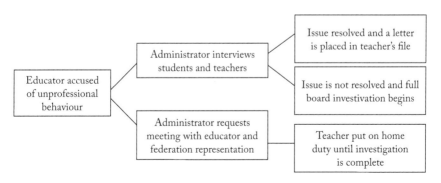

PROFESSIONAL MISCONDUCT

Educator accused of unprofessional behaviour

Administrator interviews students and teachers

Administrator requests meeting with educator and federation representation

Issue resolved and a letter is placed in teacher's file

Issue is not resolved and full board investivation begins

Teacher put on home duty until investigation is complete

In this scenario, a teacher faces a number of allegations related to professional behaviour in the school and classroom. The educator may not be following board policy, arriving late to work, leaving students alone, providing inadequate supervision on a field trip, or have poor classroom management skills. The accusation may have been made by a parent or student.

The administrator begins by taking a statement from the parent or student and then informs the educator that they need to attend a meeting with federation representation. Often these allegations do not warrant sending an educator home on paid duty; rather, an attempt is made to resolve them at the school level. If the administration and educator cannot come to an agreement, the administrator must inform the school board and the case is documented in the educator's file.

If the behaviours persist, the school board may suspend a teacher without pay, and a form of progressive discipline is applied. If the school board determines that the member continues to commit acts of professional misconduct, it refers the case to the Ontario College of Teachers, where an investigation takes place. This may lead to a disciplinary hearing, and sanctions may be placed on the educator's teaching certificate. Examples of sanctions placed on a teacher's Certificate of Qualification and Registration are reprimands (a verbal or written warning), suspension without pay for a period of time, or a requirement to complete a course on professional issues before returning to work.

Case Study: The Importance of Following Policy and Legislation
Ontario College of Teachers v. TR (2015)

TR worked in a secondary school. Allegations were brought against her from her school board stating that TR failed to report misconduct that was potentially harmful to her or her students, failed to supervise students on a field trip, and permitted students to disrupt the class on more than one occasion.

At a contested disciplinary hearing at the Ontario College of Teachers, students testified that TR's class was often loud with students yelling across the room and in the halls. In one incident a student came in to the class and refused to leave when asked by TR. The student cornered TR, threatened her if she reported the incident, and threw everything off her desk. Another student intervened and the student left.

In a second incident, students blew up a condom and proceeded to throw it around the classroom. TR did not intervene.

The incidents were brought to the attention of the administration, which questioned why a Conduct Report had not been filled out. The administration formally requested that an Incident Report be completed by TR, which they did not receive until a month later. TR stated that she chose to talk to the parents rather than fill in a Conduct Report.

The administration became aware of a third incident in which a stink bomb was released in the class, and TR once again did not fill out a Conduct Report. A fourth incident involved a poster with sexual images, which the administration confiscated during a class visit.

In a final incident, on a school field trip, TR was aware that students had engaged in theft. Students testified that some students were hanging out of the school bus yelling at people on the street. The bus driver had to stop the bus in order to gain control of the class. Students also testified that some students threw candy at TR and that she did not react.

Despite repeated communication from the administration that Conduct Reports needed to be completed as soon as possible as part of legislation requirements, TR did not do so. Instead, TR wrote emails trying to justify why Conduct Reports were not necessary.

As part of a scheduled Teacher Performance Appraisal (TPA), the administration observed TR's classroom, which was described as being in a state of "chaos," with TR not attempting to control the behaviour of the class. The administration was troubled by the lack of learning in TR's class and indicated that TR seemed "oblivious" to inappropriate comments and images in the classroom.

TR did not dispute the incidents in the disciplinary hearing but disagreed about the perception and how to manage students. After a lengthy hearing, the discipline panel found TR to be incompetent and to have displayed a lack of knowledge, skills, and judgment regarding the welfare of students.

TR was ordered to receive a reprimand by the discipline panel and complete a course in classroom management and effective student discipline. TR's name was published in *Professionally Speaking*, the College magazine, and under Disciplinary Decisions on the College's website.

This case appears in *Professionally Speaking*, June 2015.

(1) What were the main issues in this case?

(2) What legislation did TR not follow?

(3) What consequences can arise if a teacher chooses not to follow legislation?

(4) What can you learn from this case regarding classroom management?

Scenario 3: Accusation of Conduct Unbecoming
The College Investigation

Figure 3-4

CONDUCT UNBECOMING

Scenario 3 is considered one of the most controversial forms of investigation and discipline, as it involves an educator's behaviour *outside* the school and classroom hours. While many educators believe that their activity after hours does not influence their ability to teach, the Ontario College of Teachers and the Supreme Court of Canada have been very clear that it can.

Such a scenario could play out in various ways. A parent could report directly to the College an encounter with the teacher outside school hours. Or an administrator, aware of a teacher's conduct outside school hours, could investigate the allegations and discipline the teacher. If conduct persists, the administrator could refer a case to the College. A teacher may be arrested, with the police notifying the school. Even if the arrest is not related to children, the Director may inform the College.

Case Study: Respecting Professional Boundaries
Ontario College of Teachers v. RB (2014)

RB began carpooling to work with a colleague who lived close by. Shortly after, RB began to have feelings for his colleague and expressed his infatuation with her. The colleague stated that the feelings were not reciprocal, became uncomfortable, and stopped carpooling with RB. RB began to call her house despite repeated reminders by his colleague that she was married and not interested in him. At one point, her husband spoke to RB and requested that he stop calling their house and leave her alone. She also wrote RB a letter requesting that he cease all contact with her.

At a staff party several months later, RB began yelling at her. He threw the letter in her face. After being charged with harassment under the *Criminal Code*, RB pleaded guilty to repeatedly harassing his colleague over an eighteen-month period.

RB also pleaded guilty to a discipline panel of the College and was found to have committed professional misconduct—more specifically, that he:

- failed to maintain the standards of the profession;
- failed to comply with the *Education Act*, section 264;
- contravened a law;
- committed an act regarded by members as disgraceful, dishonourable, or unprofessional;
- engaged in conduct unbecoming a member.

RB was ordered to face a reprimand and take a course on appropriate boundaries with colleagues, and his name was published in *Professionally Speaking*, the College magazine, and under Disciplinary Decisions on the College's website.

This case appears in *Professionally Speaking*, September 2014.

(1) What are the issues in this case?

(2) Do you think it was right or fair that RB was disciplined by the Ontario College of Teachers for conduct outside the classroom?

(3) What does this case tell you about off-duty conduct?

The Disciplinary Hearing

Teachers summoned to attend a disciplinary hearing at the Ontario College of Teachers receive a Notice of Hearing detailing the allegations. The Notice of Hearing is also placed on the College's website and made available to the public. The disciplinary hearing follows a formal process governed by a variety of legislation and laws. All hearings follow the *Statutory Powers and Procedures Act* (1990), which outlines a fair process for those accused of professional misconduct or incompetence. This is commonly referred to as the *right* to due process and a fair trial.

The structure of a hearing is very similar to an actual court case. Three panel members function as adjudicators. All panels must be composed of one elected Member of Council and one appointed Member of Council. This ensures that both the public and the profession are represented at a hearing. To the right of the panel is a witness station and a court reporter. If young students give testimony, a screen may be put in place so that they do not have to face the accused. The member sits to the right of the panel with legal representation and often federation representation. To the left of the member is College Counsel, which often consists of one or two lawyers. To the right of the panel is Independent Legal Counsel, a lawyer who is impartial to the entire process and is present to ensure a fair trial and that everyone present follows legislation and policy. At the very back of the room is a public gallery, which may consist of the media, the member's families or friends, or parents who may have lodged the complaint against the educator.

A disciplinary hearing can last anywhere from one day to several years depending on the complexity of the case and whether the parties are able to reach an agreement on the facts and the appropriate disposition of the case.

Figure 3-5

THE DISCIPLINARY HEARING

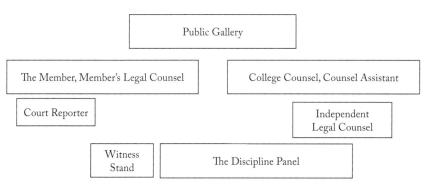

According to section 30(2) of the *Ontario College of Teachers Act*, in cases of professional misconduct:

A member may be found guilty of professional misconduct by the discipline panel, after a hearing, if the member has been guilty, in the opinion of the panel, of professional misconduct as defined in the regulations.

A wide range of possible penalties under the act include:

- revoking the member's teaching certificate;
- suspending the member's teaching certificate for up to twenty-four months;
- imposing specific terms, conditions, or limitations on the certificate;
- reprimanding, admonishing, and/or counselling the member;
- fines of up to $5,000;
- publication of the findings, including the member's name;
- fixing costs to be paid by the member.

In sentencing and assessing penalties, the panel may take into account mitigating factors (e.g., cooperation, guilty plea, or remorse) and aggravating factors (e.g., lack of remorse, degree of exploitation, or efforts to cover up). Also, all decisions are subject to appeal through the courts.

Fitness to Practise

The Fitness to Practise Committee conducts hearings into whether a member is physically or mentally incapacitated. Because incapacity does not involve culpable conduct, the committee seeks to balance protection of the public interest and the rehabilitation of the member.

The hearing procedures are similar to those employed in discipline cases. Also, the penalties are similar to those applied in incompetency cases, with the exception that the hearings are closed to the public. Cases in which the facts are disputed can involve complex medical testimony. Also, in its rulings, the panel must be careful not to violate the human rights of the member, which are protected under the *Ontario Human Rights Code* and the *Canadian Charter of Rights and Freedoms*.

Because the hearings are closed, the results of the Fitness to Practise hearings are generally unknown. If the member's certificate is restricted, then a notation is placed on the College's public register.

A case in which the member appealed the College's decision to the courts provides a useful glimpse into the workings of the panel. In *Sclater v. the Ontario College of Teachers* (2000), the member challenged the decision of the Fitness to Practise panel, which rejected a disposition of the case recommended by the member and the College lawyers prosecuting the case. The panel determined that the joint submission did not attend sufficiently either to the serious "boundary violations" committed by the teacher in her relations with students or to the concerns about her ability to "act in a position of trust." According to McIntyre & Bloom (2002), the panel ordered that, before her application for reinstatement could be considered, "she be suspended and that she undergo not less than 20 therapy sessions at her own expense" (p. 106), followed by a psychiatric evaluation, before her application for reinstatement could be considered. Ultimately, the courts sided with the Fitness to Practise panel, ruling that the teachers on the panel had sufficient knowledge of teaching to make this decision based on the evidence presented.

It is important to keep in mind that making a complaint to the Ontario College of Teachers is only one process for dealing with allegations of professional misconduct, incompetence, or incapacity. Complaints may also be pursued through internal school board disciplinary procedures, which are covered in board policy and the collective agreements made with the local affiliate of the teachers' federation.

TEACHER FEDERATIONS IN ONTARIO

The first organized labour groups of teachers were formed in 1888 by women teachers, and several of these groups banded together in 1918 to form the Federation of Women Teachers' Associations of Ontario (FWTAO). A group of secondary principals and teachers established the Ontario Secondary School Teachers' Federation (OSSTF) in 1919. The Ontario Public School Men Teachers' Federation (OPSMTF) was formed by male elementary school teachers in 1920. Established in 1939, the Association des enseignantes et des enseignants franco-ontariens (AEFO) is a French-language labour organization whose members work in Ontario's French-language Catholic public, elementary, and secondary schools and in other French-language establishments in Ontario. The Ontario English Catholic Teachers' Association (OECTA) was created in 1944. The amalgamation of FWTAO and OPSMTF created the Elementary Teachers' Federation of Ontario (EFTO) in 1998.

In 1935, FWTAO, OPSMTF, and OSSTF created the Ontario Teachers' Council (OTC), which became the Ontario Teachers' Federation (OTF) in 1944 with the establishment of the *Teaching Profession Act*. Currently, the four federations that make up the Ontario Teachers' Federation are important educational stakeholders. All four federations serve the same purpose: to protect their members. This is achieved, first and foremost, by: negotiating teachers' collective agreements with school boards (and, as of the spring of 2014, with the Ministry of Education); maintaining those collective agreements; providing ongoing support and education to its members; and supporting and upholding the public education system.

Prior to the establishment of teachers' unions, teachers often endured poor compensation and working conditions. They had no job security, no rights, no sick leave, and no pensions. Women teachers were paid considerably less than men, and could be terminated if they got married or became pregnant (Richter, 2006a; 2006b; 2007). At its second annual meeting in 1920, OSSTF became the first teachers' organization to pass a motion supporting the principle of "equal pay for equal work."

The *Teaching Profession Act* (1944) required all educators to become members of the Ontario Teachers' Federation as a condition of teaching in Ontario's publicly funded schools; however, it is the (then) five (now four) affiliates that hold the bargaining rights for their respective members. The main purpose of the federation was to protect teachers' working conditions and their salaries. As there was no legislated procedure for doing so, this initially was done on individual basis. It was not until July 1975, with the passage of Bill 100, the *School Boards' and Teachers' Collective Negotiation Act*, that a new set of fundamental principles was established to ensure that there would be no restrictions on the scope of bargaining, that the parties would be required to bargain in good faith, and, most importantly, that teachers had the right to strike and boards the right to lock them out.

Collective agreements deal with much more than salary, benefits, and class sizes. They can also include such things as:

a) Grievance procedures

b) Probationary teachers

c) Union rights and management rights

d) Pregnancy/parental leave

e) Staff allocation

f) Seniority

g) Physical environment/health and safety

h) Medical procedures

i) Salary schedule

j) Employee benefits

k) Criminal record checks

l) Performance appraisals

All unions, including teachers' unions, are charged with the "Duty of

Fair Representation" of its members under the *Ontario Labour Relations Act* (section 74):

> A trade union or council of trade unions, so long as it continues to be entitled to represent employees in a bargaining unit, shall not act in a manner that is arbitrary, discriminatory or in bad faith in the representation of any of the employees in the unit, whether or not members of the trade union or of any constituent union of the council of trade unions, as the case may be.

As such, most if not all collective agreements contain provisions that outline the teacher's right to union representation in matters related to a teacher's conduct and/or competence. The wording may vary slightly from contract to contract, but if the board requires a teacher to meet with his/her supervisor in order to answer to allegations of any kind related to possible discipline, the supervisor must inform the teacher that he/she has the right to have a union representative present. Failure by the employer to do so can result in the discipline being overturned. As such, this is an important point for teachers to know and understand regarding possible discipline or professional misconduct.

THE GRIEVANCE PROCESS

A grievance is a formal process for problem solving in which a bargaining unit can file a complaint against the employer when they believe there has been a violation of their contract. Because the bargaining unit is the official signatory to a collective agreement and the official representative of its members, only the bargaining unit may file the grievance, not an individual member.

Three forms of grievance are:

1. *Individual grievance* —an individual employee grievance may be initiated where the subject matter of the grievance is specific to the employee.
2. *Group grievance* —a group grievance may be initiated where a number of employees join together in filing their grievances.

3. *Policy grievance*—a union or policy grievance may be initiated where the subject matter of the grievance is of general interest and where individual employees may or may not be affected at the time that the grievance was filed.

In cases of some allegations against teachers, more than one investigation may occur, so it is important to note that a grievance can be initiated only to resolve a violation of the collective agreement. Grievances cannot stop an investigation by Children's Aid, the police, the Ontario College of Teachers, or a school board. However, if the matter relates to a member's conduct in relation to his/her employment, the union will still provide initial representation to ensure that his/her rights to due process are respected.

All grievances follow the same general process:

- A teacher who feels that his/her rights under the collective agreement have been violated must contact the union for advice.
- The union will gather information about the situation and, perhaps in conjunction with a grievance committee, will determine whether they feel a contract violation has taken place.
- If so, the union will proceed with the process as outlined in the collective agreement, which is commonly a multi-stage process:
  ° an informal stage in which the union tries to resolve the matter informally with the principal;
  ° if the informal stage proves unsuccessful, the union may proceed to formal step(s) in which the matter is addressed with the board—often one step with the Human Resources and, if unsuccessful there, a subsequent step with the director;
  ° if these formal stages are unsuccessful, the matter can be referred for arbitration.
- If a matter moves to arbitration, the Ontario Labour Relations Board becomes involved, and the matter is then dealt with by a single arbitrator or an arbitration panel. Matters decided by arbitration become part of the legal labour landscape and can be relied on by other arbitrators.

Not every matter that a teacher objects to, however, is necessarily a grievance. Sometimes, the union may decide not to take a matter forward through the grievance process if it believes there is no contract violation or if the matter is not of sufficient consequence to merit going to arbitration. In either case, the teacher may appeal the decision, in which case the bargaining unit or the provincial union will have an appeals process.

THE ROLE OF THE FEDERATION IN THE WORKPLACE

Although the Ontario Teachers' Federation plays no formal part in the hierarchical structure of the district school board, its local affiliates do provide the classroom teacher with advice and support, including legal support where necessary.

The collective agreement includes a salary grid for teachers based on years of experience and category placement. OSSTF has its own internal system for providing Certification Rating Statements to its members for category placement purposes. The other three affiliates require their members to apply to the Qualifications Evaluation Council of Ontario (QECO) for a Statement of Evaluation. Teachers are rated on the basis of their academic background and trade records.

Several other job-related items in addition to salary scale are typically negotiated at the bargaining table by the local affiliate. These include: insured benefits, such as coverage for prescription drugs and dental services; sick leave entitlement and retirement gratuity; working conditions, which typically cover such matters as preparation time, supervision time, and the number of hours a teacher can be required to teach in a day; provisions regarding seniority, transfer, and lay-offs; and a "just cause" clause, without which employers would be able to discipline teachers or terminate their employment far more easily.

Electing Federation Officers

Teachers' federations play a crucial role in the professional lives of their members. It is therefore important for teachers to understand their role in the negotiation of salaries, benefits, working conditions, and arbitration procedures.

It is also important for teachers to take seriously their democratic rights and responsibilities as federation members. As members, they will be called on to elect school representatives and district leaders, give a strike mandate to teams negotiating collective agreements, and vote to accept or reject contracts.

CHECKING YOUR UNDERSTANDING

- In 1998, teachers in Ontario became fully self-regulating with the creation of the Ontario College of Teachers, which has the power to issue, suspend, and revoke certificates.
- The College has one overriding duty: to serve and protect the public interest.
- The College has a Governing Council of elected and appointed members that establishes policy, works on committees, and oversees the work of the Registrar.
- The Registrar, who is directly responsible to the College council, is responsible for implementing policy, managing operations, and supervising staff.
- Since the *Education Act* defines "teacher" as a member of the Ontario College of Teachers, only persons who hold a certificate of qualification in some form from the College are permitted to teach in a publicly funded school in Ontario.
- In *Foundations of Professional Practice*, the College identifies four ethical standards (care, trust, respect, and integrity) and five standards of practice (commitment to students and students' learning, leadership in learning communities, ongoing professional learning, professional knowledge, and professional practice). It also outlines its Professional Learning Framework for the Teaching Profession.
- Acts by a member of the College of Teachers considered to be professional misconduct are defined in *Regulation 437/97: Professional Misconduct.*
- Complaints of professional misconduct or incompetence are directed to the Investigation Committee of College, which may

direct the complaint to the Discipline Committee or the Fitness to Practise Committee. A wide range of penalties are available under the act.

- Disciplinary hearings, which follow formal processes guided by law, are very similar to court cases. The accused member may have legal representation, and College counsel serves as the prosecutor. The three-person discipline panel is supported by independent legal counsel.
- Teachers have been considered professionals in Ontario since 1944, with the passage of the *Teaching Profession Act*, which established the Ontario Teachers' Federation. OTF now consists of four affiliates: AEFO, ETFO, OECTA, and OSSTF.
- The main purpose of OTF is to protect and promote the interests of teachers. Only persons employed by a board as teachers are members of OTF. Principals and vice-principals are not members.
- Collective agreements negotiated with school boards deal with salary, benefits and class sizes. They also address issues such as grievance procedures, seniority, and performance appraisal.
- Grievances are formal processes for dealing with complaints against employers.

APPLYING YOUR UNDERSTANDING

Many complaints made to the Ontario College of Teachers are not referred to the Discipline Committee but are dismissed or resolved through dispute resolution.

Before complaints proceed to the Discipline Committee, they are considered by the Investigation Committee. Complaints resolved at this level are generally not published, but samples of such complaints are published without identifying information in *Professionally Speaking* for illustrative purposes.

The summaries quoted below illustrate two cases from June 2007 that did not proceed to a hearing.

Case #1

Complaint: Unwarranted, unfair punishment of student and using "scare tactic."

Outcome of investigation: No investigation.

Parents of a grade 6 student complained about their child's teacher, who they said had "centered out [their child] for unwarranted punishment" and had "belittled" the student in a number of ways, including: not allowing the student to return to class to pick up a forgotten backpack; not allowing the student to go to the washroom; giving a detention for talking after their child said "excuse me" for bumping into another student; making the student stand by an outside wall as punishment; making the student redo an assignment, which the member could not find; sending the student to the hall after someone threw something at the teacher; etc.

The parents also alleged that the teacher used a "scare tactic" by having a lawyer write to them to cease and desist the false allegations being made against the member.

The Investigation Committee panel considering the complaint directed that the allegations not be investigated because they did not relate to professional misconduct, incompetence, or incapacity.

Case #2

Member: Not identified.

Decision: Admonished by the Investigation Committee.

Following notification by an employer, the Registrar initiated a complaint against a member of the College. The Registrar alleged that the member, an elementary teacher:

- hugged one or more students;
- held hands with one or more students;
- accessed inappropriate Internet sites on the classroom computer.

On January 26, 2006, the Investigation Committee ratified an MOA (memorandum of agreement) between the member and the College, in which the member:

- admitted the alleged conduct;
- agreed to be admonished, in writing, by the Investigation Committee;
- agreed to complete a course of instruction, pre-approved by the Registrar, regarding maintaining appropriate boundaries with students;
- agreed to provide the Registrar with a written report, prepared by the course practitioner, indicating whether the member recognized the need for teachers to establish and maintain appropriate student/teacher boundaries;
- agreed to notify the Registrar of any complaints of a similar nature made to his employer;
- agreed to a notation being placed on the public register.

PART B

TEACHERS AND SAFE SCHOOLS

CHAPTER 4

THE LEGAL DUTIES AND
RIGHTS OF TEACHERS

*After reading this chapter you will understand in broad terms the duties
of teachers and principals under the* Education Act *and its regulations.
The implications of these duties are explored by examining disciplinary
decisions of the Ontario College of Teachers, and legal cases from the
Ontario and Canadian court systems. The rights of teachers are also
delineated in relation to their duties. (Subsequent chapters address
duties and rights in specific areas of practice.)*

Case Study: Defining Boundaries with Social Media
Ontario College of Teachers v. IH (2014)

An openly gay teacher in a secondary school felt compelled to help a student who approached
him about "coming out." The teacher shared his own story and gave the student movies to
watch on sexuality, sexual orientation, and coming out. The student and the teacher then
became Facebook friends.

A second student from a different school in the school board approached the teacher
to engage in conversation on social media. This student propositioned the teacher, but the
teacher did not report this to the administration.

The teacher then exchanged personal information on social media about the second
student with the first.

The board became aware of these conversations and suspended the teacher for twenty days, and he was ordered to take a course on professional boundaries.

The incidents were reported to the Ontario College of Teachers, and a hearing was held. The discipline panel found the member guilty of professional misconduct and ordered that he receive a reprimand, be suspended for twenty days from June 27 to September 27 (already served at his board), and take a course on professional boundaries. In their decision, the discipline panel stated that "the use of electronic media is now firmly entrenched," revealing "many dangers for members of the profession, regardless of the intent."

This case appears in *Professionally Speaking*, June 2015.

(1) Why were some of the teacher's decisions considered unprofessional?
(2) In what ways was the teacher trying to be helpful to students?
(3) Do you agree with the discipline panel's penalty?
(4) What do you think would have been an appropriate penalty?

Educators are held in high regard as professionals and as people acting *in loco parentis*. They are also expected to act in a manner that befits their important roles as guardians, educators, and moral educators. This is evident in the *Education Act* and its regulations, which outline the responsibilities and duties of teachers, principals, and school boards. It is also reflected in court rulings, which defer to the judgment of educators who act reasonably and are pointed in criticisms of educators who do not. As citizens and educational professionals, teachers and principals also enjoy rights that must be protected.

DUTIES OF PRINCIPALS

Although the school board has the overall responsibility for providing instruction and adequate accommodation (*Education Act*, section 170(1)), it is the school principal who is specifically charged with the instruction and discipline of students, and for ensuring that each school is a safe and healthy place for students to learn. Section 265(1) of the act includes the following obligations for principals:

> It is the duty of a principal of a school, in addition to the principal's duties as a teacher,
>
> (a) to maintain proper order and discipline in the school; ...
>
> (j) to give assiduous attention to the health and comfort of the pupils, to the cleanliness, temperature and ventilation of the school, to the care of all teaching materials and other school property, and to the condition and appearance of the school buildings and grounds; ...
>
> (m) subject to an appeal to the board, to refuse to admit to the school or classroom a person whose presence in the school or classroom would in the principal's judgment be detrimental to the physical or mental well-being of the pupils ...

The duties of the principal are elaborated in *Regulation 298*, a regulation made under the *Education Act*.

> 11(1) The principal of a school, subject to the authority of the appropriate supervisory officer, is in charge of,
>
> (a) the instruction and the discipline of pupils in the school;
>
> (b) the organization and management of the school.
>
> 11(3) In addition to the duties under the Act and those assigned by the board, the principal of a school shall, except where the principal has arranged otherwise under subsection 26(3),
>
> (a) supervise the instruction in the school and advise and assist any teacher in co-operation with the teacher in charge of an organizational unit or program;
>
> (b) assign duties to vice-principals and to teachers in charge of organizational units or programs; ...
>
> (e) provide for the supervision of pupils during the period of time during each school day when the school buildings and playgrounds are open to pupils;

(f) provide for the supervision of and the conducting of any school activity authorized by the board; ...

(k) provide for instruction of pupils in the care of the school premises;

(l) inspect the school premises at least weekly and report forthwith to the board,

(i) any repairs to the school that are required, in the opinion of the principal,

(ii) any lack of attention on the part of the building maintenance staff of the school ...

Teachers should also be vigilant in complying with the standardized testing procedures of the Education Quality and Accountability Office (EQAO) when providing supports for students taking provincial tests. In this regard a principal was reprimanded, suspended for six months, and required to complete a course on professional ethics for not following EQAO legislation. The case below demonstrates a lack of professional judgment and perhaps a realization that standardized, legislated, testing is part of the law in Ontario.

Case Study: Not Following EQAO Legislation
Ontario College of Teachers v. RJC (2013)

During a three-year period, a principal at an elementary school did not follow proper procedure when instructing his staff on how to administer the EQAO test. He removed test materials from the package and provided them to teachers prior to the day of the assessment; modified the multiple choice answer sheet of at least one student; permitted or directed students who did not meet the requirements for accommodations to have scribes assist them with the test, and allowed students who did not have an Individual Education Plan or other permitted circumstances to leave the classroom to assist them with the test. He also told his staff that he had discretion over administering the test, which was not true.

RJC's school board investigated the matter, and the principal received a written warning. The EQAO withdrew its reporting of the school's results from 2007 to 2010, as the results were not valid.

RJC pleaded guilty of professional misconduct in front of a discipline panel of the Ontario College of Teachers. He was found guilty of: failing to maintain the standards of the profession; falsifying records; failing to comply with the *Education Act*; issuing a document that contained false information; and committing acts that would be seen as unprofessional, disgraceful, and dishonourable.

The discipline panel ordered that RJC receive a reprimand, that the Registrar suspend his licence for six months, that he complete a course in professional ethics at his own cost, and that his name appear in *Professionally Speaking*.

This case appears in *Professionally Speaking*, September 2014.

(1) What effect do you think the principal's actions had on the school community?

(2) The school board issued a warning while the discipline panel issued a six-month suspension on the member's teaching certificate. What sort of penalty would you issue?

(3) What is the significance of EQAO protocol?

As the principal teacher and the person charged with the management and organization of the school, the principal assumes wide-ranging authority and obligations. Recognizing the broad scope of the principal's duties, the act requires teachers to assist the principal in various ways. The case above illustrates not only the seriousness of following EQAO protocol but also the amount of responsibility bestowed on principals to supervise their teachers and make sure they follow legislation as well.

THE DUTIES OF THE PRINCIPAL UNDER THE OCCUPATIONAL HEALTH AND SAFETY ACT

Schools are considered places of employment, and all staff within a school are considered employers or employees. Principals are considered employers, and under the *Occupational Health and Safety Act* (1990), Section 25, all employers must ensure that:

(a) the equipment, materials and protective devices as prescribed are provided;

(b) the equipment, materials and protective devices provided by the employer are maintained in good condition;

(c) the measures and procedures prescribed are carried out in the workplace;

(d) the equipment, materials and protective devices provided by the employer are used as prescribed; and

(e) a building, structure, or any part thereof, or any other part of a workplace, whether temporary or permanent, is capable of supporting any loads that may be applied to it,

> (i)　as determined by the applicable design requirements established under the version of the Building Code that was in force at the time of its construction,
>
> (ii)　in accordance with such other requirements as may be prescribed, or
>
> (iii)　in accordance with good engineering practice, if sub clauses (i) and (ii) do not apply. R.S.O. 1990, c. O.1, s. 25 (1); 2011, c. 11, s. 9.

Principals must ensure that all equipment in classrooms are safe and checked on a monthly basis. Special attention is given to workshops, science labs, cooking facilities, and gym equipment.

Principals must also ensure that teachers and teacher candidates who work with any form of chemicals must be trained according to Health Canada's *Workplace Hazardous Materials Information System (WHMIS)* and all chemicals must have a WHMIS label to clearly identify what is contained in jars, containers, etc.

DUTIES OF TEACHERS

Teachers employed by school boards assume statutory and regulatory duties as outlined in the *Education Act* and *Regulation 298*. These broad duties may be further defined—narrowed or expanded—in the collective agreement between a board and a teachers' federation.

In addition, the duties outlined in the regulations made under the *Teaching Profession Act* and *Ontario College of Teachers Act* apply to teachers by virtue of their membership in the Ontario Teachers' Federation and the Ontario College of Teachers. (See chapter 1.)

Teachers are charged with the duty of maintaining a safe and supportive learning environment within their classrooms. This responsibility also extends to their duties in other parts of school.

Section 264(1) of the *Education Act* states:

It is the duty of a teacher and a temporary teacher:

teach

(a) to teach diligently and faithfully the classes or subjects assigned to the teacher by the principal;

learning

(b) to encourage the pupils in the pursuit of learning;

religion and morals

(c) to inculcate by precept and example respect for religion and the principles of Judaeo-Christian morality and the highest regard for truth, justice, loyalty, love of country, humanity, benevolence, sobriety, industry, frugality, purity, temperance and all other virtues;

co-operation

(d) to assist in developing co-operation and co-ordination of effort among the members of the staff of the school;

discipline

(e) to maintain, under the direction of the principal, proper order and discipline in the teacher's classroom and while on duty in the school and on the school ground;

language of instruction

(f) in instruction and in all communications with the pupils in regard to discipline and the management of the school,

    (i) to use the English language, except where it is impractical to do so by reason of the pupil not understanding English, and except in respect of instruction in a language other than English when such other language is being taught as one of the subjects in the course of study, or

(ii) to use the French language in schools or classes in which French is the language of instruction except where it is impractical to do so by reason of the pupil not understanding French, and except in respect of instruction in a language other than French when such other language is being taught as one of the subjects in the course of study;

timetable

(g) to conduct the teacher's class in accordance with a timetable which shall be accessible to pupils and to the principal and supervisory officers;

professional activity days

(h) to participate in professional activity days as designated by the board under the regulations;

absence from school

(i) to notify such person as is designated by the board if the teacher is to be absent from school and the reason therefor;

school property

(j) to deliver the register, the school key and other school property in the teacher's possession to the board on demand, or when the teacher's agreement with the board has expired, or when for any reason the teacher's employment has ceased; and

textbooks

(k) to use and permit to be used as a textbook in a class that he or she teaches in an elementary or a secondary school,

(i) in a subject area for which textbooks are approved by the Minister, only textbooks that are approved by the Minister, and

(ii) in all subject areas, only textbooks that are approved by the board;

duties assigned

(l) to perform all duties assigned in accordance with this Act and the regulations.

Section 20 of *Regulation 298* supplements the duties under the *Education Act* by indicating that teachers shall also:

(a) be responsible for effective instruction, training and evaluation of the progress of pupils in the subjects assigned to the teacher and for the management of the class or classes, and report to the principal on the progress of pupils on request;

(b) carry out the supervisory duties and instructional program assigned to the teacher by the principal and supply such information related thereto as the principal may require;

(c) where the board has appointed teachers under section 14 or 17, co-operate fully with such teachers and with the principal in all matters related to the instruction of pupils;

(d) unless otherwise assigned by the principal, be present in the class-room or teaching area and ensure that the classroom or teaching area is ready for the reception of pupils at least fifteen minutes before the commencement of classes in the school in the morning and, where applicable, five minutes before the commencement of classes in the school in the afternoon;

(e) assist the principal in maintaining close co-operation with the community;

(f) prepare for use in the teacher's class or classes such teaching plans and outlines as are required by the principal and the appropriate supervisory officer and submit the plans and outlines to the principal or the appropriate supervisory officer, as the case may be, on request;

(g) ensure that all reasonable safety procedures are carried out in courses and activities for which the teacher is responsible;

(h) co-operate with the principal and other teachers to establish and maintain consistent disciplinary practices in the school;

(i) ensure that report cards are fully and properly completed and pro-cessed in accordance with the guides known in English as Guide to the Provincial Report Card, Grades 1-8 and Guide to the Provincial Report Card, Grades 9-12, and in French as Guide d'utilisation du bulletin scolaire de l'Ontario de la 1ère à la 8e année and Guide du bulletin scolaire de l'Ontario de la 9e à la 12e année, as the case may be, both available electronically through a link in the document known in English as Ontario Student Record (OSR) Guideline, 2000 and in French as Dossier scolaire de l'Ontario: Guide, 2000, online at www.edu.gov.on.ca/eng/document/curricul/osr/osr.html or www.edu.gov.on.ca/fre/document/curricul/osr/osrf.html;

(j) co-operate and assist in the administration of tests under the Education Quality and Accountability Office Act, 1996;

(k) participate in regular meetings with pupils' parents or guardians;

(l) perform duties as assigned by the principal in relation to co-operative placements of pupils; and

(m) perform duties normally associated with the graduation of pupils. R.R.O. 1990, Reg. 298, s. 20; O. Reg. 95/96, s. 2; O. Reg. 209/03, s. 1.

The *Education Act, Regulation 298*, and other legislation make it clear that teachers and principals owe a duty of care to their students due to their special relationship of trust. Since parents are required to send their children to school, they are entitled to expect that their children will receive excellent teaching in orderly and welcoming classrooms, in a safe and supportive school environment.

---

(1) What are the duties of the teacher in the classroom?

(2) What are the duties of the teacher outside the classroom?

(3) Did any of these duties surprise you? If so, why?

TEACHERS' INSTRUCTIONAL DUTIES

The primary classroom duties of the teacher are to to "teach diligently and faithfully the classes or subjects assigned to the teacher by the principal," "encourage the pupils in the pursuit of learning," and instill core values through both words and actions (*Education Act,* section 264).

What do these broad statements mean in practice?

Teach Diligently and Faithfully

Teachers are expected to be diligent and faithful in caring for students and promoting learning in their classrooms. As professionals charged with great social responsibilities, teachers are responsible for developing effective instructional resources, adapting them to the needs of their students, and evaluating the achievement of learning outcomes. This diligence and faithfulness is directed two ways. First, teachers are to show due care for the well-being and learning of students put into their charge by parents/guardians in a particular community. Second, they are to teach within the constraints of board and provincial curriculum guidelines and assess student achievement in relation to determined standards.

As professionals, teachers are charged with the task of adapting the curriculum to meet the needs of the students in their classes. This means that they have academic freedom in making judgments concerning the best ways to deliver the curriculum in particular teaching and learning contexts.

So long as they can demonstrate that their conduct is professional and their intentions thoughtful, most teachers are not likely to run into trouble for the decisions they make in their classroom teaching.

The effectiveness of teachers is being increasingly scrutinized. The appraisal processes for new and experienced teachers, which are outlined in chapter 10, identify competencies that teachers should demonstrate. Teachers who fail to meet minimal standards on the various competencies are given opportunities to improve their performance.

Case Study: Weighing Different Forms of Discrimination
Ontario College of Teachers v. The Teacher (2013)

In 2008, a teacher was hired to teach grades six to eight in a public school. The students alleged that he frequently began his morning with "bonjour fags and fagettes" and proceeded throughout the day to tell students to "shut up" or that they were "stupid." The students also alleged that the teacher showed a lack of care for his students, laughing when one student fell backwards and hit his head and showing little tolerance for a student with Tourettes.

The teacher was told by his administration he would be undergoing a Teacher Performance Appraisal in the fall of 2008, and it was suggested that he contact his federation about getting support with classroom management. He was also informed that parents had complained about his tone, yelling in class, lack of student engagement, and lack of knowledge regarding accommodations for students with special needs. After a series of meetings and discussions with the teacher, in which he was told he needed to review OSRs and gain a better understanding of exceptional students, he was placed on home assignment.

The teacher resigned shortly after and did not return to work. Even though the member had resigned, the allegations of his behaviour were brought forward to the Ontario College of Teachers. An investigation took place, and the first hearing was held in 2012. At the same time, the teacher brought forward a human rights case against the school board, stating they had discriminated against him based on race.

The discipline panel concluded that the member was "an inexperienced and frustrated professional educator lacking in the basic tenets of classroom management," and, further, that the teacher, rather than accept professional advice, perceived the administration as being critical and discriminatory. The teacher was unable to see his behaviour as being discriminatory toward exceptional students and toward sexual orientation. The teacher was found guilty of professional misconduct and directed to take a course on classroom management.

The teacher then brought forward a human rights case against the Ontario College of Teachers, stating that the investigation and disciplinary process were discriminatory and racist. The teacher's case was denied on the basis of a lack of evidence. The teacher was ordered to pay the College's legal fees for this lengthy case.

This case appears in *Professionally Speaking*, without the member's name, in March 2016.

(1) What evidence is there that this teacher was not diligent or faithful in his practice?

(2) What other duties of teachers under the *Education Act*, section 264(1), or *Regulation 298*, section 20, did he fail to meet?

(3) Do you think the penalty imposed by the discipline panel was appropriate?

(4) What role did the Ontario Human Rights Commission play in this case?

Encourage Pupils in the Pursuit of Learning

Effective instruction should also lead to evidence of student learning. The wording of this duty stresses *encouragement* in the *pursuit* of learning. It does not require concrete evidence of learning. Implicit in this phrasing is a recognition that there is not a clear causal relationship between diligent or competent instruction and student learning. Indeed, much depends on the individual student, other students in the class, and the learning community.

Teacher competence, then, is not judged simply on the basis of student achievement, though students' success in meeting learning expectations may certainly be taken into account. Teachers are accountable to the principal to report on the progress of pupils. They are also required to report to parents or guardians at regular intervals. These reporting requirements point to teachers as professionals accountable for their actions. The teacher in the OCT case above, in addition to his other professional lapses, failed to meet standards of the profession by being dismissive of concerns raised by students, parents, and the administration. By calling his students names, yelling at them, and laughing at them, the teacher did not create a positive learning environment. He also failed to understand the importance of following Individual Education Plans and being respectful of exceptional students. Students in a classroom can have difficulty learning when teachers do not perform their duties properly. This case is an example of how student learning is affected when a teacher fails to set the right tone and lead by example.

In this era of increased accountability, which has been accompanied by increased assessment of students and use of standardized tests, teachers should maintain an effective system for recording student progress and should keep samples of student work. Teachers should also be able to demonstrate to administrators and parents, particularly in schools performing poorly on standardized tests, how they are working to improve student learning.

The professional misconduct case listed below lists some ways in which teachers may fail to encourage learning, and how they can go about improving their practice.

Case Study: Losing Control
Ontario College of Teachers v. CMB (2012)

CMB was a teacher in a large urban high school. In a single incident, a student threw a pop can in a garbage can instead of the recycling bin. CMB repeatedly asked the student to remove the can from the garbage. She then grabbed his sweater. causing it to rip. Another student took out a cell phone to record the interaction, and CMB told the student to put the cell phone away. When the student refused, CMB attempted to grab the phone. The student walked away, but CMB followed and grabbed the student by the shoulder, causing the student to fall. CMB then attempted to lock her classroom door. The student with the pop can tried to enter, and CMB replied, "Shut up and get the ___ out."

CMB was suspended for fifteen days by the school board, and the incident was reported to the Ontario College of Teachers. CMB attended her disciplinary hearing and pleaded guilty to allegations that she:

- failed to maintain the standards of the profession;
- abused a student or students verbally;
- abused a student or students physically;
- failed to comply with the Act;
- committed acts that would be regarded by members as disgraceful, dishonourable, or unprofessional;
- engaged in conduct unbecoming a Member.

CMB received a reprimand and was ordered to take a course on boundary violations and anger management.

This case appears in *Professionally Speaking*, December 2013.

(1) What were some of the issues presented in this case?

(2) Do you think that a fifteen-day suspension and taking a course on boundary violations and anger management were appropriate consequences for CMB's actions?

(3) What should teachers do if they do lose their temper?

Instill Core Values Through Both Words and Actions

Education is an ethical enterprise in which teachers play a major role in developing the character of students and, by extension, contribute to the development of good democratic citizens.

Even though they are no longer expected to adhere to the Judeo-Christian religious belief system, teachers should demonstrate in their classroom conduct that they respect the ethical principles and virtues conveyed in section 264 of the *Education Act*. The language may be old-fashioned, but the call to be virtuous in one's classroom conduct is clear both from the law itself and from cases that arise from it.

The case above highlights three issues. First, the teacher had the opportunity, for example, to address the importance of recycling but failed to do so when she lost her temper instead. Second, technology has changed the way teachers and students are held accountable, and everyone in a school needs to be aware that their behaviour can be recorded. Teachers should conduct conversations on the ethical use of cell phones in classrooms rather than attempting to control situations such as in the case above. These examples are not about teaching curriculum but about having discussions about issues that affect society, education included. Finally, teachers need to exercise a great deal of caution when touching students, especially in heated exchanges. By modelling self-control, teachers can demonstrate to students how to deal with conflict and anger.

Teachers can save themselves and their students much grief by recognizing the power of their words and actions and conducting themselves with appropriate prudence and care. Even the most sincere of teachers make mistakes in judgment and are advised to be ready to apologize and make amends before an incident develops into a crisis.

This case and other discipline cases of a similar nature make it clear that the language and behaviour of teachers in the classroom should be consistent with their professional status and their duty to act as an appropriate role model for impressionable students.

Profane or vulgar language may be protected if it is used for clear instructional purposes. This means that a teacher would be protected if using an article or story containing swearing or sexual references (Brown & Zuker, 2007). Much depends, of course, on the maturity and sophistication of the students. It is still wise to consult with the principal before using such materials, particularly if you have any qualms about their appropriateness.

Similarly, the physical appearance of teachers can sometimes engender controversy. There was a time when teachers could be reprimanded for their grooming or choice of clothing. In the 1970s, for example, many schools expected male teachers to wear jackets and ties, and female teachers were sometimes reprimanded for wearing pantsuits. There seems to be a more *laissez-faire* attitude toward dress today. There have been no cases before the courts or the College recently concerning physical appearance. Nonetheless, teachers are advised to dress in a manner appropriate for a professional. It is worth bearing in mind, for example, that unkempt beards, torn jeans, miniskirts, or low-cut blouses may diminish the respect accorded teachers by students, parents, and colleagues.

Teaching Under the Authority of the Principal and the School Board
The teacher is in charge of the classroom, but this authority is subject to the authority of the principal, who in turn is under the authority of a supervisory officer and the Director of Education. The principal, as principal-teacher, is in charge of "the instruction and the discipline of pupils in the school" and the "organization and management of the school" (*Regulation 298*, section 11(1)(a)(b)).

Teachers are not islands unto themselves but members of a school community dedicated to teaching and learning within the jurisdiction of the local school board. They have considerable autonomy within their own classroom to implement the curriculum in ways that best meet the needs of their own students. Secondary school teachers do have to work with their colleagues in the same department to make sure they are teaching subjects in a similar manner. Often three grade 9 English teachers will have the same course outlines, assignments, and exams to ensure consistency in the department and subject matter.

Nonetheless, teachers have a clear professional and legal obligation to be consistent with school expectations, and to follow board policies and provincial guidelines. Teachers are usually most effective when working collegially with other professionals as part of a learning community to develop effective educational programs for students.

The case below illustrates some of the complexities regarding the academic freedom of teachers.

Case Study: Choosing and Preparing Assignments Carefully
Morin v. Prince Edward Island Regional Administrative Unit (2002)

Morin was a junior high language arts teacher in his second year as a probationary teacher. He showed his grade 9 class a documentary exploring the influence of Christian fundamentalism on American politics. This video was related to a class project he was about to begin on the meaning of religion in different societies.

This documentary upset some students and parents, who complained to the principal. The principal told Morin not to show the video again and cancelled the class project.

Morin was placed on an involuntary paid leave of absence, and then, when asked to return, went on sick leave. When he did go back, parents pulled their children from his class. At the end of the year, his probationary contract was not renewed.

Morin, believing that the decision to forbid the film and the subsequent hiring decision constituted violations of his human rights, filed a court action. He accused the school board of:

- breach of his right to freedom of expression under the *Charter*;
- wrongful dismissal;
- defamation (of professional status).

Morin argued that he had a satisfactory performance evaluation by the principal, and that the decision not to renew his contract constituted wrongful dismissal. The administration argued, first, that there had been issues with Morin's teaching ability before the incident, for which they presented documentation. Second, as Morin was on a probationary contract, they claimed that his contract had simply not been renewed.

Another issue that was debated during the trial was Morin's overall professionalism. The administration produced evidence that demonstrated Morin was argumentative and "insubordinate." Morin denied these allegations.

Morin lost at trial, and both he and the school board appealed the decisions back and forth many times. In the end, the Supreme Court agreed that his *Charter* right to freedom of expression had been violated.

On the other hand, the court stated that there was no proof that the school board wrongfully dismissed Morin since he was not a full-time teacher. After examining numerous appeals and counter-appeals by the Board, the Supreme Court awarded Morin a small amount of financial compensation for legal costs relating to the case solely on the grounds of a violation of a freedom of expression. The court dismissed Morin's claims of wrongful dismissal and defamation of professional character.

---

(1) What are some reasons for protecting or limiting a teacher's freedom of expression in the classroom?

(2) How might Morin have approached this controversial topic more effectively?

(3) What are the keys issues in this case?

(4) How can teachers balance their own rights versus the rights of students, parents, and the community?

The Supreme Court judges in this case affirmed teachers' freedom of speech. However, they were clear to point out that the rights of students, parents, and the community are also very important to consider in the public education system. The majority in this split decision were critical of the principal for rushing to judgment in response to complaints. They did concede, however, that the principal had authority over the school and that free expression by teachers could lead to disruption. In this case, because of its controversy and media attention, the learning environment of the students was affected, and the overall school climate as well.

The academic freedom of teachers must be weighed in the balance with school and societal issues. Kevin A. Kindred (2006), in "Teachers in Dissent: Freedom of Expression in the Classroom," concludes his study of this and similar cases with these comments:

> The decision makers in these cases recognized that teachers are entrusted with a captive and impressionable audience, and yet they were still willing to entrust the teacher with some degree of personal control over the subject being taught. This level of trust is consistent with the notion of a professional. As well, the recognition of the degree of independent control exercised by a teacher within the classroom is relevant to other potentially significant questions in education law ... (p. 231)

While teachers enjoy a degree of academic freedom in curriculum and instruction, this freedom does not generally apply to supervisory or administrative duties.

Case Study: Be Careful What You Publish
Ontario College of Teachers v. JT (2015)

JT was a teacher in a public secondary school. Outside school hours, he co-authored a novel with his wife and son that contained sexually explicit material about teenagers, including scenes of stripping, bondage, and sexual assault. The novel also sexualized students and contained negative stereotypes about teachers and administrators. JT published the novel under his family's company.

This case is not simply about a teacher writing an inappropriate novel; it is complicated by the fact that the media revealed that JT served as Chair of the Discipline Committee for the Ontario College of Teachers. He was asked to immediately resign and placed on a one-year leave of absence from his school. Parents were extremely upset to learn that their children's teacher would have condoned a novel that was sexually inappropriate. The school board referred JT's case to the Ontario College of Teachers. In the middle of the disciplinary hearing, JT resigned from the teaching profession and signed an undertaking with the College that he agreed never to teach again.

This case appears in *Professionally Speaking*, March 2016.

(1) What connection did JT fail to make between his role as teacher and his role as author?

(2) Do you believe JT should have been penalized for his decisions?

(3) Do you think teachers should be able to publish or create art, for example, outside the profession? Should limits be placed on their forms of expression?

TEACHERS' SUPERVISORY DUTIES

Section 265(1) of the *Education Act* clearly identifies the principal as the head teacher and manager of the school. In addition to their duties as teachers, principals are required "to maintain proper order and discipline in the school" and "to give assiduous attention to the health and comfort of the pupils ..." This also entails a duty to ensure that students are properly supervised at school and in school activities (*Regulation 298*, section 11(3) (e)(f)).

These duties of the principal, and the attendant powers, are reinforced by the duties of the teacher listed in section 264(1) of the *Education Act*, which call on teachers to obey the principal's directions in the maintenance of safety, order, and discipline. Supervisory duties have often been an area of contention between school boards and teachers' federations. Federations have worked hard to negotiate limits on the number of hours teachers are required to supervise students. Recently, they negotiated a provincial framework agreement that limits assigned supervision to seventy-five minutes per week, with exceptions in cases of emergency. Some federations are seeking a supervision cap of sixty minutes in the next round of contract negotiations. The Ontario Principals' Council, on the other hand, has expressed concerns about the current level of supervision. Principals maintain that an adequate supervisory presence by teachers prevents problems. They suggest that supervision is spread too thin in some schools, which places students at greater risk of harm and school boards at greater risk of safety-related lawsuits.

In Ontario today, principals make every effort to comply with the supervisory limit of seventy-five minutes a week. There may be emergency situations in which the principal has to assign additional supervision. If asked or ordered to provide additional supervisions in order to ensure student safety, teachers should keep in mind that their professional and statutory duties and responsibilities extend beyond the terms negotiated in collective agreements. This principle was affirmed in the case of *Winnipeg Teachers' Association v. Winnipeg School Division No. 1* (1976), when the Supreme Court ruled that professional contracts should be read so that principals are able to discharge their legal and professional duties to ensure safety in schools. The court applied the following test for determining whether the assignment of supervisory duties beyond explicit collective agreement provisions was reasonable:

(a) it must be related to the enterprise of education;

(b) it must be fair to the teacher;

(c) it must be in furtherance of the principal's duties.

The length of the school day has been a particularly contentious supervision issue, particularly as it relates to when teachers must be "present in the classroom or teaching area ... at least fifteen minutes before the commencement of classes in the school in the morning" (*Regulation 298*, section 20(d)). Arbitration cases have made it clear that teachers are required not just to be present in schools (e.g., the staffroom) but in their classrooms or other areas where they may be required to supervise students. The term "instructional day" in legislation is student focused and does not define the work day for teachers. Less well defined is what constitutes instructional duties (which are covered by contractual agreements on the number of "instructional minutes" teachers are expected to work each week) versus supervisory or administrative duties. Arbitration board rulings on cases between school boards and federations are not clear on this point, because they often hinge on the precise wording of each collective agreement.

Teachers are well advised to avoid insubordination or even the impression of insubordination, because these could lead to complex grievance procedures and even dismissal. (See chapter 10 for further discussion of employer–employee relations in schools.)

TEACHERS' ADMINISTRATIVE DUTIES

As employees and professionals, teachers also have administrative duties. While this principle is widely accepted, there have been disputes regarding the nature and amount of additional work that teachers are *required* to perform.

Case Study: Issues Heard by Arbitrators
St. Clair Catholic District School Board v. OECTA (2001)

Many issues between school boards and teachers' federations are heard by arbitrators under provisions in collective agreements. Generally, the decisions of arbitrators resolve the issues, though decisions could be appealed to the courts. Arbitrators' decisions, which are based on points of law, often set important precedents concerning the professional lives of teachers.

In this case, the school board directed that teachers must attend an asbestos aware-ness training session "… after the regular business day of the teachers." The teachers sought additional pay for attending the workshops. The training sessions were offered either before or after school, or during the teachers' lunch break.

Arbitrator Watters found that the school board was entitled to schedule asbestos train-ing sessions outside the instructional day and that the teachers were obliged to attend them as part of their professional duties, without additional compensation. Watters, citing the Winnipeg Teachers' case (1976), wrote:

> I am satisfied that the Asbestos Awareness Training was in "furtherance of [one of] the principal duties" to which the teacher is committed … [T]he Association did not seriously challenge the fact the training had to occur. Its complaint, rather, was that it was scheduled outside of the instructional day and that teachers were not provided with additional compensation for their attendance. It is, therefore, necessary to determine whether the Employer could properly schedule the train-ing outside of the instructional day and, if so, whether it was obligated to pay the teachers for their attendance. I can find nothing in the collective agreements, the Education Act, or the Regulations that would obligate the Employer to schedule the training within the hours of the instructional day …
>
> Under the terms of their collective agreements, teachers in both the Elementary

and Secondary Units receive an annual salary. It is clear that this salary encompasses the performance of certain duties outside of the instructional day, such as staff meetings after school and parent-teacher interviews after school or in the evenings. I consider it significant that health and safety issues are addressed in the after school staff meetings and that teachers do not receive extra compensation for their attendance at same. In the final analysis, I have not been persuaded that good reason exists to treat the training sessions in a different fashion for purposes of compensation. I think that the training sessions were analogous to a single issue staff meeting. The only difference is that, instead of providing a forum for discussion of, or reporting on, issues, the meeting focused on the delivery of formal training ...

Given the nature of the latter group's [teachers'] professional obligations, it is difficult to speak in terms of a regular or clearly defined workday.

Mr. Watters did, however, rule that it was unreasonable to require teachers to participate in professional development during their lunch period.

---

(1) What was the statutory basis for the arbitrator's decision?
(2) How would you interpret the last sentence of the quotation in relation to teaching as a profession?
(3) What are the implications of this decision for teachers?

Professional Development

The above case affirms that teachers are expected to participate in a range of professional development activities as part of their responsibilities as employees and professionals.

Legislation also clearly states that teachers must "participate in professional development days" (*Education Act*, section 264(1)(h)) in their school boards. It is also expected that teachers will volunteer to participate in additional training without compensation, because annual salaries denote flexibility and professionalism involves a commitment to ongoing professional development.

Other Administrative Duties

Preparation Time. Teachers are provided with paid preparation time during the school day. While they are afforded considerable flexibility in how they use this time, they are generally expected to be available in the school in case they are asked to assist the principal by performing supervisory duties.

Parent–Teacher Interviews. Teachers are expected to "participate in regular meeting with [pupils'] parents or guardians" (*Regulation 298*, section 20(j)). This was confirmed in an arbitration case, *Durham Catholic District School Board and Ontario English Catholic Teachers' Association* (1999). The arbitration board found that the school board had the right to require teachers "to report to parents by attending evening parent-teacher interviews." The arbitration board reached this decision despite the fact that neither statute law nor contracts expressly state that teachers must participate in evening interviews.

Attending Graduation. Teachers are also obliged to attend graduation. *Regulation 298*, section 20(m) requires teachers to engage in "duties normally associated with the graduation of pupils." This duty, like parent–teacher interviews, has a long history in Ontario education. It is also a duty that most teachers assume gladly.

Delegation by Principals. The principal may delegate to a teacher in the school any of his powers and duties under Part XIII of the act, dealing with student discipline. This delegation may occur only in the absence of both principal and vice-principal and must be in accordance with board policy.

CONCLUSION

Teachers need to be aware of their legal duties with regard to instruction, supervision, and administrative tasks. Legislation and legal cases also make it clear that teachers as professionals are held to a higher standard than non-professional employees.

While collective agreements limit the additional work principals may assign teachers, teachers are advised to comply with their principal's directions. If they feel the directions are excessive, they can confer with their federation representatives and, if necessary, grieve the principal's order. Employer–employee relations are examined further in chapter 10.

CHECKING YOUR UNDERSTANDING

- As a result of being *in loco parentis*, educators are considered under common law to owe their students a "fiduciary duty."
- The *Education Act* and its attendant regulations provide the statutory basis for public education in Ontario.
- The principal is responsible for the organization and management of the school and the instruction and discipline of students.
- The principal is also the person charged with ensuring that the school is a safe and healthy learning environment.
- Teachers have a number of duties outlined in the *Education Act* and *Regulation 298*. These duties may be further defined in collective agreements.
- Teachers' instructional duties include: teaching the classes assigned by the principal; encouraging students in the pursuit of learning; and acting as an appropriate role model for students both on and off duty.
- Teachers have considerable autonomy in their own classroom but are expected to teach in a manner consistent with school expectations, board policy, and provincial guidelines.
- Teachers must carry out the supervisory duties assigned by the principal within the limitations established by their collective agreement.
- Teachers' administrative duties include: attending workshops and training sessions; participating in professional activity days; attending parent–teacher meetings; and assisting with graduation ceremonies. These duties could be scheduled outside the regular school day.

APPLYING YOUR UNDERSTANDING

Case Study: The Importance of Appropriate Teaching Tools
Ontario College of Teachers v. PS (2015)

PS decided to show his students a movie about the life of a famous painter. The Ontario Film Review Board rated the movie: "PG, Parental guidance is advised. Themes or content may not be suitable for all children." Some of the students in the class were disturbed by the sexually aggressive content of the film, and PS agreed it probably was not a wise choice to have shown it.

In a second incident, PS distributed postcards with famous paintings and drawings to his class, some which contained nude images. He distributed 584 postcards, of which 37 depicted nudes, both male and female. PS told the students in advance that some of them contained nude images and that they did not have to look at them if doing so made them uncomfortable. Despite this warning, the students were disturbed by the images. PS stated that the exercise was looking at the elements and principles of design, and he agreed perhaps the students were too young to view the nude images on the postcards.

In a third incident involving drawing, the member referred to a circle as a "hairy ball."

In a fourth incident, the member put a paper tube between his legs in order to cut it, and the girls in his class thought he was simulating masturbation.

PS was suspended twenty-five days without pay by his school board and was required to go for professional counselling. His actions were also reported to the Ontario College of Teachers, and PS attended a disciplinary hearing.

PS admitted that he was guilty of professional conduct, and allegations of sexual abuse of students were dropped by the discipline panel. The panel concluded that there were several incidents of poor judgment and inappropriate behaviour by PS, and that after one incident, he should have known how to speak and behave in front of younger students.

The panel ordered that PS receive a reprimand, twenty-five days of suspension (already served), and complete a course on adolescent development and professional boundaries, and that his name be published in *Professionally Speaking*, the College magazine, and under Disciplinary Decisions on the College's website.

This case appears in *Professionally Speaking*, December 2015.

(1) Should the teacher have shown the video? What might PS have done instead?

(2) How would an art teacher know when it is acceptable to show images of nudity?

(3) Do you think PS needed to be reported to the Ontario College of Teachers?

(4) Do you think PS deserved a twenty-five-day suspension?

CHAPTER 5

ENSURING SAFE CLASSROOMS AND SCHOOLS

After reading this chapter, you will have a better understanding of the ways teachers, principals, and other members of the school community can ensure the safety of classrooms and schools. In particular, you will learn about:

- *the importance of developing classroom management strategies and making sure the classroom is safe for all students at all times;*
- *the consequences of misconduct by students with regard to suspension, expulsion, and criminal charges;*
- *the implications of the principal's statutory duty to maintain order and discipline in the school.*

Case Study: Jordan Manners and the Impact of School Violence

Jordan Manners, a fifteen-year-old student at C.W. Jefferys Collegiate Institute, was shot dead in a stairwell at school in June 2007.

While youth violence was not uncommon in this north Toronto neighbourhood, citizens were outraged that the sanctuary of the school had been so horribly violated. Students were terrified by the severity of the incident and teachers traumatized.

Schools are not entirely safe places for students. Teachers, students, and intruders sometimes act in ways that put students at risk. One teacher at C.W. Jefferys characterized the school as a "war zone" in which teachers and administrators were reluctant to discipline students for fear of reprisals from parents, lawsuits, and human rights complaints.

Several weeks after the incident, the Toronto District School Board commissioned human rights lawyer Julian Falconer to investigate safety concerns in Toronto schools—more specifically, the schools in the Jane-Finch corridor. As he interviewed students, a fourteen-year-old girl disclosed that she had been sexually assaulted in a school washroom earlier in the school year and nothing had been done about it. As part of his legal duty to report, Falconer exposed the fact that the vice-principal and principal knew about the sexual assault and did not report it to the police, Children's Aid, or the student's parents. Both administrators were fined by Children's Aid Society and charged by the police, and the vice-principal was reported to the Ontario College of Teachers. The charges were eventually dropped by the Crown, but vice-principal Silvio Tallevi was found guilty of professional misconduct by a discipline panel of the Ontario College of Teachers.

This was one of several sexual assaults that had occurred at the school for which little or no action was taken to protect the victims or punish the assailants, according to the report of the School Community Safety Advisory Panel (2008), generally known as the Falconer Report. This report also exposed a "culture of silence" within the Toronto District School Board; while 61% of the teachers from C.W. Jefferys had witnessed a student threaten another teacher in a two-year period. Many teachers described witnessing drug trafficking, physical threats, sexual harassment, and students with weapons. Teachers felt that the administration was not protecting students or teachers, and administrators admitted to feeling pressure from the board not to suspend students. The pendulum had swung from "zero tolerance" to "zero accountability."

The Falconer Report contained 126 recommendations and led to an increased awareness of school safety issues and to many administrative reforms. Recommendations in the report also led to the introduction of community police officers into Toronto schools and the development of the Gender-Based Violence Prevention Program in the TDSB.

(1) Was the school responsible for the murder of Jordan Manners?
(2) Was the school responsible for the sexual assault?
(3) Did the school have effective disciplinary processes?
(4) Was the school a positive and safe place for students?

The case above illustrates that school safety is a systemic issue that must be examined from every angle and with every stakeholder. The Falconer Report was significant in capturing the voice of students, teachers, administrators, parents, and the community. It was not one issue, but many, that led Falconer to write such an extensive and lengthy report.

SAFETY AND CULTURE OF SCHOOLS

Teachers work with young people on a daily basis yet often know little about what really matters to the students and what influences them. In *Freaks, Geeks and Cool Kids* (2004), sociologist Barry Milner, Jr., notes:

> In large part, teachers and administrators tend to ignore subtle forms of cruelty when they can because they lack the knowledge and power they need to deal with them. More specifically, the way schools are organized means it is hard for them to know what is going on in the peer culture and that they have few effective sanctions to use against those who abuse others. (p. 186)

It is important for teachers and administrators to understand the underlying interactions of school life and, in particular, the nature and impact of peer dynamics. In his sociological study of student culture in schools, Milner examines how the elements of teenager, school, and consumerism interact.

> Our educational system plays a central role, not just in giving people technical skills, but also in molding their desires and ambitions. Life with one's peers, in and out of the classroom, powerfully shapes people's world views and personalities. (p. 169)

After studying 304 retrospective accounts by college and university students and observing students in schools, Milner was particularly struck by the profound importance of status differences in high school peer relations. Social standing in schools, he discovered, is a function of *coolness* derived largely from the display of consumer goods. Toward the top are athletic males and attractive females; toward the bottom are "geeks" and "nerds." Cliques and social marginalization are the natural result.

Teachers and administrators who have their finger on the pulse of student culture are better able to influence that culture and, by doing so, make schools safer places for students. While Milner's focus is on understanding school culture, he notes that one school in his study was very successful in breaking down these informal power structures. In this school, as one student wrote, "The goal of administration was to break up cliques throughout our four years in high school so that we would all become friends."

SAFE SCHOOLS LEGISLATION IN ONTARIO

Keeping students safe while in school has always been an important issue for teachers and administrators. Over the years, legislation has varied in its approach on how to control the behaviour of others in order to keep large numbers of students safe. *Part 8, Behaviour, Discipline and Safety* of the *Education Act* addresses these issues. Discipline and safety provisions are periodically updated through new legislation. These regular updates can change in tone and direction depending on which political party is in power.

BILL 157, KEEPING OUR KIDS SAFE AT SCHOOL ACT

Student safety is a major concern of parents and policymakers. On February 1, 2010, Bill 157, *Keeping Our Kids Safe at School Act* was enacted by the Ontario government, with significant changes to student conduct and consequences. It put more responsibility on all school staff to report incidents of bullying and school violence.

Following are excerpts from *Keeping Our Kids Safe at School: Reporting and Responding to Incidents* (OME, 2009):

- all school staff to *report* to their principal incidents that can lead to suspension or expulsion
- principals to contact the parents of victims of these types of incidents

- staff who work directly with students to respond to incidents that have a negative impact on the school climate.

These could include racist or sexist comments, graffiti or vandalism—incidents that are unacceptable in our school...

Student behaviours that can lead to suspension include:
- Uttering a threat to inflict serious bodily harm on another person
- Possessing alcohol or illegal drugs
- Being under the influence of alcohol
- Swearing at a teacher or at another person in a position of authority
- Committing an act of vandalism that causes extensive damage to school property at the pupil's school or to property located on the premises of the pupil's school
- Bullying
- Any other activities identified in school board policy.

Student behaviours that can lead to expulsion include:
- Possessing a weapon
- Using a weapon to cause or to threaten bodily harm to another person
- Committing physical assault on another person that causes bodily harm requiring treatment by a medical practitioner
- Committing sexual assault
- Trafficking in weapons or in illegal drugs
- Committing robbery
- Giving alcohol to a minor
- Any other activities identified in school board policy.

These behaviours can lead to suspension or expulsion and must be reported when they occur at school, at school-related activities, or off school property where it can have a negative impact on school climate.

Who has to report an incident?

All school board employees are required to report in writing to their principal any incident that must be considered for suspension or expulsion. Board employees include:

- vice principals
- teachers and educational assistants
- all non-teaching staff, such as those involved in social work, child and youth work, psychology and other related disciplines
- administrative and custodial staff
- school bus drivers ...

The principal can inform parents or guardians about:

- the incident
- the harm their child suffered
- what steps were taken to protect their child's safety, including any disciplinary measures taken in response to the incident.

The principal cannot name or provide any identifying information about the aggressor ...

A principal is not permitted to call the victim's parents or guardian if:

- the student is 18 years or older or is a 16- or 17-year-old student who has withdrawn from parental control
- the principal believes that telling the parent(s) would put the student at risk of harm from the parent(s).

A principal must call [the parents or guardians] if the incident leads to a suspension. The *Education Act* already requires the principal to inform the aggressor's parents within 24 hours of the incident. Parents also receive written notice telling them the reason for and duration of the suspension and outlining the appeal process.

Depending on the incident, police may be called. Principals must follow their local police/school board protocols when involving police.

When board employees believe that a student may be in need of protection, they must continue to follow the usual procedure and call the Children's Aid Society ...

If a teacher or any other school staff learns of an incident that will have a negative impact on school climate and could lead to a student being suspended or expelled it must be reported ...

If a principal learns that any member of the school staff has not reported a serious incident that could lead to a student being suspended or expelled, the matter could be dealt with as a human resource issue, consistent with school board human resources policies and collective agreements.

As well, all staff that hold teaching certificates, including teachers, principals and superintendents, are governed by the *Ontario College of Teachers Act*, which sets out activities that are defined as professional misconduct and outlines sanctions.

Supporting Victims

School staff who work directly with students are required to support all students, including those who either instigate or are victims of serious student incidents. They will provide contact information about professional supports—such as public health units, child and youth workers, help phone lines —or other community agencies that offer the appropriate type of confidential support. This could include, for example, a sexual assault centre, Kids Help Phone, or the Lesbian Gay Bi Trans Youth Line ...

School staff who work directly with students will provide those students wishing to discuss such issues as healthy relationships, gender identity, and sexuality with contact information about professional supports available in their community.

ADDRESSING BULLYING: BILL 13, THE ACCEPTING SCHOOLS ACT

Despite the good intentions of Bill 157, issues relating to bullying and homophobic bullying continued to be a problem in Ontario schools. The consequences of bullying were becoming more extreme, as illustrated in the high-profile suicides of Jamie Hubley (2011) and Amanda Todd (2012), who used social media to publicly end their life.

Jamie Hubley, a fifteen-year-old student from Ottawa and son of a city councillor, was the victim of ongoing homophobic bullying. At one point, students tried to shove batteries down his throat on a school bus. He was repeatedly teased and called names at school over being openly gay. Jamie posted on social media that his battle with bullying was over, that he was "Tired of life, really. It is so hard ..." On Friday, October 14, 2011, Jamie killed himself.

Allan Hubley, Jamie's father, became an advocate to end homophobic bullying in schools. He spoke at conferences, to the media, and to other politicians in an effort to raise awareness and to push for changes in the legislation.

Amanda Todd was a fifteen-year-old teenager from Port Coquitlam, British Columbia. After being blackmailed on social media, bullied at school, cyber bullied by fellow classmates online, and physically assaulted at school, she chose to end her life, in October 2012, one year after Jamie Hubley.

Politicians began to discuss the possibility of a federal anti-bullying law, but to date, one does not exist. Instead, the RCMP began encouraging teenagers and adults to use the sections of the criminal code that could apply, on threats, assaults, harassment, and sexual exploitation.

In a provincial study on Gay Straight Alliances (GSA) and their advisors, Kitchen and Bellini (2013) found that schools that had a GSA and a GSA advisor who was a strong advocate were perceived as safer. The study also revealed what many LGBTQ students had been saying for years, that teachers were ignoring homophobic bullying both in the classroom and in the halls.

The Ministry of Education acknowledged that homophobic bullying had largely been ignored by teachers and administrators. They referenced EGALE Canada's (Taylor & Peter, 2011) national survey, *Every Class in Every School: The First National Climate Survey on Homophobia, Biphobia, and Transphobia in Canadian Schools*. The report exposed an education system that ignored certain types of bullying while addressing others. This "pick and choose" attitude toward student safety is highly discriminatory. The Ministry of Education took into consideration the devastating effects of teen suicide related to cyber bullying and homophobic bullying. The new laws meant teachers and administrators were now legislated to keep all students safe.

Bill 13, *Accepting Schools Act* was enacted in 2012, and for the next year, teachers across Ontario participated in professional development on homophobic bullying and cyber bullying. All secondary schools, including Catholic public, had to allow the formation of Gay Straight Alliances. Catholic schools, especially at the Archdiocese level, initially protested the act, claiming religious rights. However, in this case student rights and safety prevailed.

The act also mandated all staff, including bus drivers, to report incidents of bullying and cyber bullying to the school administration as soon as possible. Cyber bullying received more attention, and under the act, students could now be suspended for cyber bullying even if it took place off school property.

The act built on the Ontario Ministry of Education's *Equity and Inclusive Education Strategy* (2009) and strategies that help make schools safe. The legislation looked at student behaviour through many different lenses. Some of the recommendations made (pp. 18–23) were:

- To include mental health workers in schools and increase counselling options for students.
- To direct changes to the curriculum so that issues regarding equity, inclusion, and bullying prevention be part of student learning.
- A public awareness campaign that included reaching out to parents and the community.
- An emphasis on a whole school approach including bullying and homophobic bullying prevention and intervention.
- The establishment of Gay Straight Alliances in every secondary school in Ontario to support LGBTQ students.

The amendments to the *Education Act* in Bill 13 resulted in a revised *Code of Conduct* in 2012. The memorandum gave direction to school boards to review their own codes of conduct and ensure that they were consistent with the revised provincial *Code of Conduct*.

Section 301(2) of Part XIII of the *Education Act*, which outlines the purposes of the provincial *Code of Conduct*, was revised to include prevention of bullying in schools. If a board enters into an agreement with a third party with respect to rental of school space, the board must include in the agreement a requirement that the other party follow standards that are consistent with the provincial *Code of Conduct*, in accordance with section 301(3.1).

The standards of behaviour in school board codes of conduct must be consistent with the requirements set out in this memorandum. In reviewing their codes of conduct, school boards must consult with school councils and stakeholders, including: parents, principals, teachers, and students; Parent Involvement Committees; Special Education Advisory Committees; community partners; community-based service providers; and members of First Nations, Métis, and Inuit communities (e.g., Elders) and other relevant groups (e.g., providers of child care) that are traditionally not consulted. School board codes of conduct must:

- include the standards stated in the provincial *Code of Conduct*;
- set out standards of behaviour for all members of the school community (e.g., parents, students, staff, visitors, volunteers);
- link locally developed standards to the relevant provincial standards (e.g., school board rules for the use of electronic devices such as cell phones could be linked to the provincial standard requiring those at school to "respect the need of others to work in an environment that is conducive to learning and teaching");
- indicate where and/or when these standards will apply (e.g., in school sports activities, on school buses, at offsite school-sponsored activities, or in circumstances where engaging in an activity could have a negative impact on the school climate);
- include procedures and timelines for review (reviews should be conducted at least every three years).

All forms of bullying are more likely to occur when teachers and administrators fail to understand and address student conduct in schools. The tragedies listed above, whether the murder of Jordan Manners, or the suicides of Jamie Hubley and Amanda Todd, should never have happened in the first place. They are reminders for teachers of the seriousness of their role as *in loco parentis.*

Case Study: Understanding Homophobic Bullying
Jubran v. School District No. 44 (North Vancouver) (2005)

Azmi Jubran was a secondary student at Handsworth Secondary School from 1993 to 1998. Jubran was the victim of relentless bullying. He was repeatedly called *queer, homo,* and *fag* despite the fact that his offenders knew he was not gay. He was physically assaulted, spit on, and continually punched and pushed in the halls. Jubran reported this abuse to the school administrators who did little to help him.

In 1996, while he was in grade 10, Jubran filed a Human Rights Complaint against North Vancouver District School Board. He won his case, and the Tribunal stated the school board was responsible for not helping him, not providing comprehensive discipline plans for students, and "not providing a learning environment free of discrimination." The school board never denied Jubran's story; in fact, they willingly admitted to knowing that he had been the victim of homophobic bullying.

The school decided to appeal the decision based on the fact that Jubran was not gay and therefore the bullying was not homophobic bullying. The British Columbia Supreme Court overturned the Tribunal's decision, finding its case flawed.

Jubran decided to appeal the decision of the British Columbia Supreme Court, and, in 2005, he won.

His case gained media attention for several reasons. Many found it appalling that a school board would admit that it had let a student be bullied for five years and did little to help.

The following is quoted from the province's *Code of Conduct.*

> A positive school climate and a safe learning and teaching environment are essential if students are to succeed in school. A positive school climate means everyone feels they are welcome and respected.
>
> All students, parents, teachers and staff have the right to be safe, and feel safe, in their school community. With this right comes the responsibility for everyone to be accountable for their actions and contribute to a positive school climate.

PROVINCIAL CODE OF CONDUCT

WHY IS THERE A PROVINCIAL CODE OF CONDUCT?

Ontario's provincial code of conduct sets clear standards of behaviour for individual school boards to follow, so that they can develop their own codes of conduct. The standards of behaviour in school board codes of conduct must be consistent with the requirements outlined in the provincial code of conduct.

WHO IS INCLUDED IN THE CODE AND WHERE DOES IT APPLY?

The code of conduct applies not only to students, but to everyone involved in the publicly funded school system, including parents or guardians, volunteers, teachers and other staff members. The code applies whether on school property, on school buses, at school-authorized events or activities, or in other circumstances that could have an impact on the school climate.

FUNDAMENTAL BELIEFS

- Everyone has a responsibility to promote a safe environment.
- Everyone should be aware of their rights, as active and engaged citizens. More importantly, everyone should also accept responsibility for protecting their rights and the rights of others. Responsible citizenship involves taking part in the civic life of the school.
- All members of the school community are to be treated with respect and dignity, especially those in positions of authority.
- Everyone has a responsibility to resolve conflicts in a way that is civil and respectful. Insults, hurtful acts and a lack of respect for others disrupt learning and teaching in a school community.
- Everyone is expected to resolve conflicts without using violence. Physical aggression is not a responsible way to deal with other people. No one should use an object to injure another person, or even threaten to use an object to injure another person. This is unacceptable and puts everyone's safety at risk.

STANDARDS OF BEHAVIOUR

Respect, civility and responsible citizenship

All school members must:

- respect and follow all applicable laws;
- demonstrate honesty and integrity;
- respect differences in people;
- treat one another with dignity and respect at all times, especially when there is disagreement;
- respect and treat others fairly, regardless of race, ancestry, place of origin, colour, ethnic origin, religion, gender, sexual orientation, age or disability;
- respect the rights of others;
- show care and respect for school property and the property of others;
- take the proper steps to help those in need;
- respect all members of the school community, especially those in a position of authority;
- respect the need of others to work in an environment that encourages learning and teaching;
- seek help from school staff, if necessary, to resolve conflict peacefully;
- not swear at a teacher or at another person in a position of authority.

Safety

School community members must not:

- engage in any form of bullying, whether it is in person or through technology, like email or cell phones;
- commit sexual assault;
- traffic weapons or illegal drugs;
- commit robbery;
- give alcohol to anyone under the legal drinking age;
- be in possession of a weapon, including firearms;
- use any object to threaten or intimidate another person;
- injure anyone with an object;
- be in possession or under the influence of alcohol or illegal drugs, or give them to anyone else;
- inflict or encourage others to inflict bodily harm;

- engage in hate propaganda or other types of behaviour caused by hate or bias;
- commit an act of vandalism that causes extensive damage to school property at the student's school or to property on the school premises.

Roles and Responsibilities

School boards provide direction to their schools to ensure opportunity, excellence and accountability in the education system. School boards must:

- develop policies that set out how their schools will implement and enforce the provincial code of conduct and all other rules that they develop as related to the provincial standards that promote and support respect, civility, responsible citizenship and physical safety;
- seek input from school councils, Parent Involvement Committees, the Special Education Advisory committee, students, staff, parents or guardians, volunteers and the community;
- review these policies regularly with students, staff, parents, volunteers and the community;
- establish a process that clearly communicates the provincial code of conduct to all parents, students, staff and members of the school community to gain their commitment and support;
- ensure an effective approach to intervene and respond to all violations that relate to the standards for respect, civility, responsible citizenship and physical safety;
- provide opportunities for all staff to gain the knowledge, skills and attitudes they need to develop and maintain academic excellence and safe learning and teaching environments.

Principals, under the direction of their school board, take a leadership role in the daily operation of a school.

They provide this leadership by:

- demonstrating care for the school community and commitment to academic excellence in a safe teaching and learning environment;
- holding everyone under their authority responsible for their behaviour and actions;

- empowering students to be positive leaders in their school and community;
- communicating regularly and meaningfully with all members of their school community.

Teachers and school staff, under the leadership of their principals, help maintain order in the school and are expected to hold everyone to the highest standard of respectful and responsible behaviour. As role models, staff uphold these high standards when they:
- help students work to their full potential and develop their self-worth;
- empower students to be positive leaders in their classroom, school and community;
- communicate regularly with parents on important issues;
- maintain consistent standards of behaviour for all students;
- show respect for all students, staff, parents, volunteers and members of the school community;
- prepare students for the full responsibilities of citizenship.

Students are to be treated with respect and dignity. In return, they must demonstrate respect for themselves, for others and for the responsibilities of citizenship through acceptable behaviour. Respect and responsibility are demonstrated when a student:
- comes to school prepared, on time and ready to learn;
- shows respect for himself/herself, for others and for those in authority;
- refrains from bringing anything to school that may put the safety of others at risk;
- follows the established rules and takes responsibility for his/her own actions.

Parents play an important role in the education of their children and can support the efforts of school staff in maintaining a safe and respectful learning environment for all students. Parents fulfill this responsibility when they:
- show an active interest in their child's school work and progress;
- communicate regularly with the school;

- make sure their child is neat, properly dressed and prepared for school;
- ensure that their child attends school regularly and on time;
- inform the school promptly about their child's absence or late arrival;
- become familiar with the provincial code of conduct, the board's code of conduct and school rules;
- encourage and help their child follow the rules of behaviour;
- help school staff deal with disciplinary issues involving their child.

COMMUNITY PARTNERS AND THE POLICE

Partnerships already in place may be enhanced and new partnerships with community agencies and members of the community may also be created. Community agencies are resources that school boards can use to deliver prevention or intervention programs. Community members need to support and respect the rules of their local schools.

The police play an essential role in making our schools and communities safer. Police investigate incidents in accordance with the protocol developed with the local school board. These protocols are based on a provincial model developed by the now Ministry of Community Safety and Correctional Services and the Ministry of Education.

THE CONDUCT OF STUDENTS

Random acts of violence, such as the Brampton Centennial Shooting (1978), École Polytechnique Massacre (1989), and the Dawson College Shootings (2006), have raised public awareness of the fact that students in schools are not entirely safe from terrible crimes. The sexual assault and murder at C.W. Jefferys Collegiate Institute reinforced these perceptions and prompted calls for increased efforts to make schools safe from violence.

What is violence? Lawyer Eric Roher (1997), in *An Educator's Guide to Violence in Schools*, writes:

> Many people believe that violence always involves some sort of physical contact or assault. In fact, conduct which does not involve physical

contact with another person may be described as violent. For example, a black student who is subjected to racially motivated threats may be a victim of violence. Similarly, a gay or lesbian student who is teased, taunted or intimidated by homophobic classmates may be a victim of violence. Students who find themselves being bullied, harassed or subject to acts of extortion by older or larger students are also possible victims of violence. None of these acts involves physical contact but they all result in the victimization of a particular student. Violence, in a school context, has been defined as "anything that jeopardizes the climate for an effective learning and working environment". It can include abusive language, disruptive or aggressive behaviour in the classroom, assaults, the carrying and use of weapons, and emotional and verbal abuse. (p. 1)

It has long been understood that children and youth, while they do commit crimes, deserve to be treated differently from adult offenders. This was recognized in our society with the *Juvenile Delinquents Act* of 1908. The *Young Offenders Act* of 1984 added to the protection afforded young offenders but was soon criticized for being soft on youth who commit serious crimes. In 2003, the *Youth Criminal Justice Act (YCJA)* became the new law governing youth crime in Canada.

Children under the age of twelve are seen as not criminally responsible for their actions, since they are deemed unable to appreciate fully the consequences of their actions. "Refractory behaviour by children," according to the authors of *Children's Law Handbook* (Zuker, Hammond & Flynn, 2005), "is typically addressed as a matter of child protection legislation and/or intervention by the school system" (p. 162).

Youths between the ages of twelve and eighteen are seen as bearing some responsibility for their actions. The *YCJA* governs how the justice system balances their vulnerability as youth with their responsibilities as members of society. As a general rule, it encourages the resolution of offences without the formal involvement of the youth justice system. In particular, "extrajudicial measures" are encouraged so youth can be held accountable for their misconduct without having to enter a courtroom. The intention is to prevent crime by addressing young students' circumstances and to rehabilitate these students before they become caught up in a cycle of criminal behaviour.

This extrajudicial and rehabilitory concept is in tension with other aspects of the act that seek to ensure that young people are subject to meaningful consequences, including serving adult sentences for serious crimes of violence.

What are the implications for schools? The preference for extrajudicial measures means that the police and the courts are increasingly likely to defer to the authority of principals in cases that take place in schools, especially when the offences are relatively minor or involve first-time offenders. *Ontario Schools Code of Conduct* serves as a guide to conduct, discipline, and punish offences in schools. The safe schools provisions in the *Education Act*, particularly the power to suspend or expel students, are critical tools for law and order in schools.

SAFE SCHOOLS PROVISIONS IN THE EDUCATION ACT

The primary responsibility for safety in schools rests with the principal as the primary parent and disciplinarian. The principal is expected to exercise careful judgment in ensuring that young people conduct themselves appropriately within a safe school environment.

While principals have less severe punishments at their disposal than the police do, this is offset by a lower evidentiary standards to meet in determining misbehaviour. Also, principals and teachers, as substitutes for parents, are more interested in remedying behaviour than meting out severe punishments.

Two of the most common forms of punishments are suspension or expulsion. There have been major shifts since the 1990s in how schools administer suspensions and expulsions. Students who are suspended for one to five days are given homework packages to complete and bring back to school. Students suspended for longer than five days are expected to attend a suspension program that includes coursework and workshops on anger management, substance abuse, or conflict resolution.

Students who are expelled from a school are placed in a different school within the same board. If the student is expelled from the board, the board is responsible to help the student find alternative education options.

SUSPENSION

While *Ontario Schools Code of Conduct* applies to all participants in public schooling, the consequences listed for violating the code apply only to students. Section 306(1) of the *Education Act* reads:

Activities leading to possible suspension
306. (1) A principal shall consider whether to suspend a pupil if he or she believes that the pupil has engaged in any of the following activities while at school, at a school-related activity or in other circumstances where engaging in the activity will have an impact on the school climate:

1. Uttering a threat to inflict serious bodily harm on another person.
2. Possessing alcohol or illegal drugs.
3. Being under the influence of alcohol.
4. Swearing at a teacher or at another person in a position of authority.
5. Committing an act of vandalism that causes extensive damage to school property at the pupil's school or to property located on the premises of the pupil's school.
6. Bullying.
7. Any other activity that is an activity for which a principal may suspend a pupil under a policy of the board.

Mitigating factors
The principal must take into account the following mitigating factors:
1. The pupil does not have the ability to control his or her behaviour.
2. The pupil does not have the ability to understand the foreseeable consequences of his or her behaviour.
3. The pupil's continuing presence in the school does not create an unacceptable risk to the safety of any person. O. Reg. 472/07, s.2.

Other factors
Under *Regulation 427/07*, the principal must take into consideration the following mitigating factors when suspending or expelling a student:

1. The pupil's history.
2. Whether a progressive discipline approach has been used with the pupil.
3. Whether the activity for which the pupil may be or is being suspended or expelled was related to any harassment of the pupil because of his or her race, ethnic origin, religion, disability, gender or sexual orientation or to any other harassment.
4. How the suspension or expulsion would affect the pupil's ongoing education.
5. The age of the pupil.
6. In the case of a pupil for whom an individual education plan has been developed,
    i. whether the behaviour was a manifestation of a disability identified in the pupil's individual education plan,
    ii. whether appropriate individualized accommodation has been provided, and
    iii. whether the suspension or expulsion is likely to result in an aggravation or worsening of the pupil's behaviour or conduct.

If the principal decides to suspend the student, the student is suspended from the school and from all school-related activities for a period of one to twenty school days. Students who are suspended for one to five days are expected to receive homework packages from the school prepared by their teachers.

The board is required to provide an academic program for students who are suspended for six to ten days, while those who are suspended for eleven to twenty days must be offered an academic program and various supports to promote positive behaviour.

The principal is required to inform teachers of the suspension. Written notice of the suspension is to be given "promptly" to the student and the parent (unless the student is over the age of eighteen and/or has withdrawn from parental control). The notice must include the reason for the suspension, the duration, information about any program for suspended students, and information concerning the right of appeal.

The principal must also notify as soon as reasonably possible the parents of a student who has been harmed as a result of the activity leading to the suspension, unless the student is an adult or unless such notification would not be in the student's best interests. When so notifying parents, the principal must be careful to protect the privacy of the student who has been suspended.

Students, parents, or guardians may appeal a suspension within ten school days by giving written notice to the appropriate supervisory officer. The school board must then hear and determine the appeal within fifteen school days of receiving the written notice, unless both sides agree to a later deadline.

Appeals must be heard by a panel of at least three school board trustees. In the meantime, the student remains suspended. The standard of proof at the hearing is a "balance of probabilities" rather than "beyond a reasonable doubt," and the school board's decision on an appeal of a suspension is final. The board may confirm the suspension, confirm the suspension but shorten its duration, or quash the suspension and expunge the record.

EXPULSION

Expulsion from school is a severe form of punishment meted out for very serious offences by students. Section 310(1) of the act reads:

SUSPENSION, INVESTIGATION AND POSSIBLE EXPULSION

Activities leading to suspension

310. (1) A principal shall suspend a pupil if he or she believes that the pupil has engaged in any of the following activities while at school, at a school-related activity or in other circumstances where engaging in the activity will have an impact on the school climate:

1. Possessing a weapon, including possessing a firearm.
2. Using a weapon to cause or to threaten bodily harm to another person.
3. Committing physical assault on another person that causes bodily harm requiring treatment by a medical practitioner.

4. Committing sexual assault.

5. Trafficking in weapons or in illegal drugs.

6. Committing robbery.

7. Giving alcohol to a minor.

7.1 Bullying, if,

    i. the pupil has previously been suspended for engaging in bullying, and

    ii. the pupil's continuing presence in the school creates an unacceptable risk to the safety of another person.

8. Any other activity that, under a policy of a board, is an activity for which a principal must suspend a pupil and, therefore in accordance with this Part, conduct an investigation to determine whether to recommend to the board that the pupil be expelled.

The principal is to undertake a thorough investigation into the circumstances of the offence in order to determine whether to recommend to the board that the pupil be expelled. In the meantime, the student is placed in a program for suspended students and has no immediate right to appeal the suspension. The requirements for the principal to report to teachers and parents are the same as those described above under suspension protocols.

If the principal, on concluding the investigation, decides not to recommend expulsion, the original suspension is either confirmed, modified, or withdrawn. If the principal decides to recommend expulsion, then the principal must prepare a report for the school board summarizing his or her findings and recommending whether the student be expelled from his or her school only, or from all the schools of the board. In considering whether to recommend expulsion, the principal has to take into account any mitigating factors. The principal also must make a recommendation on the type of school or program that might benefit the student.

On receiving a principal's recommendation to expel a student, the school board holds an expulsion hearing with the principal, the student's parents (or the student, if an adult), and any other persons specified by board policy. After hearing submissions from all parties, the board may decide to expel the student either from the student's own school or from all the schools in the board. Students expelled from their own school are assigned to another school in the board; students expelled from all schools of the board are assigned to a program for expelled students operated by the board. There is no time limit for an expulsion from all the schools of a board, but a student is not entitled to be readmitted to a school until he or she has successfully completed a program for expelled students. The program consists of an academic and non-academic component. This helps ensure that expelled students have the opportunity to continue their education and develop "long-term positive attitudes and behaviours by identifying and addressing the underlying causes of the behaviour that led to the expulsion" (Policy/Program Memorandum 142: School Board Programs for Expelled Students, 2007).

If the school board decides not to expel the student, it may uphold, modify, or expunge the original suspension.

Case Study: Failing to Take Bullying Seriously
Karam v. Ottawa-Carleton District School Board (2014)

A student in an Ottawa school became friends with two boys, but their relationship quickly turned to one in which he was bullied by them. While "play fighting," the boys often placed the student in chokeholds. They also called him names, and the student began to feel trapped. He complained to the principal and vice-principal that the boys were being physically aggressive with him and were stealing from him. He claimed that nothing was done to help him or stop the bullying

The bullying culminated in a dramatic event in which the student suffered an episode of difficulty breathing and non-responsiveness in class following an argument with the two other male students. It appeared to his classmates that he was suffering a seizure, but the teacher did not call for an ambulance.

The student's doctor diagnosed his reaction as a panic/anxiety attack and suggested that he consider removing himself from the school. His mother arranged for him to be home schooled and eventually enrolled him in a new school.

The student and his parents claimed that, although the staff had responded to individual incidents of theft or "play fighting," more could have been done to help foster healthy relationships. The parents believed that the lack of documentation, and the school's failure to request an ambulance when the student fell ill in class, were evidence that the school had ignored the student.

Mr. and Mrs. Karam argued in small claims court that the board failed to exercise the required duty of care toward their son, which is that of a reasonably prudent parent.

The principal claimed that he believed that all reported incidents had been dealt with. Neither he nor any of the teachers had received any reports of the student being choked. The teachers described certain problematic incidents between the boys, but the teachers believed that, in each case, the boys remained friends and resolved any issues between them. The teachers denied having received any complaints about bullying.

The court considered whether this case was appropriate for damages based on the standard of care and alleged negligence in meeting that standard of care, and whether, but for the alleged negligence, the student would not have suffered damages.

The court confirmed that the standard of care owed to a student was that of a careful or prudent parent. It found that the student had complained about minor incidents to the vice-principal, who should have been aware of the situation. However, it would not have been apparent to the students, other than the two other male students, or to the rest of the teachers or the principal that the student felt bullied, because he continued to sit near the bullies and to play sports and associate with them. On the face of it, they still appeared to be friends.

However, following the student's panic attack, it became apparent to everyone that he was a victim of bullying. At that point it was necessary to separate the student from the two male students, and homeschooling was appropriate.

The court awarded $5,000 in damages to the student and considered these to be reasonable expenses.

This decision is not significant in terms of monetary impact; however, boards should be aware of liability for failure to respond to a student's needs and the consequences of ignoring bullying.

THE ROLE OF THE CRIMINAL JUSTICE SYSTEM

While the school system is better equipped to protect students from harm and to punish and reform student offenders, the police and the courts continue to play an important role in ensuring student safety.

The purpose of criminal law is to protect individuals and maintain order in society. Students, teachers and other people in schools are protected from violence and other offences by criminal law, and may themselves face criminal charges for violating the law of the land.

VIOLENT CRIMES

Violent crimes committed by students, particularly homicide or aggravated assault, are taken very seriously by the police and the courts. The *Youth Criminal Justice Act* has increased the number of violent offences for which youth can be sentenced as adults.

The killing of another human being—directly or indirectly, intentionally or not—is a *homicide*, which may be deemed murder (first-degree or second-degree murder) or manslaughter.

Murder is the intentional killing of another individual. According to section 231(1) of the *Criminal Code* a charge or conviction of first-degree murder pertains to situations in which:

- the murder is planned and deliberate;
- one person hires another to commit murder;
- the victim is a law enforcement officer;
- the murder is caused while committing another serious offence, such as aggravated assault, sexual assault, or forcible confinement.

"Second-degree murder" refers to murders that do not fit the situations listed above. "Manslaughter" is defined as a killing resulting from a wrongful act, even if the killing was unintentional.

Criminal assault, the most common form of violent crime, refers to threatened or actual physical contact without consent. There are several levels of assault under the *Criminal Code*:

Level 1:   Threatening or pushing accompanied by (a) intentionally applying force; (b) attempting or threatening force by act or gesture; (c) accosting or impeding someone while openly wearing or carrying a weapon or imitation weapon.

Level 2:   Assault with a weapon or causing bodily harm, such that there are serious consequences for the victim's health or comfort.

Level 3:   Aggravated assault, which is defined as wounding, maiming, disfiguring, or endangering the life of the victim.

While relatively minor Level 1 assaults in the school may be handled using the powers of the principal under the *Education Act*, weapons offences and more serious allegations of assault will be referred to the police as well. This does not mean that the principal will not take action against a student who has committed a serious criminal assault. The *Education Act* is clear that the principal is responsible for suspending such a student immediately, and possibly, after a thorough investigation, for recommending that the student be expelled.

Sexual assault, another very serious violent crime, ranges in severity from unwanted sexual touching to aggravated sexual assault. Teachers who witness these crimes must report them immediately to the principal and, possibly, the police.

Teachers and principals play important roles in preventing violence by creating positive learning environments and enforcing the school's code of conduct. Natural consequences and rehabilitation at the school level also serve a critical function in the justice system because the courts defer to the judgment of educators in minor cases.

OFFENCES AGAINST PROPERTY

Canadian society takes a dim view of crimes against property, such as theft, robbery, and vandalism.

Theft, which is the taking of property, permanently or temporarily, without the owner's permission, is the most common criminal offence. It is also very common in schools, though the items taken may be of relatively low value. Nonetheless, these are serious crimes that merit the school's, and possibly the police's, attention. For the most part, the police do not become involved in theft cases unless the items stolen are of high value. Robbery that includes violence or the threat of violence will nearly always involve the police.

Another common property crime in schools is vandalism: the intentional destruction of property. Examples of vandalism in schools include graffiti, damage to classroom fixtures, breaking windows, stopping up toilets, and setting potentially serious fires. Vandalism, which is very often a sign of larger discipline problems within the school, is a significant problem that is best handled internally, though the police may be called in to investigate serious cases. Again, extrajudicial measures by the principal are critical to reducing vandalism.

ALCOHOL AND DRUG OFFENCES

The use of alcohol and illegal drugs is common among teenagers in Canada, even though alcohol is illegal before the age of nineteen and improper use of controlled drugs illegal at any age. While most students do not abuse alcohol or drugs regularly, many students do encounter problems related to their use. As a result, it is important for schools to monitor their use in school and at school events. It is also important for them to help students who exhibit dependency habits.

Generally, the police are not involved with alcohol or drug offences at school, except when they are hired to supervise school events such as dances. As with other crimes on school property, they defer to the judgment of the principal acting *in loco parentis*. Police and police sniffer dogs may be called into schools if the principal has reasonable grounds for suspecting a student of trafficking.

The youth criminal justice system's increasing reliance on extrajudicial measures is a double-edged sword for educators. On the one hand, it recognizes that educators acting *in loco parentis* are better able to understand, influence, and punish children and youth than distant officers of the court. On the other hand, along with the *Code of Conduct*, this reliance adds considerably to the responsibilities and disciplinary challenges that principals and teachers face.

THE PRINCIPAL'S DUTY TO MAINTAIN ORDER AND DISCIPLINE

The statutory duty of principals to maintain order and discipline under the *Education Act* has been an important theme throughout this chapter. Principals, working with staff members, have a key role to play in establishing a safe school culture. Principals are also responsible for determining appropriate disciplinary measures, and, where necessary, suspending a student or even recommending a student's expulsion.

After outlining the principal's responsibilities concerning visitors and trespassers, this section will examine how searches should be conducted in schools and the ways in which principals should carry out disciplinary investigations. While principals have great authority, their actions are subject to legal scrutiny.

VISITORS AND TRESPASSERS

- A non-custodial parent attempts to abduct his children from the school.
- A predator passes himself off as a student.

Although we think of schools as public places, members of the general public do not in fact have the right to enter or remain on school premises unless they are authorized to do so. Students, teachers, board employees, and parents are authorized to be on school premises on any day and at any time, within limits established by the local school board. The law also permits school trustees, local clergy, and the local member of Provincial Parliament to visit without reservation. Other people may be invited onto school premises for a particular purpose by the principal or vice-principal, or may be authorized to be on school premises by board policy. Even those people who are legally permitted to be on the property do not have access to all areas of the school. This means, for example, that parents who want to visit their child's classroom are expected to make arrangements through the principal. They do not have automatic right of entry to a particular classroom. It also means that teachers do not necessarily have free access to all areas of the school.

Volunteers and members of the community are valued partners in fostering the development of young people. Volunteers assist as tutors, helpers, and coaches. Concerns about the safety of schools have led many school boards to require that they and other regular visitors (such as student teachers) obtain criminal record checks. Other members of the public who have not been authorized by the school board or principal—for example, students from another school—do not have automatic right of access. Most schools have clear signs requiring such people to report to the main office.

While physical access to secondary schools is still relatively easy, many elementary schools began locking their doors as of January 2013 under the new Safe Welcome Program.

On December 14, 2012, Adam Lanza fatally shot twenty students and six staff in Sandy Hook Elementary School in Newton, Connecticut. In the aftermath of this tragedy, former Premier Dalton McGuinty swiftly announced that all elementary schools in Ontario would lock their doors, use security cameras, and implement a buzzer system to let people in. Despite these measures to keep students safe, it was questioned by teachers why the same level of security was not offered to Ontario's secondary schools, which leave their doors open all day.

Access to schools is at the discretion of the principal, who has the right to exclude *anyone* whose presence is considered "detrimental to the safety or well-being" of others on the premises. This could include disruptive parents and members of the public. Others who may be carefully screened or denied entry are non-custodial parents because there have been cases of attempted abduction. Students serving suspensions or who have been expelled are also not permitted access.

Case Study: The Brampton Centennial Secondary School Massacre

On the morning of Wednesday, May 28, 1975, sixteen-year-old Michael Slobodian went to school with two loaded rifles and proceeded to open fire. He killed fellow classmate and best friend John Slinger in the boys' washroom, then walked down the hall and killed his English teacher Margaret Wright in front of her class. Slobodian then proceeded to shoot thirteen other students before he turned the gun on himself. Students and teachers panicked. Some hid in closets while other students broke windows with chairs and tried to escape.

Canadian comedian Scott Thompson, who lived on the same street as Slobodian, and had been his friend since childhood, recalls walking by Slobodian's body in the hallway covered in blood. School resumed the following Monday, with no counselling support offered to students or staff.

Premier Bill Davis's daughter was a student at the school. The day after the shooting, Davis asked Attorney General John Clement to meet with Justice Minister Otto Lang to review Canada's loose gun laws. A group led by John Singer's parents petitioned Queen's Park demanding that the *Criminal Code* be changed in order to prevent further acts of gun violence in schools.

The result of the Brampton massacre was still felt forty years later when the *Toronto Star* ran a feature on it on May 28, 2015. Many of the former students, now adults, talked openly how they never got over the incident even though they were told to carry on.

Slobodian left a suicide note:

> To Whom It May Concern,
> My life is now gone to pot. I am going to eliminate certain people from this world. Those people are: Mrs. Wright, Mr. Bronson and any other sucker who gets in my way. I am then going to kill myself so as not to be imprisoned. I am not insane but just strictly fed up with life. I am not getting anywhere and it's my fault. I love my parents and my family and I know that they love me.
>
> Michael Peter Slobodian.

---

(1) What do you think were the circumstances that led to this tragedy?
(2) What has changed in forty years regarding school safety and how school boards deal with traumatic incidents?
(3) Do you think stricter gun laws in Canada have prevented further incidents of gun violence in schools?

LOCKDOWN PROCEDURES

Bill 212 amended the *Education Act* regarding the behaviour, discipline, and safety of students. Even though some boards in Ontario did have lockdown procedures, Bill 212 mandated that all school boards implement the protocol. *Lockdown* refers to an incident in which a perceived or real threat is imminent in a school and all doors and classroom doors are locked. Below are highlights from the lockdown guidelines in the Provincial Model for a Local Police/School Board Protocol (OME, 2015, pp. 32-36).

Mandatory Requirements

1. All publicly funded school boards in Ontario must establish a lockdown policy to ensure the development and implementation of individual school plans.

2. A minimum of two lockdown drills must occur each school year...
"**Lockdown**" should *only* be used when there is a major incident or threat of school violence within the school. ... "**Hold and Secure**" should be used when it is desirable to secure the school due to an ongoing situation outside and not related to the school, such as a bank robbery nearby ... "**Shelter in Place**" should be used for an environmental or weather related situation, where it is necessary to keep all occupants within the school ...

Clearly defined roles, responsibilities and expectations are critical in emergency situations. At a minimum, plans should include expectations of staff, students, parents and police.

Principal – The principal is responsible for over-all planning, the final content of the plan, scheduling of drills, inviting police, fire and Emergency Medical Services (EMS) to participate in and be aware of planning and drills, training of students and for the overall safety of staff and students. In an actual incident (not a drill), the police are responsible for management of the threat and subsequent criminal investigation, however the principal shall provide full cooperation with police.

Staff – School staff, and in particular administrators, have the overall responsibility for the training, safety and well-being of students ...

Students – Students have a responsibility to be familiar with the plan and to respond quickly to the direction of staff during a crisis situation. Any student with information or prior knowledge of an individual or a potential situation which may result in a violent incident, must come forward with that information as soon as possible ...

Police – Police are responsible to respond to and investigate violent incidents. During a violent incident, police will assume command and control of the response and investigation. Parents and guardians must be informed of the existence of this plan. Accurate floor plans are a key component of lockdown plans and are important both from a planning and response standpoint ...

It is recommended that, before locking a door, staff should gather everyone in the immediate vicinity into their classroom or other secure area, but only if it is safe to do so. Once inside a secure area, staff and students should:

- stay away from doors and windows;
- turn off lights;
- close blinds;
- be aware of sight lines;
- if there is a window in the classroom door, consider covering window;
- take cover if available (get behind something solid);
- remain absolutely quiet;
- teachers to take attendance;
- no cell phone use unless necessary to communicate regarding the incident. Cell phones should be shut off or put on vibrate ...

As washrooms cannot be locked and therefore should be identified during planning as a danger (red) area in the event of a lockdown, students need to evacuate washrooms if at all possible and get to an area which can safely be locked down (green) ...

Fire-drills have long been accepted as an important and effective tool in preparing staff and students, in the event a fire breaks out in a school. Equally important, is the practicing of lockdown drills, in preparation for a major incident of school violence ...

SEARCH AND SEIZURE

R. v. A.M., which was featured in chapter 2, made it clear that constitutional protections against unreasonable warrantless searches apply to students in school. The police officers who used a sniffer dog to help them search St. Patrick's High School in Sarnia on November 7, 2002, neither obtained a warrant from a judge nor had a reasonable basis for suspecting that drugs were present in the school. This police action, therefore, was considered unreasonable under both criminal law and the *Education Act*, since the "entire school body" was "held in detention" for a "warrantless, random search."

The court added that a warrantless search by school authorities, rather than the police, would be appropriate if based on reasonable grounds and conducted in a reasonable manner. It is important to understand why school authorities are held to a lower legal standard than police officers.

Case Study: R. v. M. (M.R.) (1998)

Mr. Cadue, vice-principal of a Halifax junior high school, had been advised on more than one occasion that thirteen-year-old M.M.R. had been dealing drugs at the school. Cadue had reason to believe his student informants: They were acquaintances of M.M.R. and a previous tip they had given him had proven to be correct.

On the day of the dance, one of the informants told Cadue that M.M.R. was "carrying" at the dance. Cadue then called the police and requested that an officer be present. He then asked M.M.R. and his friend to come to the main office. He asked them if they were in possession of drugs, then advised them that he was going to search them.

The police officer watched as Cadue conducted a search of the students. A bulge in M.M.R.'s socks was revealed to be a cellophane bag. Cadue showed the bag to the officer, who identified it as containing marijuana. The officer then arrested M.M.R. and advised him of his rights.

(1) Did the vice-principal act appropriately?
(2) Did the police officer act appropriately?
(3) Was M.M.R.'s "right to be secure against unreasonable search and seizure" (*Canadian Charter of Rights and Freedoms*, section 8) violated?

School principals and teachers have a duty to ensure that schools are safe places for learning. Common law recognizes their duty of care while acting *in loco parentis.* The *Education Act* charges them with the duty to maintain order and discipline. They must be careful, however, not to violate the legal rights of students under the *Canadian Charter of Rights and Freedoms.*

R. v. M. (M.R.) (1998) raised interesting legal points and prompted the courts to weigh the rights and responsibilities of educators and students in balance. When and under what circumstances was a search by a school administrator or teacher considered unreasonable under the *Charter?*

An earlier case had already determined that a school administrator could conduct a personal search of a student. In *R. v. G. (J.M.)* (1986), the Supreme Court held that, while the student had a legitimate expectation of privacy, the school's duty to maintain a safe and orderly learning environment was more important. As a result, the principal's search and seizure of a marijuana joint found in the student's pant cuff was deemed to be appropriate. G.J.M. was found guilty of possession of a narcotic, a charge laid by a police officer who appeared on the scene after the search.

In *R. v. M. (M.R.)*, the police officer was present for the search. As a result, the youth court judge dismissed the evidence, arguing that the vice-principal was acting as an agent of the police through an "agreed strategy" between them. The appellate courts and, finally, the Supreme Court of Canada ruled the search reasonable and legal and ordered a new trial.

First, the courts determined that the decision of the vice-principal to conduct a search was reasonable, given the information with which he was provided. The Supreme Court identified, as reasonable grounds, information from a credible student source, from more than one student or teacher, from the administrator's own observations, and from any combination of the above.

Second, the Supreme Court determined that the decision to search was consistent with Cadue's duties under Nova Scotia's *Education Act* and was not arbitrary in nature. Education legislation in both Nova Scotia and Ontario authorizes the search of students under appropriate circumstances. The search was also conducted before a witness, the police officer. School authorities should conduct searches in the presence of another staff member or a police officer.

The Supreme Court seemed reluctant to usurp the role of educators in assessing the information provided to them, concluding: "Courts should recognize the preferred position of school authorities to determine if reasonable grounds existed for a search." Indeed, students were deemed to be aware that their rights in school were more limited. Justice Cory of the court wrote:

> Students know that their teachers and other school authorities are responsible for providing a safe environment and maintaining order and discipline in the school. They must know that this may sometimes require searches of students and their personal effects and the seizure of prohibited items. It would not be reasonable for a student to expect to be free from such searches. A student's reasonable expectation of privacy in the school environment is therefore significantly diminished.

Third, the courts concluded that the police officer was not directly involved in the search. If the officer had been directly involved, and the higher legal standard for a search by an agent of the police had applied, the courts may have accepted the youth court judge's decision to dismiss the evidence.

Fourth, the courts found no evidence that there was an agreed strategy between the vice-principal and the officer.

Educators must act reasonably in exercising their greater scope in conducting searches. The case of *R. v. A.M.* made it clear that random searches in schools are not permitted. As legal scholar Greg Dickinson (2009) writes, it was not the intent of the Supreme Court "to allow a reasonably well-educated guess to constitute reasonable grounds" (p. 176). The court went even further. It expressed concern that making it easy for principals and the police to conduct such searches would send negative messages to students about their fundamental rights as citizens.

School board/police protocols instruct school personnel when conducting searches to ask students to remove items from their personal property and clothing as opposed to removing the items from the students directly. These protocols also instruct school personnel not to conduct personal searches. It is up to the police to conduct personal searches, presumably with a warrant based on evidence of probable cause.

Disciplinary Investigations in Schools

The incidents described above focus on cases that ultimately led to criminal proceedings and sanctions. Most disciplinary incidents in schools, however, are handled by the principal under the *Education Act* and Ministry of Education guidelines. Principals have both the duty and the authority to investigate all cases of student misconduct, and, in the worst cases, to suspend or recommend for expulsion students who violate the school's code of conduct or education legislation.

Principals should conduct investigations in a timely manner and interview witnesses while events are fresh in their minds. When the police are involved, such as in weapons or drug cases, principals may wish to delay their own investigations to avoid hampering the police investigation. Principals should cooperate with the police and supply them with copies of all their investigation notes. If the police are involved, principals should attempt to contact parents as soon as possible. They should also keep in mind that police investigations are separate and distinct from school investigations.

Each witness should be kept in a separate room under supervision. Each witness and victim should be asked to provide written and signed statements independently. All interviews and other sources of information should be thoroughly documented and dated. Notes should be carefully maintained in a manner consistent with the privacy rights of those involved. Language should be clear, simple, and descriptive. Opinions, subjective comments, and judgments should be avoided; adjectives and adverbs should be used with caution because they may connote judgment.

In making decisions, principals should use a balance of probabilities to weigh the evidence and explain their reasoning clearly and succinctly based on the evidence.

They should bear in mind the importance of procedural fairness under the *Statutory Powers Procedures Act*. The actions of a principal may be reviewed for procedural fairness when suspensions and expulsions are appealed to the board or a tribunal, respectively. In addition, as the search and seizure cases above make clear, the criminal courts also assess the reasonableness of school authorities' actions.

Principals and teachers who act diligently and fairly in investigating misconduct in schools are more likely to have the results of their inquiries respected by all parties.

THE ONTARIO COLLEGE OF TEACHERS ON SAFETY IN LEARNING ENVIRONMENTS

In April 2013, the College released *Safety in Learning Environments: A Shared Responsibility*, an advisory that focused on student safety. The advisory discussed places of learning both on and off school property such as classrooms, labs, gyms, schoolyards, off-site facilities, field trip locations, and school buses—largely reinforcing the points concerning safety made in this chapter.

Following are relevant excerpts from the Advisory.

- Know and apply legislation and your employer's policies with respect to student safety generally and particularly those regarding codes of conduct, reporting and responding to incidents of violence and abuse, lockdown procedures and safe school protocols.
- Know and apply legislation and your employer's policies regarding the specific activity you are conducting with students.
- Be aware of legislation and your employer's policies about intervening in violent or aggressive behaviour by and among students.
- Ensure that you and your students have the necessary training, knowledge and skills to undertake an activity, to respond safely and to report unsafe activities or situations.
- Model respectful behaviour and non-violent conflict resolution skills.
- Encourage healthy relationship and bullying prevention skills throughout the curriculum.
- Ensure that any intervention undertaken does not jeopardize your personal safety or the safety of others.
- Know who to contact and where to go to get help if needed.
- Know your professional responsibilities. Ontario Certified Teachers

have a professional responsibility through due diligence to safeguard and educate students who have been placed under their care. Jointly with school administrators and key stakeholders, teachers are responsible for creating safe and healthy instructional settings, integrating hazard identification, assessing the risks and controlling the situation in all aspects of the facility. Due diligence refers to taking every precaution reasonable in the circumstances to avoid injuries.

- Understand your duty and your employer's duty to contact or report to outside agencies, such as children's aid societies or the police, about concerns and/or suspicions of child abuse.
- Know your responsibility as it relates to police/employer protocols for responding to violent incidents.
- Always maintain professional boundaries with students.
- Be aware and responsive to new and emerging safety concerns that affect students (such as food allergies).
- Become familiar with individual plans for students who have health or other safety concerns.
- Ensure that areas that contain safety items such as WHMIS binders, fire extinguishers, eye wash stations, defibrillators and first aid kits are clearly marked. Report missing items.
- Interact with students appropriately.
- Understand how to support vulnerable populations such as students with exceptionalities or students who are bullied.
- Know how to recognize mental health issues, including signs and words of aggression and suicidal intent, and report them immediately.
- Learn how your school's Safe and Accepting Schools Team can be of help.

CONCLUSION

The case above is troubling on many levels and leaves us with many unanswered questions. Why were the police not involved? How could such an excessive amount of corruption occur in a school without someone with authority coming in and ending it? What happened to the students who were sexually abused?

There is no simple formula for ensuring that schools are safe places for teaching and learning. *Ontario Schools Code of Conduct* has proven a useful guide to the roles and responsibilities of all members of the school community. The increased emphasis on prevention, progressive discipline, and early intervention in the 2007 changes to the safe schools provisions in the *Education Act* reflects a growing understanding that school safety and student conduct are complex issues that are best addressed by educators who understand their students and schools.

Educators who are aware of their ethical, legal, and professional duties are best able to balance the rights of individuals with the safety of the community.

Responding and reporting any form of unethical behaviour is paramount in a profession that deals with the most vulnerable citizens of our country, our children.

CHECKING YOUR UNDERSTANDING

- *Ontario Schools Code of Conduct* sets clear provincial standards of behaviour for all people involved in the school system. It calls on everyone to contribute to fostering safe school environments.

- The principal has the overall statutory responsibility for ensuring that the school is a safe and healthy learning environment.

- School boards must create lockdown procedures for schools and train staff in how to keep children safe.

- Board employees who work directly with students must respond to any student behaviour that is likely to have a negative impact on the school climate.

- Students are also legally required to be self-disciplined, obey teachers, and accept such discipline as would be exercised by a "kind, firm and judicious parent." Such discipline does not include corporal punishment.

- The *Youth Criminal Justice Act* attempts to balance the vulnerability of young people with their responsibilities as members of society. It encourages the resolution of offences through "extrajudicial measures" without the formal involvement of the criminal justice system.

- The *Education Act* lists a number of specific activities for which the principal may suspend a student from school and from all school activities for a period of one to twenty days. Depending on the length of the suspension, the student may be assigned to a special program for suspended students.

- The *Education Act* also lists a number of specific activities for which the principal must immediately suspend a student and then carry out an investigation with a view to possibly recommending that the school board expel the student.

- According to Bill 13, employees, including school bus drivers, who become aware that a student may have engaged in an activity that could lead to suspension are required to report the matter in writing to the principal as soon as possible.

- A board may expel a student from the student's own school or from all the board's schools. If from the student's own school, the student is assigned to another school in the board. If from all the board's schools, the student is assigned to a special program for expelled students that the student must successfully complete before being readmitted to a school.

- Parents (or the student if an adult) may appeal a suspension or expulsion to the school board or to a specially convened tribunal, respectively.

- Violent crimes committed by students will inevitably lead to police involvement as well as school-imposed sanctions. Less serious offences may simply be dealt with by the principal under the *Education Act*.

- Only certain people are legally authorized to be on the school premises. Other people may be invited by the principal. The principal has the authority to exclude anyone whose presence is detrimental to the safety and well-being of others. Even those permitted to be on the premises do not have access to all areas of the school.

- Students' expectation of privacy in schools is significantly diminished. School authorities may search a student's property and person if they have reasonable grounds to do so. A search should be non-intrusive and be conducted with a witness present.

- The Ontario College of Teachers' advisory on school safety focuses on a wide variety of best practices for teachers.

APPLYING YOUR UNDERSTANDING

Conduct Unbecoming of Students or Teachers

A fourteen-year-old student, Sheldon, was in the school library playing computer games when a teacher, Mr. Hage, entered and told him to leave because he should not be playing computer games during school time. According to Mr. Hage, Sheldon got upset when Mr. Hage moved his chair to encourage him to leave. Mr. Hage said the student grabbed his hand and twisted it before stomping out of the room. Mr. Hage suffered a fracture of his hand.

Sheldon's story is somewhat different. He said that Mr. Hage yelled at him and another student, telling them to stop playing computer games. He claimed that the teacher pulled the chair out from under him, causing him to fall to the floor. Sheldon, bruised and seething, left the lab and marched into main office to speak to the principal.

(1) What are the main facts in the case?

(2) What are the main issues?

(3) What areas of education law are relevant to this case?

(4) What advice would you offer the principal in dealing with this case?

(5) What is the likely outcome for Sheldon? For Mr. Hage?

CHAPTER 6

AVOIDING NEGLIGENCE: ACTING AS A CAREFUL AND PRUDENT PARENT

After reading this chapter, you will understand:
- *the importance of the educator's role of acting as a careful or prudent parent in order to ensure that schools are safe places for students to learn.*
- *the definition of negligence in civil law and the four elements necessary for a finding of negligence;*
- *the legal consequences when educators breach their duty of care, as laid out in education statutes;*
- *legal concepts such as foreseeability, reasonableness, vicarious liability, voluntary assumption of risk, and contributory negligence (illustrated through legal cases);*
- *ways in which educators can avoid negligence through professionalism and risk management.*

Case Study: A Failure of Care in PHE
Hussack v. Chilliwack School District No. 33 (2009)

Devon Hussack, a student with a record of chronic absence, had missed all the Physical and Health Education classes in which field hockey skills were taught. On the day he returned, the class was divided into teams to begin play. While the teacher considered not permitting

Hussack to play due to his lack of preparation, he ultimately decided that the student would benefit from participating because he had experience in ice, floor, and roller hockey and could be quickly brought up to speed by listening to the teacher's verbal instructions to the class about what they had learned to date.

Unfortunately, Hussack attempted to check a player from behind, something the teacher had specifically instructed should not be done. The other student raised her hand backward, striking Hussack in the face. He suffered lacerations, bruising, swelling, and a concussion and developed headaches, disturbed sleep, and sensitivity to light. He was later diagnosed with somatoform disorder and became increasingly housebound, qualifying for a disability pension.

Hussack, the plaintiff, sued the teacher and school district, the defendants, for a breach to the standard of care. His lawyer argued that the teacher had endangered the defendant by failing to ensure that he was progressively trained. It was argued that past experience in hockey actually increased Hussack's risk, as he needed opportunities to unlearn habits acquired on ice.

Counsel for the defendants suggested that Hussack had been contributorily negligent, but this was dismissed by the court. Also dismissed were allegations about possible pre-existing conditions and subsequent harm caused by an over-protective parent.

As a result, the school district was held liable for $1,365,000 in damages, which included $1 million for future loss of income.

---

(1) What acts or omissions by the teacher contributed to the accident?

(2) Do you think that the court ruling was fair? Why or why not?

(3) Think about this case in relation to a school situation in which you are likely to be involved (e.g., an art activity, science lab, or field trip). How might the lessons learned from this case inform your actions?

Educators must always be aware of potentially hazardous situations and think carefully when planning any activities that have an element of risk. By ensuring that adequate safety precautions are taken, they reduce the risk of harm for everyone and the likelihood of being sued.

NEGLIGENCE

Negligence is defined as the failure to use reasonable care. Police can bring charges of criminal negligence when actions are considered to be grossly negligent. It is much more likely that negligence by an educator would lead to civil law proceedings. A teacher could be found guilty if his or her unintentional actions were judged to have contributed to an injury. Depending on the circumstances, both the teacher and the school board, who as the teacher's employer could be found vicariously liable, could be required to compensate the victim financially.

NEGLIGENCE IN CRIMINAL LAW

In order for someone to be guilty of a crime, there must be evidence of both *actus reus* ("the guilty act") and *mens rea* ("the guilty mind"). Generally, a crime requires a deliberate intention to commit a wrongful act or knowledge that the act was against the law. Even though negligence is generally thought of as an unintentional act, the Crown can also establish *mens rea* by proving that the accused was criminally negligent. According to the *Criminal Code*, section 219(1), a person is criminally negligent who:

(a) in doing something, or
(b) in omitting to do anything that is his duty to do, shows wanton or reckless disregard for the lives or safety of other persons.

For example, when a five-year-old was run over while riding his bike unsupervised, his parents were charged with failing to provide the necessities of life to their son. Though they intended no harm, they were found guilty due to their wanton and reckless disregard for their son's safety. The judge was particularly upset that the parents had failed to heed previous warnings and sentenced the father to one year in jail and the mother to a conditional sentence of seven months.

Similarly, when a street race led to the deaths of two pedestrians, the two drivers were charged with criminal negligence.

Criminal negligence cases do not feature in education law, so it is highly unlikely that a teacher will ever be found criminally negligent. Civil cases against educators and school boards are very common, however.

NEGLIGENCE IN CIVIL LAW

The failure to use reasonable care is often the basis for lawsuits in civil law. Negligence becomes the basis for lawsuits in civil law if the failure to act as a reasonably prudent person would do in such circumstance results in damage or loss to another person. This standard was established in 1856 in England (*Blyth v. Birmingham Water Works Co.*).

Negligence became recognized as a tort due to a landmark case in Scotland. In *Donoghue v. Stevenson* (1932), a brewer, Stevenson—the defendant—was found to owe a duty of care to Mrs. Donoguhe—the plaintiff. His failure to notice a snail at the bottom of a bottle of ginger beer was a breach of that duty. This breach of duty was responsible for Mrs. Donoghue's subsequent illness. Stevenson was required to compensate her for the injury she sustained. The highest court identified the *neighbour principle*, which states, "You must take reasonable care to avoid acts or omissions which you can reasonably foresee would be likely to injure your neighbour."

The standard of care for teachers is even higher. Teachers must take reasonable care to avoid acts or omissions that could harm students, toward whom they have a duty to act as a careful or prudent parent would do.

ELEMENTS OF NEGLIGENCE

Four elements are necessary for a finding of negligence in a civil suit:

(1) The plaintiff is owed a duty of care by the defendant.
(2) The defendant breached that duty of care.
(3) Actual damage or loss was sustained.
(4) The breach of duty was the proximate cause of damage or loss by the defendant.

In the *Hussack* case, the student was owed a duty of care by his teacher. This duty of care was breached by the teacher's failure to properly train a student who had been absent. This failure to act *in loco parentis* led to significant harm, as reflected in the award by the court. Finally, the lack of appropriate instruction was considered the proximate cause of the blow to the head and subsequent infirmity.

Cases of negligence fall under civil law, which operates under a set of principles collectively known as the law of *tort*. In tort law, redress for damages to the plaintiff takes the form of a financial award. Torts can be intentional (e.g., assault or sexual misconduct) or unintentional (e.g., negligence). The plaintiff's burden of proof is lower in a civil case than in a criminal case. The onus of proof is "a balance of probabilities" rather than "beyond a reasonable doubt."

DUTY OF CARE IN CIVIL LAW

Teachers and schools have a fiduciary relationship with students and the parents who entrust their children to the school. As a result of being *in loco parentis*, teachers and schools have an obligation to conduct themselves in a manner consistent with this trust. Generally the standard of a careful or prudent parent is used in assessing *fault* for an *act* or *omission*.

The duty of care of teachers and school boards is well established in law. The expectation that teachers in Canada act as prudent parents was established in *Williams v. Eady* (1893). In that case, a boy was severely burned in a flash fire caused by a boy lighting a bottle of phosphorous with a match. The teacher was deemed negligent for leaving the bottle of phosphorous in the conservatory where students could find it. While both sides in negligence cases tend to accept that there is a duty of care, they may dispute the nature of the duty given the specific facts of the case.

In Ontario, the duties of boards, principals, and teachers are set out in statute law. The *Education Act* and its associated regulations reflect the high standards set by society for educators.

DUTIES OF SCHOOL BOARDS

The school board assumes the overall responsibility for ensuring a safe and healthy learning environment for the schools in its jurisdiction. Section 170(1) of the *Education Act* delineates the following obligations for school boards:

> Every board shall,
> 6. provide instruction and adequate accommodation during each school year for the pupils who have a right to attend a school under the jurisdiction of the board; ...
> 8. keep the school buildings and premises in proper repair and in a proper sanitary condition, provide suitable furniture and equipment and keep it in proper repair, and protect the property of the board;
> 9. make provision for insuring adequately the buildings and equipment of the board and for insuring the board and its employees and volunteers who are assigned duties by the principal against claims in respect of accidents incurred by pupils while under the jurisdiction or supervision of the board.

DUTIES OF PRINCIPALS

Similarly, principals are charged with the day-to-day responsibility of ensuring that each school is a safe and healthy learning environment. Most notably, Section 265(1) of the *Education Act* lays out the following obligations:

> (a) to maintain proper order and discipline in the school; ...
> (j) to give assiduous attention to the health and comfort of the pupils, to the cleanliness, temperature and ventilation of the school, to the care of all teaching materials and other school property, and to the condition and appearance of the school buildings and grounds; ...

As the person charged with the responsibility for maintaining discipline and order in the school, the principal assumes wide-ranging authority and obligations. The act, recognizing the broad scope of the principal's duties, requires teachers to assist in keeping the school safe and orderly under the principal's direction.

DUTIES OF TEACHERS

Teachers are charged with the duty of maintaining a safe and healthy learning environment within their classrooms. This responsibility also extends to their duties in other parts of the school, as noted in chapter 1.

Section 264(1) of the *Education Act* states:

It is the duty of a teacher and a temporary teacher: ...

(d) to assist in developing co-operation and co-ordination of effort among the members of the staff of the school

(e) to maintain, under the direction of the principal, proper order and discipline in the teacher's classroom and while on duty in the school and on the school ground.

The *Education Act* and other legislation make it clear that teachers, principals, and boards all owe a duty of care to their students because of their special relationship of trust. Since parents are required to send their children to school, they are entitled to expect that reasonable precautions will be taken to ensure that they will be safeguarded from all foreseeable risks.

Case Study: The Duty of Care of School Districts
Paquette (Litigation guardian of) v. Surrey School District No. 36 (2014)

A vice-principal, after hearing footsteps on the school roof, yelled at the two boys from an open window. A twelve-year-old boy, afraid of getting caught, jumped from a height of twenty feet on to a cement surface and was injured.

The student sued the school district for negligence and sought an award of damages.

The British Columbia Supreme Court held the school board liable to the plaintiff for injuries he suffered when he fell off the roof of his school.

In the court case, the defendant had acknowledged ongoing problems with students accessing the roof by climbing trees in close proximity to the building. To impede access to the roof, branches had been cut from many trees, but not from the cherry tree that had been climbed by the plaintiff.

The judge's ruling found that it was *foreseeable* that the cherry tree might also be used, and that students could be put at risk. Thus, the school district was deemed negligent for breach of its duties under the *Occupiers' Liability Act*, not under its duties *in loco parentis*. The judge, acknowledging contributory negligence on the part of the student, apportioned 75 percent of the liability to the school district.

This case was appealed to the British Columbia Court of Appeal. In dismissing the appeal, the appeals court found that the school board, "an institution charged with the care of children and obliged to take reasonable steps to ensure the safety of its premises, ought to have brought a greater degree of thought and care to the risk posed by children getting onto the roof than did the children doing the climbing."

(1) What acts or omissions by the school district contributed to the accident?

(2) Do you think that the court ruling was fair? Why or why not?

(3) The judge found the school district negligent under the *Occupiers' Liability Act*. Why?

(4) Think about this case in relation to a school situation in which you are likely to be involved. How might the lessons learned from this case inform your actions?

OCCUPIERS' LIABILITY

School boards, like all property owners, are responsible for ensuring that appropriate care is taken to prevent accidents to anyone using the property. This is why it is important for homeowners to ensure that their premises are safe (e.g., by keeping sidewalks clear of snow and ice). School boards own large amounts of property that are regularly used by students, staff, and members of the public. For this reason, board personnel, particularly principals and custodial staff, should pay attention to the condition of the premises at all times.

Section 3 of Ontario's *Occupiers' Liability Act* states that the occupier of the land and structures owes a duty to

> take such care as in all the circumstances of the case is reasonable to see that persons entering on the premises, and the property brought on the premises by those persons are reasonably safe while on the premises.

School boards must meet this standard in relation to regular users (e.g., staff and students during the school day), people who use the premises at other times (e.g., children using the playground after hours or adults cutting across the schoolyard), and even people using the property illegally (e.g., trespassers).

In *Kennedy v. Waterloo (County) Board of Education* (1999), the school board was sued after Kennedy crashed into a bollard while riding his motorcycle at a high speed. The plaintiff successfully sued the school board for failing to take reasonable care in not removing the bollards from that location. The school board was apportioned 75 percent of the costs, with the plaintiff being found contributorily negligent. Since school premises are regularly used by the public, appropriately or otherwise, school boards as occupiers must exercise a duty of care to anyone who might enter the grounds or buildings. As noted above, they are not considered to be *in loco parentis* for school-age children who use the premises outside school hours or activities.

Occupiers' liability may also be an issue in cases of injury to students, especially when they are under the care of educators. In *Cox (Litigation Guardian of) v. Marchen* (2002), the student litigant injured her Achilles heel while leaving the building through an emergency exit door. Although the student knew that this locked door was not to be used, she and others regularly used it to go to the parking lot. The principal did not conduct regular inspections of the door, and it was not repaired until after the incident. The Ontario Superior Court found that although the student violated school rules, she had a reasonable expectation that the door would be safe. The court found the principal at fault based on both the standard of care in the *Education Act* and the standards contained in the *Occupiers' Liability Act*.

In the *Hussack* case, the judge chose to focus on occupiers' liability, but, in upholding the ruling, the appeals court used language relevant to the standard of care in the *Education Act*.

BREACH OF DUTY OF CARE

For a finding of negligence, the defendant must owe a duty of care. In addition, there must be evidence that this duty of care was breached due to an act or omission on the part of the defendant.

Case Study: Moddejonge v. Huron County Board of Education (1972)

A tragic accident occurred during a field trip. The outdoor education instructor permitted a group of students to go swimming in a reservoir. The instructor had warned the students about the drop-off under the water, but the drop-off was irregular and poorly marked with buoys. A sudden breeze caused a student who could not swim to move beyond the drop-off. The student drowned, as did another student who attempted to rescue him.

The court ruled that a reasonably prudent parent would guard against these risks, which it regarded as foreseeable. Among the factors taken into account were: the instructor permitted students to go into water where there was a drop-off; he did not swim, and did not provide sufficient life-saving equipment; once the wind came up, he did not take safety measures; the death of the rescuer was a foreseeable response to an emergency created by the instructor's negligence.

(1) Did the outdoor education instructor breach his duty of care to the students?

(2) Had he warned them sufficiently?

(3) Was he responsible for the death of the boy who attempted a rescue?

Teachers are held to a very high standard of care. Teachers and school boards have to make an effort to foresee a wide range of consequences of their acts or omissions. Adopting risk-management strategies can limit the chances of injury and reduce the chances of successful negligence suits. While the standards are high, they are not unreasonable, as the following excerpt from the Supreme Court of Canada ruling in *Stewart v. Pettie* (1995) makes clear:

> One of the primary purposes of negligence law is to enforce reasonable standards of conduct so as to prevent the creation of reasonably foreseeable risks ... Tort law does not require the wisdom of Solomon. All it requires is that people act reasonably in the circumstances. The "reasonable person" of negligence law ... is not an extraordinary or unusual creature; he is not superhuman; he is not required to display the highest skill of which anyone is capable; he is not a genius who can perform uncommon feats, nor is he possessed of unusual powers of foresight. He is a person of normal intelligence who makes prudence a guide to his conduct. He does nothing that a prudent man would not do and does not omit to do anything a prudent person would do ... His conduct is the standard "adopted in the community by persons of ordinary intelligence and prudence."

Modified Standard of Care

In the *Hussack* case, the court applied the standard of care of a careful and prudent parent. Courts, however, modify the required standard of care depending on the circumstances of the case.

In *McKay v. Board of Govan School Unit 29 of Saskatchewan* (1968), a student was severely injured when attempting a dismount from the parallel bars. The physical education instructor had not demonstrated the dismount to students, and McKay had minimal experience with this exercise. The Court of Appeal determined that the careful parent standard did not apply to the facts of this case. Justice Woods wrote:

> A physical training instructor in directing or supervising an evolution or exercise is bound to exercise the skill and competence of an ordinarily competent instructor in the field. The standard of the careful

parent does not fit a responsibility which demands special training and expertise.

The careful parent standard continues to be used, but the courts have adapted it to recognize the higher level of expertise expected of teachers as professionals. This is most clearly expressed in the case of *Brown v. Essex (County) Roman Catholic Separate School Board* (1990). In this case, the plaintiff was using a sewing machine when the cloth bunched, causing the needle to stay in one spot. Because the teacher had not explained what to do if the cloth bunched, the student did not turn off her sewing machine. As a result, the needle broke into three pieces, one of which became imbedded in the student's eye. The court found that the sewing teacher "did not act as would a careful or prudent parent with her background and knowledge of sewing." The judge argued that "a *reasonably prudent sewing teacher* owed students the duty of care to have warned them of the particular dangers involved in sewing on the spot." This ruling elegantly acknowledges the careful and prudent parent standard while elevating the standard to acknowledge the additional expertise of a professional educator.

LIMITS TO FORESEEABILITY

The standard of care does not require school boards or teachers to take precautions against accidents that are not reasonably foreseeable. As the court noted in *Ramsden v. Hamilton* (1942):

> Human prudence would be taxed beyond reason, were it to endeavour to foresee every possibility of human ingenuity, or boyish mischievousness, in its search of opportunities to get into trouble, in even the remotest and most unlikely corners, nooks, or crannies.

Here are some unfortunate incidents that the court decided were not results of negligence:

- *Fraser v. Campbell River (Board of School Trustees of School District No. 72) (1987)*: A student jumped head-first into the snow in the schoolyard and injured himself. The teacher had conducted the class in a manner that was controlled and disciplined. The plaintiff's action was sudden and could not have been foreseen.

- *McCue v. Etobicoke (Board of Education) (1982)*: A high school student sustained an eye injury when another student flicked a paperclip before class began. It was not reasonable to expect the teacher to be present or to foresee this incident.
- *Crouch v. Essex County Council (1966)*: A student deliberately sprayed caustic soda into the eyes of another student. The teacher had warned of the dangers of caustic soda, maintained reasonable classroom management, and could not have foreseen such a deliberate act.

NEGLIGENCE OUTSIDE SCHOOL HOURS

It is clear that during the course of the regular school day teachers and schools have a duty of care to students. But what if an incident occurs during a special activity, or off campus, or outside school hours?

Note that students participating in authorized and approved school activities, such as field trips and intercollegiate sports events, remain under the care of the supervising teacher wherever they are and whatever time it may be. Students may need to be reminded that all the normal expectations of the school's code of conduct apply during activities like school dances or concerts. Overnight and extended trips can also present special problems, and supervising teachers should ensure that parents and students clearly understand that participants remain responsible to the principal for their behaviour just as if they were at school.

Schools need to be explicit in stating school opening and closing times so students and parents know not to presume that schools will provide supervision outside those times. Schools also need to be consistent in applying these rules; otherwise they may be viewed as negligent should an accident occur when the school was open unofficially.

It is crucial for teachers to avoid sending young students into danger. Consider a grade 1 student who is stranded at school due to a family emergency. It would be negligent to send her home at 4 p.m. so the teacher can get home. In-school detentions that cause students who are bused-in to miss their normal transportation home could also be deemed negligent.

What if a student is injured on the playground on the weekend? While the school has a duty of care to *students,* they are not students when playing on school property at night or on the weekend and the school is not responsible for their supervision. They are children, not students, during that time. The duty of the school board is simply to ensure that the condition of the grounds is not hazardous and that any equipment is properly maintained. If they do not do this, then the common law standard of occupiers' liability is used against them rather than the standard of care of a prudent parent.

ACTUAL DAMAGE OR LOSS

While negligence is a failure to use reasonable care, not all negligent acts cause actual damage or loss. Courts will award a claim only to a plaintiff who can demonstrate that the breach of care has caused actual harm or loss. If Hussack had not been hit by a field hockey stick, for example, there would have been no loss, and legal action would not have succeeded.

Fortunately for everyone, most negligent acts do not lead to significant harm. Nonetheless, with over 236,000 teachers in Ontario, there are numerous negligence cases every year that do result in significant damage or loss.

CAUSATION

Once it is established that the defendant has breached the standard of care required of a teacher, the plaintiff must prove that the defendant's negligent act caused the harm sustained by the plaintiff.

In the case of *Hussack v. Chilliwack School District No. 33*, the court carefully assessed the degree to which the school board's negligence contributed to Hussack's injury. They applied the "but-for" test that courts often apply in negligence cases. If suitable training had been used, would Hussack have sustained fewer injuries? Would the proper training have altered Hussack's behaviour or the actions of the spotter? In ruling in Hussack's favour, the court decided that causation was likely. Similar questions led the court to conclude that Moddejonge's swimming death was caused by the outdoor education instructor's failure to foresee the consequences of his own acts and omissions.

VICARIOUS LIABILITY

A person or organization that did not directly cause the plaintiff's injury may be found liable in tort law. This is known as the principle of *vicarious* (substitute) *liability.* For example, if the person who caused a car accident did not own the vehicle, the owner could be held vicariously liable for lending it to someone not competent to drive safely. This is intended to ensure that owners exercise care in lending their vehicles. It also enables the plaintiff to obtain money from the insurance policy of the owner if the driver is not insured sufficiently.

In civil suits, the plaintiff tends to include as defendants anyone who could have played a role in the incident. Anthony Brown (2004), in *Legal Handbook for Educators,* writes:

> In many instances, the defendants in a tort action are the teacher involved, the principal (whether directly involved or not), and the school board. The plaintiff's lawyer will issue a statement of claim against everyone who is potentially liable because one cannot always predict how a judge or jury will find or apportion liability. (p. 110)

You may have noticed that the school board is one of the defendants named in all of the cases cited in this chapter. While the board as a corporate entity may have done nothing wrong, the board is often sued along with the teacher accused of negligence. The school board may have had clear guidelines in place, which a teacher, other employee, or volunteer disregarded. Nonetheless, the board may be found vicariously liable and required to pay the plaintiff. For example, in *Bain v. Calgary Board of Education* (1994), the teacher was found negligent in the serious injury of a student on a field trip. While the board was not negligent in its actions, it was found vicariously liable and thus required to compensate the plaintiff. If the teacher had been the only party responsible in law, Bain would not have collected significant damages, given the defendant's meagre assets.

The prospect of having to pay significant damages caused the board to pursue this case vigorously. The board could have sought indemnity from its employee, but this is rarely done because boards usually have much deeper pockets than their employees.

DEFENCES AGAINST NEGLIGENCE

The best defence against a negligence claim is that negligence did not exist or that the defendant did not owe the plaintiff any duty of care. The plaintiff, even if negligence is proved, may not be able to recover as much as expected if the court finds that the accident was unavoidable or that the plaintiff voluntarily assumed the risk or had also been negligent in the incident.

Unavoidable Accident

Injury or loss may result from a situation that is unavoidable, no matter what precautions a reasonable person might take.

- A school bus driver lost control of the vehicle because it was struck by lightning:
    - The unavoidability of the situation could be a full or partial defence against a negligence claim.
- A piece of ice fell from a passing plane and struck a student playing at recess:
    - The airline, not the school, would be liable for this unforeseeable event.
- A student suffers a brain aneurysm while at school:
    - The school would not be liable for a random and unavoidable event such as this.

Voluntary Assumption of Risk

For a *voluntary assumption of risk* defence to succeed, the defendant must prove that the plaintiff clearly knew of the risks of his or her action and made a choice to assume those risks. Negligence cases involving sports injuries often hinge on questions regarding the voluntary assumption of risk inherent in the particular sport.

Case Study: Thomas v. Hamilton (City) Board of Education (1994)

Thomas, an athletic grade 11 student, executed a routine tackle during a school football game. Unfortunately, as Thomas hit the ball carrier on the thigh with his head down, his helmet dislodged. Despite prompt medical attention, Thomas was rendered a quadriplegic by the incident.

Thomas sued, among others, the coach and the school board, arguing that their negligence caused his injuries. Much of the trial revolved around the question of voluntary assumption of risk. The plaintiff argued that he and his parents had not been warned of the risks inherent in football. It was further alleged that the coach had not trained Thomas in proper tackling technique and should have known that the plaintiff's "long, lean, swan neck" rendered him more susceptible to injury.

The defendants noted that Thomas, his parents, and his doctor had completed forms giving their informed consent. The court, in finding in favour of the defendant, stated that Thomas voluntarily assumed the risk, and that the coach and the school board had exercised appropriately the duty of care of a careful and prudent parent. Nor could they have reasonably anticipated the long-neck theory, which may or may not have been a factor.

The case eventually made its way to the Ontario Court of Appeal, which made the following statement about participation in dangerous sports:

> The appellant participated in his high school's junior football program of his own free will. He was aware of the risk of injury, even serious injury, that is inherent to participation in a contact sport such as football. However, he did not, through his consent to participate (and that of his mother), assume all risk of injury to the extent that school authorities were relieved of the duty of care that they owed to him.
>
> The appellant was not incapacitated, let alone obviously incapacitated ... He had his mother's consent, and his family doctor's certificate stating that he was fit to play football. He knew that football was a contact sport which carried with it the risk of serious injury. He wore a "horse collar" because he was aware of the fact that his neck was exposed to injury. He said, as the trial judge noted in his reason for judgment, that even if he had specifically contemplated the risk of a catastrophic neck injury, he would probably have continued to play.
>
> The appellant was appropriately and progressively coached. He was an

excellent athlete who excelled in a number of sports, including football. His equipment was adequate. The injury he sustained occurred during a routine play and, although the consequences of his injury were, and continue to be devastating, the injury came within the ambit of those risks inherent in a contact sport such as football. He did not, of course, give a consent which would overcome negligent conduct on the part of the Board or his coaches. However, I agree with the trial judge that neither the Board nor the coaches were negligent and that his mother "consented to the normal risks of the game". I am not prepared to say that the trial judge was wrong in reaching that conclusion.

(1) Why were the coach and school board not found negligent for their actions or omissions in practice or during the game?

(2) Why did the plaintiff introduce the long-neck theory?

(3) Did the plaintiff and his family understand the risks they were assuming?

(4) What do you think of the statement by the Ontario Court of Appeal?

(5) As a result of this decision, Thomas received no money to assist him in his life as a quadriplegic. Was this fair?

While Thomas was ultimately unsuccessful, his case illustrates the scrutiny under which school boards and their employees are placed when it came to negligence cases.

First, it is incumbent on school boards to ensure that every reasonable safety measure is taken. In the McKay case, inadequate coaching and the lack of proper supervision led to findings of negligence against the school board. In *Thomas*, close scrutiny failed to reveal any negligent acts on the part of board employees.

Second, it is essential for teachers, schools, and school boards to obtain informed consent from students and their parents or guardians before students participate in activities such as extracurricular sports or trips off school property. In the *Thomas* case, the forms signed by the student, parents, and doctor left no doubt that they had been fully informed of the inherent risks before the student was permitted to play football. If the board had not obtained informed consent, this failure in itself could have constituted a form of negligence.

Bain v. Calgary Board of Education (1994), which is summarized below, illustrates that an act must be voluntary and that the assumption of risk must be explicit. Although nineteen-year-old Bain had gone on a voluntary, unsupervised hike on his own initiative, the court ruled that he had not given express or implied agreement to assume risk of injury; nor had he waived his right to claim damages due to a breach of care on the part of the instructor.

Teachers should exercise great care to ensure that informed consent forms are completed. This gives students and parents the opportunity to voluntarily assume the risks inherent in a particular activity. It is wise, in requesting and obtaining waiver forms, to include all potential risks, so students and parents cannot argue that they were unaware of them. Students should not be permitted to participate without written consent, because this could be grounds for a successful negligence suit. At times, teachers accept consent over the phone; this could be problematic because it leaves the school board open to a claim that the parent was not informed of all of the risks. On school outings, teachers should stick to the agreed itinerary and outline of activities and diligently follow school board policies and procedures. Finally, educators should remember that the purpose of informed consent is to address the potential hazards inherent in a particular high-risk activity. Informed consent does not absolve the supervising teacher from the duty to take all reasonable care to prevent foreseeable accidents. Waiver forms will not protect a teacher if it can be shown that an accident was caused by the teacher's negligence rather than by the natural risks inherent in the activity.

Contributory Negligence

At one time, under common law, a plaintiff found to be in any way at fault was denied the right to claim damages. Since then, common law has developed the notion of shared responsibility.

If both the plaintiff and the defendant are deemed to be negligent to some degree, damages are divided between them according to the principle of *contributory negligence*. Whereas normally the plaintiff must prove negligence against the defendant, in these cases the defendant assumes the burden of proof in asserting a defence of contributory negligence. The judge then apportions liability in accordance with Ontario's *Negligence Act*.

While teachers have a duty of care toward students, students also have a duty to conduct themselves responsibly and demonstrate reasonable care for their own safety. This is reflected in the duties of students in the *Education Act*. Section 23 of *Regulation 298* requires pupils to:

> (b) exercise self-discipline;
>
> (c) accept such discipline as would be exercised by a kind, firm and judicious parent;
>
> (d) attend classes regularly and punctually;
>
> (e) be courteous to fellow pupils and obedient and courteous to teachers;
>
> (f) be clean in person and habits;
>
> (g) show respect for school property.

As this section indicates, a pupil

> is responsible for his or her conduct to the principal of the school that the pupil attends,
>
> (a) on the school premises;
>
> (b) on out-of-school activities that are part of the school program; and
>
> (c) while travelling on a school bus that is owned by a board or on a bus or school bus that is under contract to a board.

The degree of care on either side will vary, depending on factors such as the age and mental ability of the students.

In *Brown v. Essex (County) Roman Catholic Separate School Board*, the school board was considered largely responsible even though the girl injured by the sewing needle was found partly responsible. On the other hand, in *Marshall (Litigation Guardian of) v. Annapolis (County) District School Board*

(2009), a four-year-old kindergarten student hit by a school bus was considered too young to be held responsible for his injuries.

Case Study: Bain v. Calgary Board of Education (1994)

Bain, a nineteen-year-old grade 11 student at a vocational school for the learning disabled, was participating in a school-sponsored outdoor education activity. In the evening, a group of students asked permission to go on an evening hike rather than watch a movie as planned. The defendant teacher, after initially refusing, gave them permission and drove them to the start of the trail. The boys were poorly dressed and provisioned for the hike. Bain lost his grip at a rock face and fell off the cliff headfirst, sustaining serious permanent injuries. The school board countered Bain's claim for damages by arguing that he had voluntarily assumed risk (see above), was an adult, and contributed to his injuries by failing to take appropriate precautions.

The court ruled that the age of the student did not detract from the duty of care of the teacher, especially given the student's learning disability. In its decision, the court wrote:

> The forestry tour was an extension of the classroom, occurring during the school year, with the specific authorization of the school board and subject to its rules and regulations. The defendant teacher remained in control of the students to the same extent as if they were in the classroom, and he owed them the same or a higher duty of care ... The defendant teacher could have avoided the injury simply by following the agenda authorized by the school board and approved by the parents for that evening's activities. The risk of harm was foreseeable.
>
> As a result, the teacher and school board were found 75 percent liable. Because Bain failed to "take proper steps for his own safety," he was held contributorily liable for 25 percent of the damages.

(1) What factors did the court need to factor into its decision to apportion responsibility between the plaintiff and the defendants?
(2) Do you agree with the court's decision?
(3) Although the board's rules and regulations were clear, it still had to pay damages. Why?

NEGLIGENCE AND THE
ONTARIO COLLEGE OF TEACHERS

Assessing negligence is often a matter for the courts, but it can lead to a finding of professional misconduct under *Regulation 437/97: The Ontario College of Teachers Act, 1996*. In fact, in some cases it is much easier to prove professional misconduct compared with negligence, which requires that some form of harm actually occur. Item 11 states that "failing to supervise adequately a person who is under the professional supervision of the member" may constitute misconduct.

A failure to adequately supervise students in a classroom, school, on a school trip, on a team, or in a club, can be interpreted as a form of negligence. In the case below, no harm came to the students, but the teacher clearly left the students unsupervised for hours. Many things could have gone wrong.

Case Study: Failing to Supervise
Ontario College of Teachers v. KSP (2014)

A teacher agreed to supervise secondary students on an overnight trip to a conference in a large city. On the first evening the teacher let students use his room to iron clothes. At 11 p.m., he left the students and did not tell them where he was going, nor did he tell any other teachers that he would be leaving students alone. The students needed assistance and tried to reach the teacher but could not for several hours. When the school trip was over, the administration suspended the teacher for five days without pay and reported him to the Ontario College of Teachers.

During a disciplinary hearing, KSP pleaded guilty to professional misconduct in that he "failed to supervise a person who is under his supervision." As well, he admitted that he was guilty of failing to maintain the standards of the profession, emotionally and psychologically abusing students, disgraceful and dishonourable behaviour, and conduct unbecoming of a member.

The discipline panel ordered that KSP receive a reprimand immediately following the hearing, complete a course on effective supervision and boundaries, receive a five-day suspension without pay retroactively, and have his name published in *Professionally Speaking*, the College magazine, and under Disciplinary Decisions on the College's website.

This case appears in *Professionally Speaking*, June 2015.

The College's (2013) professional advisory, *Safety in Learning Environments: A Shared Responsibility*, includes several pieces of advice that reinforce points made in this chapter:

- Identify and report deficiencies in the environment or equipment you use with students.
- Determine whether parental consent is required before beginning an activity so that parents or guardians authorize students' safe use of tools, materials, and equipment.
- Identify what resources are necessary to take suitable precautions within the given learning environment.
- Assess whether the activity is appropriate given the number of students and their relative abilities, disabilities, and ages.
- Determine whether additional supervision may be needed.
- Monitor, modify, or stop an activity you think is unsafe.
- Establish and monitor sound and consistent safety procedures in your classroom or teaching area and review these procedures with students.
- Be aware and responsive to new and emerging safety concerns that affect students (such as food allergies).
- Become familiar with individual plans for students who have health or other safety concerns.

RISK MANAGEMENT

By being prudent and careful, teaching professionals can enhance student safety and avoid negligence claims. School boards, too, can be proactive in avoiding negligence. In fact, the high cost of litigation and successful claims for damages have led school boards to make every effort to act defensively in order to reduce the risk of harm and potential lawsuits. In the lingo of liability insurance, this is known as *risk management*. It has two benefits:

- Safety and training lead to fewer accidents.
- It is easier to defend a lawsuit when reasonable safety measures and appropriate training are in effect.

School boards and their employees can take many risk-management measures. These include:

- identifying potential dangers through "safety audits";
- current training of teachers and coaches;
- staff training in first aid and CPR;
- maintenance on a fixed schedule;
- safety equipment in labs and gyms;
- safe vehicles and transportation plans;
- adequate supervision ratios in playgrounds and on field trips;
- appropriate reporting and record keeping;
- controlling communication after incidents occur.

The Ontario School Board Insurance Exchange (OSBIE), the self-funded non-profit insurer for 90 percent of the school boards in Ontario, offers a wide range of risk-management materials and services. (Go to www.osbie.on.ca for more information.)

As part of your duty of care to your student, take time to foresee risk and consider how you can make the learning environment safer for your students. Here are some practices to consider:

(1) Monitor your teaching area on a daily basis for potential hazards (e.g., damaged outlets, frayed cords, unsafe wall fixtures or loose ceiling tiles).

(2) Report any problem to the principal in writing on the same day, keeping a copy for your own records.

(3) Until the problem has been fixed, take whatever measures are necessary to keep the area safe for your students.

(4) If you come across a potential hazard in the school at large, report it to the principal.

(5) If you are supervising a field trip or other off-campus activity, make sure you follow board policy meticulously and know what to do in case of an accident or other emergency (always take a cell phone with you).

(6) If you are the teacher of a high-risk activity, such as technological studies, physical education, or science, be sure to follow all the appropriate safety protocols and procedures that apply in your subject area.

CHECKING YOUR UNDERSTANDING

- In tort law, negligence is the failure to use reasonable care. It can result from an act or an omission.

- Teachers are considered to be *in loco parentis* and therefore are expected to act in the role of a "careful or prudent parent" toward the students in their care.

- A modified standard of care means that in certain circumstances the standard of a careful or prudent parent is replaced by the standard of a careful or prudent expert teacher.

- The standard of care is influenced by the age of the students, the training they have received, the nature and condition of any equipment, and the number of students being supervised.

- Teachers are unlikely to be held liable for accidents that were not reasonably foreseeable.

- The four elements of negligence are: (1) the plaintiff is owed a duty of care by the defendant; (2) the defendant breached that duty of care; (3) actual damage or loss was sustained; and (4) the breach of duty was the proximate cause of the damage or loss.

- The burden of proof in a negligence case lies with the plaintiff.

- The duties of the school board include providing a safe and healthy learning environment.

- Principals must ensure a school environment in which order is well maintained and attention is paid to the health and comfort of students.

- Teachers, under the direction of the principal, are responsible for appropriate supervision of students, as well as for maintaining a safe learning environment.

- Teachers and schools are responsible for incidents that occur during school trips or during after-school activities.

- *Vicarious liability* means that school boards may be held legally liable for the actions of their teachers, even when the board did nothing wrong.

- As property owners, school boards are also responsible for ensuring that reasonable measures are taken to prevent accidents from happening to anyone entering their property.

- Two possible defences against negligence suits are unavoidable accident and voluntary assumption of risk.

- At times plaintiffs' own actions are regarded as contributing to their injury or loss.

- Negligence by a teacher could also lead to a complaint to the Ontario College of Teachers that the teacher failed to "supervise students."

- School boards should promote risk-management strategies in order to reduce the risk of harm and, by extension, litigation.

APPLYING YOUR UNDERSTANDING

One Teacher's Excursion into the Garden of Negligence

Ms. Patel, a second-year teacher, was very excited about taking her grade 5 class on a field trip to the Royal Botanical Gardens (RBG). She had planned this activity as the culmination of her unit on the season of spring. The tulips and flowering trees would beautifully illustrate spring renewal while letting students enjoy the fresh air after a long winter of being cooped up in the classroom. As her twenty-six students jostled one another and spoke loudly while boarding the bus, it was evident that they shared her excitement.

Ms. Patel was relieved that she had not cancelled the trip due to the heavy rainfall overnight. She believed that everything would be fine as long as students stayed on the paths and followed the rules.

The two parent volunteers sat behind Ms. Patel, who herself sat beside Veronica. Veronica, who needed a wheelchair to get around, had been helped onto the bus by the driver.

As the bus pulled into the RBG driveway, Ms. Patel loudly reminded the rambunctious students that they needed to obey the guide and chaperones at all times. She also asked them to stay on the path and be extra careful because of the damp conditions.

After the guided orientation tour, students were free to roam through a couple of the gardens. A number of the boys ran around and played roughly. The chaperones tried to keep the students under control, but it was difficult to identify them because they were not wearing name tags. It was also difficult to distinguish them from students from other schools. One parent noticed later that she had lost an earring while breaking up a scuffle.

Meanwhile, Veronica's wheelchair, pushed by a student, slipped off the path, causing her to fall into the mud. Her feet remained soaked until her return home at the end of the day; she would remain in bed sick for two weeks as a result of the incident.

To make matters worse, the shop was demanding that the school reimburse it for a vase that a student had accidentally broken and some candy that it said had been shoplifted.

While Ms. Patel was disappointed that the field trip had not gone entirely as planned, she was proud of how she handled Faria's apparent anaphylactic (allergic) reaction. She had grabbed Paul's EpiPen and stabbed it into Faria's thigh. Faria was rushed to hospital where, according to a call from her parents, she was recovering well.

The next day, Ms. Patel was shocked to learn that the principal had received complaints from many parents. Veronica and Faria's parents were particularly upset. They were threatening to involve lawyers.

(1) Should the field trip have been cancelled, given the conditions?

(2) Was there adequate supervision for the field trip?

(3) Should Veronica, Paul, and Faria have been permitted to go on the field trip? If so, under what conditions?

(4) Could Veronica or Faria's families sue the school board?

(5) What is the responsibility of the school board to the gift shop?

(6) What is the effect of the "consent and waiver" forms signed by the parents?

(7) Is there a basis for a complaint to the Ontario College of Teachers?

(8) What is the principal's responsibility?

(9) If you were running this field trip, what procedures would you put in place to avoid these problems?

CHAPTER 7

THE CONDUCT OF TEACHERS AT SCHOOL AND IN THE COMMUNITY

After reading this chapter, you will have a deeper understanding of the professional and legal expectations for teacher conduct in the following areas: (1) classroom management, (2) sexual conduct, (3) contact with students outside school, (4) use of technology, and (5) teachers as role models.

"Be a wonderful role model because you will be the window through which many children will see their future."
—Thomas McKinnon

"In their position of trust, teachers must teach by example as well as by lesson, and that example is set just as much by their conduct outside the classroom as by their performance within it. The misconduct which occurs outside regular teaching hours can be the basis for discipline proceedings."

—Ontario Court of Appeal, *Toronto (City) Board of Education v. O.S.S.T.F., District 15*

Case Study: Hands Off
Ontario College of Teachers v. MS (2013)

A veteran teacher received a suspension and reprimand from a discipline panel of the Ontario College of Teachers for inappropriately disciplining his students.

In one incident, MS grabbed a male student by the shoulders and pushed him. The student reported the incident, and CAS investigated, confirming that MS's use of force was unacceptable.

The member continued to use inappropriate force with students. He grabbed a male student by the shoulders, and he yelled at a male student, grabbed him by the arm, and pushed him against a blackboard. In that same incident, MS pushed another student with his hand.

The students reported the incidents, and CAS once again investigated and determined that MS was physically inappropriate with students. The school board referred the case to the Ontario College of Teachers.

The member attended a disciplinary hearing and pleaded guilty to all allegations. The discipline panel ordered that MS receive a reprimand and take courses on appropriate boundaries, boundary violations, and classroom management.

MS was also suspended from teaching for thirty days.

This case appears in *Professionally Speaking*, June 2014.

---

(1) Do you think the decision made by the discipline panel was appropriate and/or fair?

(2) What other strategies could MS have used with students?

(3) What do you think happens if Children's Aid determines a teacher's conduct is unsafe with students?

The legal rights and duties of teachers have implications for teachers' behaviour both in school and in the community. The behaviour of teachers, as professionals, should be appropriate, even exemplary, in school and in society. Teachers who exercise poor judgment or behave inappropriately either in school or in the public realm risk losing the respect of students and parents, and may also face professional or legal sanctions.

CLASSROOM MANAGEMENT AND DISCIPLINE

According to the *Ontario Schools Code of Conduct* (p. 5):

Teachers and school staff, under the leadership of their principals, maintain order in the school and are expected to hold everyone to the highest standards of respectful and responsible behaviour. As role models, staff uphold these high standards when they:

- Help students work to their full potential and develop their self-worth;
- Communicate regularly and meaningfully with parents;
- Maintain consistent standards of behaviour for all students;
- Demonstrate respect for all students, staff and parents;
- Prepare students for the full responsibilities of citizenship.

Teachers have a special role at schools and in society. This is evident in the duties of teachers in educational legislation, the high standards to which they are held in criminal and civil law, and the professional standards established by the Ontario College of Teachers. All of these have implications for how teachers manage their classrooms and discipline students.

CORRECTIVE FORCE AND PHYSICAL RESTRAINT

Section 43 of the *Criminal Code* states:

> Every school teacher, parent or person standing in the place of a parent is justified in using force by way of correction toward a pupil or child, as the case may be, who is under his care, if the force does not exceed what is reasonable under the circumstances.

This provision in the *Criminal Code* protects parents, teachers, and other caregivers from criminal sanction for using force when correcting a child's behaviour.

The Canadian Foundation for Children, Youth and the Law asked the courts to repeal this section of the *Criminal Code*, arguing that it violated the best interests and constitutional rights of children. Among those defending the law were representatives of parents who were proponents of corporal punishment and representatives of teachers who believed they might need to apply corrective force or physical restraint in the course of their duties. Those in favour of maintaining section 43 argued that it protects teachers from charges of criminal assault for using physical restraint to break up a fight, manage a student with behavioural/development issues, guide a child by the arm to the office, or defend themselves. The parents involved argued that a parent who mildly spanks a child on the leg was protected by section 43 from criminal assault charges.

Section 43 provides teachers with a special defence against charges of criminal assault. The Canadian Teachers' Federation, while supportive of the Canadian Foundation for Children, Youth and the Law's desire to protect children from abuse, opposed the foundation's argument for the elimination of this special defence for teachers against assault charges. Removal of this section, the federation argued, would result in a dramatic increase in the number of assault charges filed and prosecuted. As a result, the federation continued, teachers would hesitate to respond to innapropriate student behaviour that might require the use of reasonable force, and students most likely to disrupt may interpret the removal of section 43 as freedom to do so without consequences.

The Ontario Court of Appeal in *Canadian Foundation for Children, Youth and the Law v. Canada* (Attorney General) (2002) rejected the claim that this section constituted cruel and unusual punishment for children. It concluded that Parliament had enacted this provision so "parents and teachers have a protected sphere of authority within which to fulfil their responsibilities" for nurturing and educating children. It also saw no benefit to criminalizing non-abusive corporal punishment used by parents and others for purposes of discipline and instruction.

The court disagreed that section 43 was inconsistent with the principle of "best interests of the child," saying that this is a principle that informs legal and policy initiatives rather than a principle of fundamental justice under the *Charter.*

The Supreme Court in 2004 upheld this ruling in a split decision. Justice Arbour, in her dissent, argued that judicial attitudes toward discipline had evolved significantly over time and that section 43 was no longer appropriate. The majority, while upholding the section, made it clear that "the substantial social consensus on what is reasonable correction, supported by comprehensive and consistent expert evidence on what is reasonable presented in this appeal, gives clear content to s. 43." The list provided of harmful corporal punishment situations made it clear that the courts are unlikely to tolerate severe corporal punishment.

The Supreme Court decision also established clear directions for teachers:

> Contemporary social consensus is that, while teachers may sometimes use corrective force to remove children from classrooms or to secure compliance with instructions, the use of corporal punishment by teachers is not acceptable. Many school boards forbid the use of corporal punishment, and some provinces and territories have legislatively prohibited its use by teachers … This consensus is consistent with Canada's international obligations, given the findings of the Human Rights Committee of the United Nations … Section 43 will protect a teacher who uses reasonable, corrective force to restrain or remove a child in appropriate circumstances.

PROFESSIONALISM IN CLASSROOM MANAGEMENT

Section 43 offers special protection for teachers who may need to use corrective force or physical restraint in managing student behaviour. The court rulings on the constitutionality of section 43 also offer insights into types of teacher conduct that are considered unreasonable, such as the use of corporal punishment or force that results from the teacher's anger or frustration.

The *Ontario Schools Code of Conduct* outlines broad standards for respectful and responsible classroom management and discipline by teachers. The recent amendments to the safe schools provisions in the *Education Act* emphasize prevention, progressive discipline, and early intervention. Many books and manuals are available to guide teachers in developing positive classroom management practices.

Recent rulings by the discipline panel of the Ontario College of Teachers also help educators to determine what constitutes effective professional conduct in managing students and classrooms. As the cases make clear, despite the legal protection provided by section 43 of the *Criminal Code* from charges of criminal assault, society increasingly expects teachers to manage conflict situations without resorting to physical force.

Case Study: Discipline Cannot Equal Violence
Ontario College of Teachers v. VDP (2014)

VDP was a seasoned teacher who had been teaching for twenty years. One day a student walked into his room and swore at another student. VDP took offence to the student's language and slapped the student across the face with an open hand. Approximately three weeks later, VDP was charged under the *Criminal Code of Canada* with assault. He was found guilty and was granted a conditional discharge, placed on nine months' probation, and required to complete twenty community service hours. VDP appealed the decision but lost.

VDP pleaded guilty in front of a discipline panel of the Ontario College of Teachers. He admitted that he physically abused a student, failed to maintain the standards of the profession, contravened a law, and committed acts that were dishonourable, disgraceful, and unprofessional.

The discipline panel ordered that VDP receive a reprimand and take a course in boundary issues and boundary violations, and that his name would be published in *Professionally Speaking*, the College magazine, and under Disciplinary Decisions on the College's website.

This case appears in *Professionally Speaking*, June 2014.

MAINTAINING BOUNDARIES IN SCHOOL AND BEYOND

MAINTAINING BOUNDARIES IN SCHOOL

The student–teacher relationship is critical to classroom learning. Students are more likely to learn when they have a positive rapport with teachers and teachers are genuinely interested in making learning personally meaningful for them. In order to personalize and promote effective learning, teachers will sometimes use colloquial language, make references to popular culture, tell jokes, gently tease students, ask personal questions, or share their own personal stories. Teachers as professionals must exercise great caution in their efforts to develop positive relationships with students. A remark or strategy that seems appropriate from the teacher's adult perspective may be interpreted quite differently by students, who are both younger and less sophisticated. Irony, for example, is frequently misunderstood by children, who not only tend to have a literal view of the world but also are used to respecting what their teacher tells them.

It is important, then, for teachers to stand back and consider beforehand the implications and appearance of what they say and do in the classroom. Teachers are advised to err on the side of caution. Like teachers in the previous section who were too severe in their classroom management practices, teachers who become too familiar with their students risk transgressing the professional boundaries established to protect students. Understanding these boundaries enables teachers to maintain positive and educative relationships with students that are free from inadvertent or intentional harm.

One area of concern is verbal and non-verbal communication in the classroom. Although the use of colloquial language by teachers in the classroom may not be inappropriate, it may well seem contrived to students or cause them to lose respect. It is also important to remember that as role models teachers should help their students develop proficiency in the conventions and standards of language usage. Teachers should never swear or make sexually suggestive comments. Not only is such language entirely inappropriate for a teacher, it is likely to be offensive to many students and could well lead to disciplinary action by the Ontario College of Teachers. Teachers should also avoid making personal comments about students even if they are intended in jest. The College cautioned a teacher who made personal and inappropriate comments about a student and the student's family and ordered the teacher to complete a course of instruction on appropriate boundaries. The College also reprimanded a teacher who gently stroked a student's arm while praising the student's clothing.

Teachers are expected to establish positive relationships with students but must maintain the highest standards of respectful and responsible behaviour at all times. Novice teachers should exercise discretion in communicating with students. Observing master teachers who effectively establish rapport while respecting boundaries will help them.

MAINTAINING BOUNDARIES OUTSIDE SCHOOL

Teachers and students typically interact within the milieu of the school and school-related activities. Teachers who exercise good judgment will generally avoid contact with students outside this milieu. Those who live in the same community as their students are likely to meet students in other settings.

While this should be no cause for alarm, they should keep these interchanges pleasant yet short, particularly if other people are not present.

In *Professional Advisory: Professional Misconduct Related to Sexual Abuse and Sexual Misconduct* (2002), the Ontario College of Teachers encourages teachers to avoid:

- inviting students into their homes;
- seeing students in private and isolated situations;
- exchanging personal notes, comments, or e-mails;
- personally becoming involved in students' affairs;
- giving personal gifts to students;
- sharing personal information about themselves;
- making physical contact of a sexual nature.

By knowing and understanding the reasons for these limits, teachers protect the interests of students and demonstrate sound professional judgment.

Case Study: Trying to Sound Cool
Ontario College of Teachers v. JB (2014)

A veteran teacher was reported to the College of Teachers for referring in class to a female student as a "b__ch" and a male student as a "cocky son of a b__ch."

During a viewing of a movie in class, JB yelled out, "You are so f___ing ugly" and "You are so f___ing gay." The students felt uncomfortable and reported the incident.

The member also took students off school property without parental or administrative consent.

The school board issued three letters of reprimand, suspending JB's employment as a result of these incidents.

JB pleaded guilty in front of a discipline panel of the Ontario College of Teachers and was found guilty of professional misconduct—more specifically, that he failed to maintain the standards of the profession, abused students verbally, failed to supervise students, failed to comply with the *Education Act*, and committed acts considered disgraceful, dishonourable, and unprofessional.

JB was ordered to receive a reprimand and take a pre-approved course on professional ethics and boundaries at his own expense, and his name was published in *Professionally Speaking*, the College magazine, and under Disciplinary Decisions on the College's website.

This case appears in *Professionally Speaking*, September 2015.

---

(1) List some of JB's conduct that was considered unprofessional.

(2) What are some of the dangers of taking students off school property without parental consent?

(3) What other sanctions could the discipline panel have imposed on JB's certificate?

Socializing with a student over a hamburger, while perhaps innocent enough, raised reasonable concerns about propriety. Driving the student to and from the restaurant showed even worse judgment, because the teacher was alone with a student in a private space. The telephone calls of a personal nature further transgressed professional boundaries. The College, taking all of these acts together, determined that they constituted serious professional misconduct according to the Ontario College of Teachers. Adults who abuse children often begin to *groom* their victims through such interactions. Teachers are expected to maintain a professional relationship with students outside the classroom and school setting.

THE SEXUAL CONDUCT OF TEACHERS

Case Study: Crossing the Line
Ontario College of Teachers v. TPK (2012)

TPK was a principal responsible for helping elementary students in his school deal with bullying. TPK began corresponding via email to the student on a frequent basis and provided the student with a board laptop so they could Skype while he vacationed in Mexico. He and the student exchanged cards and gifts, and on one occasion the student and her mother stayed overnight at his house. As well, with the mother's permission, TPK took the student out for dinner. It was noted that on numerous occasions he and the student met for long periods of time behind closed doors. Eventually TPK quit being a principal in his school board and has not worked in a school since.

It was not revealed in the disciplinary decision how the Ontario College of Teachers was notified. TPK pleaded guilty to emotionally abusing a student, failing to maintain the standards of the profession, engaging in behaviour that was unprofessional, and conduct unbecoming of a member.

The discipline panel ordered TPK to receive a reprimand and not be allowed to return to the profession until a psychiatric assessment was completed and stated that TPK would not harm a student or put them at risk, and that his name be published in *Professionally Speaking*, the College magazine, and under Disciplinary Decisions on the College's website. The panel noted that TPK had received counselling already and had completed a course in professional boundaries.

The discipline panel felt quite strongly about publishing TPK's name, despite the fact that the student was under sixteen. The decision states:

> Given that the Member had recently completed the Principal's Qualification Program, which outlines the responsibilities of an administrator entrusted with the care and protection of students, his actions are especially troubling to the Committee.

The panel also "felt there were compelling reasons to publish the Member's name":

> In his role as an advocate for this vulnerable student, the public would expect that he would intervene with an appropriate strategy and behave in a responsible and respectful manner. Instead, the Member initiated an inappropriate personal relationship with the Student, which increased the emotional and psychological stress on the Student, putting her at greater risk for victimization. The Member's actions comprised a serious breach of trust and showed a blatant lack of professional judgment. Publication with name is warranted and appropriate.

This case appears in *Professionally Speaking*, December 2012.

While most people take sexual misconduct seriously, many are unaware of the prevalence of unwanted or inappropriate sexual activity in the lives of school-aged children. Sexual abuse, according to conservative research estimates, affects more than twenty-five percent of girls and ten percent of boys by the age of eighteen. Sexual harassment, which includes objectionable comments, is even more prevalent. As Cook & Truscott (2007) say:

> There are *no* circumstances in which sexual activity between a teacher and a student is acceptable. Sexual activity between a student and teacher is always detrimental to the student's best interest, regardless of what ratio- nale or belief system a teacher might choose to excuse it. (p. 87)

Sexual activity between teachers and students is deemed particularly unacceptable due to the duty of care teachers owe parents and students and the position of authority they hold as professional educators. According to *Protecting Our Children,* a report by Justice Robbins (2000), such a betrayal of trust by a teacher can be particularly harmful to students:

> The impact is often less correlated with the severity or intrusiveness of the sexual behaviour than with the pre-abuse relationship to the abuser, the vul- nerability of the victim or the way in which the disclosure of the abuse was responded to. Accordingly, a seemingly minor incident of sexual touching by a close and trusted adult can have a profound and lasting impact. (chapter 3)

Teachers who violate this trust through non-consensual or consensual sexual contact with students risk severe criminal and professional consequences. Teachers who engage in sexual harassment may also face disciplinary action from their employer or the Ontario College of Teachers.

THE CRIMINAL CODE

The *Criminal Code* sets out several sexual offences that are particularly rel- evant to sexual misconduct in the school context:

Sexual Interference (Section 151)

Every person who, for a sexual purpose, touches, directly or indirectly, with a part of the body or with an object, any part of the body of a person under the age of 16 years is guilty of an indictable offence and is liable to imprisonment for a term not exceeding ten years … or is guilty of an offence punishable on summary conviction …

Invitation to Sexual Touching (Section 152)
Every person who, for a sexual purpose, invites, counsels or incites a person under the age of 16 years to touch, directly or indirectly, with a part of the body or with an object, the body of any person, including the body of the person who so invites, counsels or incites and the body of the person under the age of 16 years, is guilty of an indictable offence and is liable to imprisonment for a term not exceeding ten years … or is guilty of an offence punishable on summary conviction …

Sexual Exploitation (Section 153)
Every person commits an offence who is in a position of trust or authority towards a young person [defined as "a person 16 years of age or more but under the age of eighteen years"], who is a person with whom the young person is in a relationship of dependency or who is in a relationship with a young person that is exploitative of the young person, and who

    (a) for a sexual purpose, touches, directly or indirectly, with a part of the body or with an object, any part of the body of the young person; or

    (b) for a sexual purpose, invites, counsels or incites a young person to touch, directly or indirectly, with a part of the body or with an object, the body of any person, including the body of the person who invites, counsels or incites and the body of the young person.

Every person who commits an offence under subsection (1) [Sexual Exploitation described above] is guilty of an indictable offence and liable to imprisonment for a term not exceeding ten years … or is guilty of an offence punishable on summary conviction …

Simply put, teachers should never engage in sexual activities with students. "Sexual interference" applies to the activity of any adult who touches a child under the age of sixteen for sexual purposes. "Invitation to sexual touching" occurs when an adult invites a victim under the age of sixteen to touch a part of the body with a sexual purpose. The sentences for these offences involving children under the age of sixteen are severe, since young children are considered vulnerable and dependent on the protection of adults, particularly their teachers. Avoiding "sexual exploitation" is particularly important for secondary schools: This clause provides young adults over the age of sixteen but under the age of eighteen with the same protection from sexual misconduct by their teachers and others who may be in a position of trust or authority.

It should be noted that consent is no defence in all three of these offences. Although students over the age of eighteen are not covered by the preceding sections of the *Criminal Code*, the general charge of sexual assault (section 271) could still apply, particularly if the consent of the student is judged to have been given "by reason of the exercise of authority" of the teacher (section 265). In addition, as will be discussed later in this chapter, sexual misconduct with a student of any age is considered by the Ontario College of Teachers to be professional misconduct.

The following case suggests that the scope of a teacher's position of trust and authority extends beyond his or her own students.

Case Study: R. v. Audet (1996)

Mr. Audet, a twenty-two-year-old physical education teacher, had sex with a fourteen-year-old female former grade 8 student whom he encountered by chance during the summer vacation. The teacher accompanied the former student and her two cousins to a party where the girls consumed alcohol. The teacher left the party and lay down in a bedroom of the cottage in which the party took place. His former student subsequently joined him and they engaged in oral sex; when the former student became uncomfortable, the teacher stopped immediately.

At the trial level, the court acquitted Audet, noting that the incident took place during the holidays and that the teacher did nothing to instigate the sexual encounter. This decision was upheld by the New Brunswick Court of Appeal.

The Supreme Court of Canada upheld the appeal made by the Crown in a split decision. Whereas the lower courts viewed the circumstances as mitigating the actions of the teacher, the Supreme Court interpreted section 153 of the *Criminal Code* on sexual exploitation literally. Because Audet was in a position of trust and authority and did engage in sex with a former student who had just turned fourteen, he was ultimately held responsible for the sexual activity that took place and guilty of sexual exploitation. (It should be noted that at the time of this case, "sexual exploitation" applied to young people over the age of fourteen but under the age of eighteen.)

Justice LaForest, writing for the majority, emphasized the responsibility of the teacher: "I am of the view that in the vast majority of cases teachers will indeed be in a position of trust and authority towards their students."

While some teachers who engage in sexual conduct with students are sexually aggressive or predatory, most appear to have personal problems, poor judgment, or an inability to understand the professional boundaries that exist between teachers and students. A recent study of discipline cases from the Ontario College of Teachers revealed that the majority of teachers who engaged in sexual conduct with students are male (Zuker, Redmond & Gannon, 2013). There are, however, a number of high-profile instances of female teachers becoming romantically involved with male or female students. The case below is an example of what can go wrong when a teacher's boundaries begin to slip and sexual lines are then crossed.

Case Study: Blurred Lines
Ontario College of Teachers v. AHC (2013)

AHC initially approached her administration with concerns over rumours circulating among students regarding her relationships with some students. She stated that she was afraid of the career repercussions of these rumours. As well, a colleague raised the same concern about AHC's relationships with students and her "youthful attire." A second colleague at a neighbouring school expressed her concern regarding AHC's desire to "friend" her son on Facebook. The administration met with AHC and suggested she not be friends with students on Facebook. She agreed.

Approximately six months later, AHC went to the administration with another problem—

that students were trying to extort money from her. During the course of a school investigation, one of the students told the administration he had proof that AHC was still on social media with students. He also produced twenty sexually revealing photos that AHC had sent him and stated that he had had sexual relations with AHC.

At this point, the administration contacted the Children's Aid Society and the police. AHC was told of the allegations and was put on leave. She resigned from her position as teacher, but her case was still referred to the Ontario College of Teachers for further investigation and a disciplinary hearing.

AHC did not attend the hearing, and she did not send a legal representative. Instead, a letter from her lawyer was read aloud stating that the member denied the allegations set out in the Notice of Hearing—more specifically, that AHC denied having sex with students, sending one student twenty sexually explicit photos of her, showing a student a tattoo on her upper thigh, and engaging in sexual dialogue with students on social media. AHC did admit that she gave out her cell phone number to students.

During the contested hearing, the discipline panel heard testimony from the student who was sent the sexually explicit photographs who stated that he had had sexual intercourse with AHC. The student submitted both sexually explicit emails and the photos as evidence.

School administrators gave testimony that this was a very bizarre situation that started with the teacher approaching the administration. On more than one occasion, AHC lied to the administration and acted as the victim. The administration did have proof that students were trying to extort money from AHC, but she did not tell the administration that this was due to the sexually explicit photos she had sent a student.

Administrators further testified that they believed the students and felt they had sufficient evidence to prove their credibility. They had confiscated cell phones, had seen the photos, had read the texts, and had seen the Facebook comments.

The discipline panel did not accept the testimony of the student who stated he had had a sexual relationship with AHC since he was unable to give any details. However, they did find the testimony of both administrators to be credible and reliable. The sexually explicit photos were clearly of AHC, who appeared scantily clad and in one photo was baring her breasts.

The committee found AHC guilty of professional misconduct in that she continued to have inappropriate electronic communication with students, the content of her conversations were sexual in nature, and she did send sexually explicit images of herself to one student.

AHC's certificate was immediately revoked and it was ordered that her name appear in *Professionally Speaking*, the College magazine, and under Disciplinary Decisions on the College's website.

This case appears in *Professionally Speaking*, March 2016.

An accusation of sexual abuse can be very damaging for teachers, even if the accusation is subsequently proven false. Michael Hanson of St. Andrew's College waited fifteen months to have his name cleared after a false accusation of sexual abuse was publicized in the media. Mr. Hanson suffered the stress of not knowing about his future, even though he was on paid leave and enjoyed the support of former students, parents, and colleagues. This underscores how important it is for teachers to conduct themselves professionally at all times and avoid placing themselves in situations that could lead to false allegations of sexual misconduct.

According to a data analysis of disciplinary decisions from 1997 to 2011, the top three categories of complaints were abuse of a student, unprofessional behaviour, and conduct unbecoming. During this period, 202 out of 55,129 male teachers and 16 out of 135,949 female teachers were found guilty of sexually abusing students (Zuker, Redmond & Gannon, 2013). Even though these numbers are very small compared with the number of teachers, it still should be seen as a warning, more so for male teachers, to remain professional at all times. Further, these numbers should be a concern for all teachers since even one case of sexual abuse of a student should never happen.

Students are more likely to be victims of sexual harassment by peers. Nonetheless, sexual harassment by teachers—objectionable comments or conduct of a sexual nature—can be particularly harmful to the security and sense of integrity of students. Such behaviour may be overtly sexual or be based on gender, sexual orientation, or perceptions about gender-appropriate behaviour. If students state to a teacher or administrator that they have been sexually harassed by a teacher—including sexual comments—the allegations must be conveyed to Children's Aid Society (if the student is under 16) and, possibly, the police. While sexist and homophobic comments do not fall under the *Criminal Code of Canada*, they do violate the Ontario Human

Rights Code. In all instances, teachers can be reported to the Ontario College of Teachers and face disciplinary measures.

SEXUAL CONDUCT BETWEEN TEACHERS

Teachers are allowed to have relationships with each other, but should always keep in mind how a relationship may affect their working environment if it ends.

Teachers need to pay special attention to amendments made to the *Occupational Health and Safety Act* in 2005. These now include Part V.1, Harassment.

Harassment includes "sexual harassment and harassment because of race, ancestry, place of origin, colour, ethnic origin, citizenship, creed, sexual orientation, age, marital status, same-sex partnership status, family status or disability."

"'Sexual harassment' means a sexual or gender-related comment, advance, proposition, solicitation, assault or other conduct or behaviour, whether explicit, implicit, direct or indirect," and harassment specifically refers to "harassment by a worker's employer or supervisor or by another worker, whether or not the harassment occurs at the workplace."

Schools boards must have Workplace Violence and Harassment policies and review them annually with all workers. Each board has a different version of the policy. Teachers who feel harassed by a colleague should speak directly with their principal. School boards may consequence teachers if harassment is ongoing despite warnings to stop. In extreme cases, boards can notify the Ontario College of Teachers and teachers may face a professional misconduct investigation.

DUTY TO REPORT SUSPICION OF ABUSE

Case Study: Duty to Report Allegations of Sexual Abuse
Ontario College of Teachers v. KAR (2009)

In the summer of 2005, two female teachers took two female students they had coached on an overnight shopping trip in another city. Although parental permission had been received, the parents did not know that the husband of one of the teachers would be accompanying them. Later, one of the students, who was under sixteen at the time, informed both teachers that she had been touched sexually at the hotel by the husband. The teachers did not report the allegation to the parents, school board, or the Children's Aid Society.

Both teachers were charged under the *Child and Family Services Act*, but the courts dismissed the charge. The discipline panel of the College found both teachers guilty of professional misconduct. In the summary of its ruling against KAR in *Professionally Speaking* (March 2010), the discipline panel wrote:

> The member had a duty to report allegations of child abuse and this did not occur. On two separate occasions, over a period of approximately 10 days, the student disclosed to the member that she had been sexually touched by the colleague's husband. By failing to report the disclosure, the member did not follow the written policy of the Durham DSB to report a case of suspected child abuse.
>
> Teachers are expected to protect students in their care at all time. By not reporting allegations of sexual abuse, the member failed to maintain the standards of the profession and failed to comply with the *Education Act*. Her conduct was unprofessional and unbecoming of a member. (pp. 69–70)

KAR was reprimanded and ordered to complete a course on professional ethics at her own expense. The other teacher who was involved, the wife of the alleged abuser, faced further penalties, because she was also found guilty of fostering an inappropriate relationship with the student. Not only was she reprimanded and required to take the same course in professional ethics, but her certificate was suspended for three months.

This case appears in *Professionally Speaking*, March 2010.

---

(1) Why was KAR disciplined by the discipline panel? Do you think the decision was fair?

(2) Why did KAR's colleague receive a suspension? Do you think the decision was fair?

(3) What is the significance of the College taking action even though the courts dismissed the case?

The abuse of children is a matter of the utmost gravity. This makes it vitally important that all members of society and, particularly, professionals who work closely with children, report any suspicions to the authorities in a timely fashion. Too often individuals ignore signs of abuse, which can lead to further abuse of the child and the abuse of more children.

This prompted the Ontario College of Teachers (2015) to issue *Professional Advisory: Duty to Report* to alert educators of their legal and professional duty. The advisory begins:

> Each of us has a responsibility to protect children and youth from harm. As a professional educator working directly with students and supporting others who are, you have a legal and ethical duty to report to a children's aid society when you have reasonable grounds to suspect that a child is in need of protection. (p. 1)

The advisory also reminded teachers that failure to report could lead to consequences such as fines under the *Child and Family Services Act* and discipline by the College for professional misconduct.

REPORTING SUSPICIONS OF SEXUAL MISCONDUCT BY TEACHERS

A teacher who has reasonable grounds to suspect another teacher of sexual misconduct with a student under the age of sixteen, even in the absence of concrete evidence, is legally obligated to report the suspicion directly to the Children's Aid Society or the Catholic Children's Aid Society, since such behaviour could qualify as child abuse (sexual molestation or exploitation) under the *Child and Family Services Act.*

It would also be prudent for the teacher to inform the principal of the suspicions and action taken. If the student is over the age of sixteen, the teacher who suspects possible sexual abuse should report the matter to the principal or other school board personnel.

When suspicions are reported, the appropriate authority is to collect information, ensure the student's safety (possibly by removing him/her from the classroom), and then inform the teacher of the accusation. The teacher would likely be suspended with pay until the complaint has been fully investigated. The teacher should contact the appropriate teachers' federation immediately to obtain legal advice and, possibly, retain a lawyer. Depending on the circumstances and outcome of the investigation, the matter could also be referred to the police and the Ontario College of Teachers.

There have been concerns that teachers are reluctant to report suspicions of colleagues due to section 18 of the *Teaching Profession Act*, which warns against "interfering in an unwarranted manner between other teachers and pupils" and requires that the teacher making such an "adverse report on another member, furnish him with a written statement of the report at the earliest possible time and not later than three days after making the report." (See chapter 1 for further information on adverse reports.)

In *Protecting Our Children*, Justice Robbins (2000) recommended that teachers be able to make an anonymous adverse report of another teacher if sexual abuse of a student is suspected. Since the passage of the *Student Protection Act* in 2002, this exception has been permitted.

REPORTING SUSPICIONS OF ABUSE BY PARENTS OR GUARDIANS

Teachers in Ontario, as part of their duty of care, also have a statutory obligation to report suspicions of child abuse that may occur in the home or elsewhere. This is because the *Child and Family Services Act* gives primacy at all times to the child's best interests, protection, and well-being. This protection is viewed as more important than the protection of parental freedom from state intervention and the awkwardness for teachers and other caregivers who may be required to report suspicions of abuse to the proper authorities. It is worth noting, as well, that teachers cannot stop at reporting these suspicions to the principal, although it is wise to notify principals in advance.

Child abuse occurs when someone under the age of sixteen suffers physical harm, sexual molestation or exploitation, emotional harm, or neglect, caused by an act or omission by the person in charge of the child. Teachers, particularly elementary teachers, are often well positioned to notice physical and behavioural signs of abuse.

For example, signs of physical abuse include bruises, cuts, fractures, burns, and malnutrition. While one bruise or one fall down the stairs may not be the basis of a reasonable suspicion of physical abuse, the regular appearance of these signs should lead to suspicion, especially if they are accompanied by changes in behaviour.

Signs of sexual abuse—crying, changes in behaviour, inappropriate sexual knowledge, fear of physical contact—are harder to discern but may become apparent to teachers who know their students well.

Similarly, signs of emotional abuse, such as decline in self-confidence and over-aggression, may be difficult to detect.

Signs of neglect—the failure to adequately care for or protect a child—may include fatigue, lack of sleep, and malnutrition.

Note also that students often confide information to teachers that may lead the teachers to suspect abuse. Even if students offer information to teacher in confidence, a teacher's duty to report overrides confidentiality. Some teachers, with this in mind, advise students that they cannot promise confidentiality.

As caregivers who work closely with children, teachers are well placed to notice child abuse and to help children live safer and happier lives by reporting suspicions.

Teachers who suspect abuse may wish to review school board resources or reputable websites that can help them better identify the signs of abuse. They are also advised to record their observations. It is important to remember that teachers are only reporting suspicions, not rendering judgment. The teacher's duty to report overrides the potential for strained relationships with parents.

How to Report Suspicions of Abuse

While it is the duty of all citizens to report suspected child abuse and neglect immediately, educators have a heightened legal and professional expectation to notice signs of possible abuse and to report their suspicions. Keep in mind that educators are only to report grounds for suspicion and leave further investigation to others.

Students Under the Age of Sixteen

Under Section 72 of the *Child and Family Services Act, Duty to Report* (1990), it is a teacher's *legal duty* to call Children's Aid Society immediately regarding suspected abuse or neglect of students under the age of sixteen. A teacher cannot ask another teacher to call or expect administrators to call on his or her behalf. Section 22 of the act states:

> *Person must report directly*
> A person who has a duty to report a matter under subsection (1) or (2) shall make the report directly to the society and shall not rely on any other person to report on his or her behalf.

Calling CAS can be stressful for teachers, so it is best to have names and dates prepared before the call. The CAS intake worker will ask if you are calling from a school or community, or are a family member. If a teacher or administrator chooses to give their name to CAS, they will receive a follow-up call; if they do not, CAS will not inform the school of the results of the investigation.

Examples of when a teacher would call CAS are:

- A seven-year-old student comes to school with bruises on his or her arms and refuses to say what happened.
- A teacher witnesses a parent slapping and screaming at a five-year-old student in a car.
- A twelve-year-old student discloses to a teacher she is having a sexual relationship with a sixteen-year-old student.
- A ten-year-old student repeatedly comes to school without lunch and asks other students for part of their food.
- A teacher witnesses another teacher kissing a fourteen-year-old student in the parking lot.

Under the *Child and Family Services Act*, if educators fail to call CAS, they can be fined up to $50,000 or face up to two years in prison. As well, they can be reported to the Ontario College of Teachers to face professional sanctions, as happened in the case of KAR. In the most severe cases, a teacher or administrator who knew about ongoing abuse or neglect that led to death could be charged with criminal negligence under the *Criminal Code of Canada*.

Students over the Age of Sixteen

If a student is over the age of sixteen, and a teacher has *evidence of or witnesses a student over the age of sixteen* being physically or sexually abused by another student, parent, or other adult, it is the teacher's *professional duty* to call the police. Also, if a student discloses that they are being abused physically or sexually, it is the teacher's duty to call the police immediately. Failure to protect a student can result in sanctions being brought against a teacher by the Ontario College of Teachers.

Consequences for Reporting

Educators are often reluctant to grapple with suspicion of possible abuse, as they may be challenged or confronted by individuals who have been investigated by CAS or the police. It is important for teachers to bear in mind that reporting suspicion of possible abuse is a prudent act to ensure that students are safe. It is also important that a factual description of what was observed is not an accusation of abuse.

Nonetheless, people can be so upset at a report to CAS or the police that they file a complaint against the teacher with the College of Teachers. After outlining two such complaints in *Professionally Speaking,* the Investigations Committee (2015) of the College wrote that

> members … are obligated to contact CAS if they believe a child may be in need of protection. As a result, the complaints were not investigated; the members were advised of the complaints and their outcome, but were not required to provide a response to the complaints. (p. 69)

TEACHERS AND TECHNOLOGY

We live in an increasingly wired world. Many teachers now rely on cyberspace for information, entertainment, communication, and social networking.

Many people, however, are unaware of potential problems associated with information technology. Because of their public profiles and duty of care to students, teachers need to be particularly mindful of the ethical and legal dimensions of new technologies.

Case Study
R. v. Cole (2009)

A sixteen-year-old female grade 10 student sent nude photographs of herself to another student. Cole, a computer science teacher and supervisor of his school's computer network, found the file on the school computer network and copied the photographs to the laptop computer that had been assigned to him by the Rainbow District School Board.

In the course of his duties, another information technology specialist monitoring the school system discovered a hidden file on the teacher's e-drive that contained 379 nude and/or sexually explicit photographs. The technician also found 12 other hidden folders with pornographic material, photographs of other students, and links to pornographic movies. The technician was also able to produce times and dates where it appeared that Cole had been downloading pornography during his teaching hours.

The principal then notified the police. The police, however, did not obtain a search warrant because the school authorities indicated that they were the owners of the materials.

After he was charged with possession of child pornography, Cole argued that his *Charter* right to be protected from unreasonable search and seizure had been violated when the police searched the laptop and its contents.

A lower court sided with Cole's claim to a reasonable expectation of privacy, comparing the password-protected computer files to a locked office credenza containing personal items.

On appeal, the court concluded that Cole had no reasonable expectation of privacy and ruled that the laptop and its files were admissible as evidence. The court concluded that the teacher's expectation of privacy was unreasonable because (a) the school board provided the laptop, (b) the user agreement he had signed stated that files stored in the system should not be considered private, (c) the teacher knew that accounts were accessible by other IT personnel, and (d) school board policy stated that school board employees were prohibited from using the equipment provided to post or access sexually explicit material.

In 2014, Cole appeared before a discipline panel of the Ontario College of Teachers and pleaded guilty to professional misconduct. The panel ordered the Registrar to immediately revoke his teaching certificate and that his name be published in *Professionally Speaking.*

This court and tribunal decision reminds teachers that they need to exercise prudence when using technology in schools or storing information on school networks. Employment law and the professional standards of the College make it clear that viewing inappropriate materials in the workplace is problematic and that those who do so may be subject to sanction. This particular case also draws attention to the fact that teachers do not have a reasonable expectation of privacy while using technology in a school setting, especially during work hours. While this case does not address wireless access, it is our opinion that it would also be unreasonable to expect privacy when using a school board wireless system. Finally, regardless of the circumstances, the possession of child pornography is a criminal offence that is always viewed as a serious violation of professional standards—and even more so when the images are of students.

Teachers should exercise care in their personal use of the Internet. Jiri Tlusty of the Toronto Maple Leafs suffered public embarrassment when nude photos of himself that he had included on his Facebook page were posted on a public website and received considerable media attention. Tlusty's experience should serve as a caution to all people in the public eye, including teachers, who have a particular responsibility to model positive behaviour and to maintain appropriate boundaries on social networking sites. Teachers are advised to maintain high-privacy settings on their social networking accounts and to avoid posting images or words that could prove embarrassing or unprofessional.

A similar case involving a teacher led to a caution by the Investigation Committee of the Ontario College of Teachers (December 2015):

> In 2011, the College received a letter from a school board indicating that a student had seen a teacher's photograph on her Facebook page. The teacher could be seen lying on a bed with her partner. The individuals donned minimal to no clothing from the waist up. A second student had also seen additional photographs of the teacher in sexually suggestive poses on the Facebook page of a professional photographer.
>
> The teacher explained she had hired a photographer to do a photo shoot to celebrate Valentine's Day with her partner. The teacher gave

the photographer a Facebook password to a personal account and asked him to post a non-suggestive photo from the shoot onto her Facebook page, which he did. The photographer mistakenly posted the entire photo album on his own Facebook page, which included suggestive photos.

The teacher acknowledged that it was not prudent to give the Facebook password to the photographer. (p. 54)

Teachers should also be careful when commenting on the Internet behind privacy settings, anonymously, or using a pseudonym. An Ontario teacher allegedly posted multiple anti-Muslim and racist tweets using the handle @ firstatheist on Twitter. Although he did not use his own name, the teacher left clues to his identity, which were discovered by students and reported to the school board (Bateman, 2015). After a ten-week investigation, the school board fired the teacher for the racist nature of the posts, and for references to students in some of them.

In British Columbia, a parent launched a professional complaint against a teacher after finding a nude photo of the teacher among thousands of photos posted on a personal website. While this incident blew over after brief media scrutiny, it does illustrate that teachers need to exercise greater discretion than other members of the public. Even if they avoid professional sanction, teachers who lack discretion may still have to deal with the judgment and mockery of students and parents.

Teachers should also avoid contact with students on the Internet, save for communication on approved board sites and e-mail accounts. This is consistent with the College's recommendation that teachers avoid social contact with students outside school.

Teachers should also be aware of the prevalence of cyber bullying. According to research conducted for the Ontario College of Teachers (Browne, 2007), "Cyberbullying students have targeted the vast majority of Ontario's 210,000 certified teachers, seeking to embarrass and intimidate them with criticism of their appearance and their grading skills, malicious gossip, and threats of physical harm" (p. 51). While the majority of teachers did not regard the impact as serious, teachers should be aware that they have the legal right to be protected from such abuse.

TEACHERS AS ROLE MODELS

In the 1870s a female teacher who married or engaged in unseemly conduct could be dismissed. In addition, a teacher who smoked, used liquor, frequented pool halls, or got shaved in a barber shop gave "good reason to suspect his worth, intention, and honesty."

In the 1920s, female teachers were not permitted to enter ice-cream parlours or to be courted by a man without a chaperone. Married women in the 1950s were able to teach but were dismissed once they became pregnant.

---

(1) Why do you think these rules were put in place?
(2) What do these rules reveal about society's views of teachers as role models?
(3) Do you think it was fair to deny teachers rights that were held by other citizens?

Ontario has changed considerably since those days, yet there remains a tension between the individual rights of teachers and the higher expectations that society holds for professionals entrusted to take care of children. This is reflected in the admittedly somewhat old-fashioned wording of section 264(1)(c) of the *Education Act*, which states that it is the teacher's duty "to inculcate by precept and example" respect for religion and the principles of Judeo-Christian morality and the "highest regard" for truth, justice, and other virtues.

The Supreme Court of Canada is unequivocal in recognizing teachers as role models. In the 1997 case of *Toronto (City) Board of Education v. O.S.S.T.F., District 15*, the court stated:

> The language [of section 264(1)(c) of the *Education Act*] is that of another era. The requirements it sets for teachers reflect the ideal and not the minimal standard ... However, the section does indicate that teachers are very properly expected to maintain a higher standard of conduct than

other employees because they occupy such an extremely important position in society.

The Supreme Court went on to elaborate its reasoning:

In their position of trust, teachers must teach by example as well as by lesson, and that example is set just as much by their conduct outside the classroom as by their performance within it. Thus misconduct which occurs outside regular teaching hours can be the basis for discipline proceedings.

Clearly, then, the professional responsibilities of teachers do not end once they leave the school, as has been made clear in a number of cases. For example, in *R. v. Audet* (1996), discussed earlier in this chapter, the Supreme Court ruled that sexual activity with a former student during the summer holidays constituted sexual exploitation and was therefore just cause for a teacher to be discharged. The court made it clear that the teacher "seriously prejudiced his status as a role model." Similarly, other acts of misconduct by teachers could serve as a basis for discipline or dismissal, depending on factors such as the likelihood of recurrence, the impairment of the teacher's relations with students, and extenuating circumstances.

At the same time, the courts are reluctant to encroach on the human rights of teachers, given the *Canadian Charter of Rights and Freedoms* as well as changing social norms. Judges' decisions attempt to strike a delicate balance between the individual rights of teachers and the expectation that they be role models in their actions in school and beyond.

In what follows, court decisions and professional misconduct cases are used to examine this balance between teachers' individual rights and the higher professional standard to which they must adhere.

LIFESTYLES OF TEACHERS

The challenge of striking a delicate balance between individual rights and social expectations is particularly evident in situations concerning the lifestyles of teachers.

Case Study: Revealing Pictures
Abbotsford School District 34 v. Shewan (1987)

In 1984, John Shewan submitted three pictures of his wife as part of an entry to *Gallery* magazine's Girl Next Door Amateur Erotic Photo Contest. These semi-nude pictures were subsequently published in February 1985. The entry identifying Ilze S as a teacher in Clearbrook, B.C., caught the attention of a radio reporter, who made inquiries with the superintendent of education. After an investigation and hearing, both Ilze and John Shewan were suspended without pay for six weeks. Newspaper reports of the school board decision sparked controversy regarding teachers as role models in the community.

The Shewans appealed their suspension to a board of reference. This administrative tribunal determined that the couple's behaviour fell within reasonable standards. In making this determination, members of the board decided that the standard to be applied was not whether "the Shewans' conduct fell below some of the community's standards but whether it was within the accepted standards of tolerance in contemporary Canadian society."

The B.C. Supreme Court and, subsequently, the B.C. Court of Appeal, found the Shewans guilty of misconduct and upheld suspensions of one month. The Court of Appeal found in part that "the publication of such a photograph of a teacher in such a magazine will have an adverse effect upon the educational system to which the teacher owes a duty to act responsibly." The obligation of teachers, the court explained, extends beyond the school to the profession and the community.

---

(1) What actions on the part of the Shewans caused them to be accused of misconduct?

(2) Why did the board of reference rule in favour of the Shewans?

(3) Why did the B.C. court determine that the Shewans were poor role models who deserved to be punished for misconduct?

(4) If you were charged with deciding this case, which side would you favour?

(5) What is the significance of this landmark case for you as a teacher?

Complicating this issue is a 1983 case in Quebec in which a teacher was suspended for violating the principles of Catholicism by appearing naked at a nudist camp. This was discovered when a picture appeared in a small-town newspaper. A board of arbitration and, subsequently, the courts indicated that the Catholic school board had failed to prove that the employee's behaviour violated Catholic principles. It is possible that the school board would have been successful if it had provided evidence that nudity is contrary to Catholic morals (Piddocke, Magsino & Manley-Casimir, 1997).

How can one reconcile these two cases? *Shewan* is a landmark case because it has helped define the degree to which teachers' private lives are public. Critical to this being a case of misconduct was the decision by the Shewans to place their pictures in the public domain by submitting them to a magazine. This made it a case of lewdness rather than of lifestyle alone. (Similar public–private distinctions have emerged in freedom of speech cases concerning teachers.)

The second case, which focused on lifestyle alone, suggests that lifestyle choices that are lawful and private are not the concern of public schools, professional bodies, or the community.

It is worth noting how much things have changed since the examples listed at the beginning of this Teachers as Role Models section. Behaviours that would have resulted in dismissal and community outrage in the 1870s, or even the 1960s, were debated in the 1980s as raising interesting issues about teachers' privacy rights. Also, in both of the cases discussed above, there was never a danger that the teachers would be dismissed for their behaviour.

Teachers whose lifestyles may have been deemed inappropriate in the past, such as living in homosexual or non-marital heterosexual relationships, are now protected by the *Canadian Charter of Rights and Freedoms*. Indeed, as the case of *Trinity Western v. College of Teachers (British Columbia)* illustrates, teachers are expected to be respectful of these lifestyles.

Most lawful and private lifestyle choices are accepted, or at least tolerated, by school boards, professional bodies, and many members of the public. Nonetheless, teachers are advised to be sensitive to their legal and ethical duty to be role models. There is little doubt that the personal conduct of teachers could lead, fairly or unfairly, to a loss of respect by students and confidence by the community. This is why many teachers are discreet about their personal lives and, in some cases, choose not to live in the communities in which they work.

The exception to the increasing acceptance of teachers' lifestyle choices is the sexual exploitation of minors. As a Discipline Committee panel of the Ontario College of Teachers wrote:

> A member making and possessing child pornography and obtaining the sexual services of persons under the age of 18 years is not suitable to be in a position of trust and authority over children and should not be permitted to teach in Ontario or elsewhere. (*Professionally Speaking*, June 2007)

LIFESTYLES OF TEACHERS IN CATHOLIC SCHOOLS

Although teachers in private and public schools are held to the higher standard of conduct as role models, their lifestyle choices and teaching positions are protected by the *Canadian Charter of Rights and Freedoms* and provincial human rights legislation. Teachers in Catholic schools are held to a different standard.

In *Caldwell et al. v. Stuart et al.* (1985), the Supreme Court decided that Roman Catholic schools could use conformity with Catholic religious practices as a *bona fide* requirement for teachers in Catholic schools. This decision validating discriminatory practices in Roman Catholic schools was based on denominational rights enshrined in the *Constitution Act* (or *BNA Act*), *1867*. This was reaffirmed in *Casagrande v. Hinton Roman Catholic Separate School District* (1987) when the Alberta Court of Queen's Bench upheld the right of the school board to dismiss a teacher who had premarital sex, contrary to Catholic doctrine. In this case, the court affirmed the school's expectation that Catholic teachers "are required to reveal the Christian message in their work as well as in all aspects of behavior." There are a number of cases in which teachers have been dismissed for pre-marital sexual intercourse, marrying outside the requirements of the Roman Catholic Church, and practising homosexuality.

In these early *Charter* cases, there was incontrovertible evidence to support the dismissals. A teacher dismissed for premarital sex was pregnant outside of wedlock. Two gay religion teachers in Catholic schools were dismissed after it was disclosed that they were joined together in a civil union ceremony (before same-sex marriage was legalized in 2003). A teacher was dismissed after it was discovered that she had not obtained an annulment and had remarried, outside the Roman Catholic Church.

It is safe to say that Catholic school boards in Ontario, particularly in suburban and urban areas, do not actively monitor the lifestyles of their teachers. Indeed, it would be fair to say that many administrators of Catholic boards are reluctant to pursue lifestyle cases. In general, a "don't ask, don't tell" policy prevails. While this may reflect cultural norms among contemporary Catholics, it may also be a response to concerns that the courts may now be less likely to defer to religious authority. For example, a gay laboratory coordinator in a religious college was successful in having his dismissal overturned. The court ruled in *Vriend v. Alberta* (1998) that the "law does not draw any distinction between heterosexuals and other groups."

Teachers employed in Catholic boards are advised to adhere to accepted Catholic lifestyles or, at the very least, to be discreet about their practices. Caution should especially be exercised in formalizing non-conforming relationships.

BELIEFS OF TEACHERS

Lifestyle choices are often intertwined with belief systems. And beliefs often inform practices. As a result, some employers may be reluctant to hire teachers with unconventional lifestyles or unorthodox beliefs, on the grounds that these teachers may implicitly promote their distinctive lifestyle or even explicitly teach their own personal beliefs in the classroom. This is often the basis for discrimination based on sexual orientation or religious beliefs.

A landmark case, *Trinity Western v. College of Teachers (British Columbia)*, brings together in an interesting manner the issues of sexual orientation and religious belief. The findings of the Supreme Court in this case are useful in delineating distinctions between teachers' private beliefs and public practice.

Case Study: Balancing Gay Rights and Religious Rights
Trinity Western v. College of Teachers (British Columbia) (2001)

Trinity Western University (TWU), a private evangelical Christian institution, applied to have its teacher education program accredited by the British Columbia College of Teachers (BCCT). BCCT declined to accredit the program. The reason given was that the code of conduct for students and staff at TWU, which was grounded in evangelical Christian values, embodied discrimination against gays and lesbians.

TWU took BCCT to court, arguing that its freedom of religion was violated. The Supreme Court of Canada, which had the final word in this dispute, had to determine the balance between freedom of religion and the right to equality for gays and lesbians. As Brown & Zuker (2002) write, "In deciding in favour of the university, the court found that the case could be decided in a way that was consistent with its interpretation of both these rights" (p. 308). At the heart of its decision was a distinction between off-duty beliefs and on-duty conduct.

TWU's admissions policy and code of conduct were found to be discriminatory. The court decision stated that "a homosexual student would not be tempted to apply for admission, and could sign the so-called student contract at a considerable personal cost."

The court also recognized BCCT's duty to respect equality in Canadian society and to adhere to the public interest section of the *Teaching Profession Act,* which contains language prohibiting discrimination.

The court also noted that TWU is a private religious institution and that as such its freedom of conscience and religion should be protected. As a result, unlike public schools and universities, it was entitled to discriminate on the basis of religion in its admissions policy and code of conduct.

The challenge for the Supreme Court was balancing these two fundamental rights. Underpinning its ruling was a commitment to pluralism. The Court quoted Justice Dickson's reasoning in an earlier Supreme Court decision: "A truly free society is one which can accommodate a wide variety of beliefs, diversity of tastes and pursuits, customs and codes of conduct." Given the rights of TWU under human rights legislation, the court continued, "[w]hat the BCCT was required to do was determine whether the rights were in conflict in reality." In the absence of concrete evidence to the contrary, the court concluded that TWU graduates would not have a detrimental effect on the learning environment in public schools. "Instead, the proper place to draw the line in cases like this ... is generally between belief and conduct." Thus, BCCT was wrong to make the assumption that discriminatory beliefs would lead to discriminatory conduct. BCCT should address only professional conduct that is discriminatory. Then it would be entirely appropriate for that teacher to be subject to disciplinary proceedings.

---

(1) Summarize the case.

(2) What is the Supreme Court's understanding of the equality rights of gays and lesbians?

(3) What is the Supreme Court's understanding of freedom of religion and conscience?

(4) How does the Supreme Court attempt to balance these competing rights?

(5) Do you agree with the decisions? Why or why not? Do you see any limitations or problems with the decision?

TEACHERS' FREEDOM OF SPEECH ON EDUCATIONAL ISSUES

A major area of debate has been the balance between teachers' right to freedom of speech and their responsibilities as role models. A number of court cases have helped delineate a path between these two important principles. In this section, the focus is freedom of speech as it pertains to educational issues.

Case Study: Federations Advocating Policy
British Columbia Public School Employers' Association v. British Columbia Teachers' Federation (2005)

The British Columbia Teachers' Federation (BCTF), which was opposed to major education reforms proposed by the provincial government, created a report to parents outlining its opposition to larger class sizes and the loss of resources to teachers. Teachers distributed these documents at parent–teacher interviews. School districts opposed this strategy, which resulted in a labour grievance that eventually found its way to the British Columbia Court of Appeal.

   The court recognized that the teachers' right to express their opinion on political issues could undermine public confidence in the education system and negatively affect parent–teacher meetings. Nonetheless, in a split decision, the majority of the justices found that the board had unreasonably curtailed the teachers' right to freedom of expression. The rights of teachers to free speech could exist alongside their obligation to conduct themselves professionally with students and parents.

(1) Summarize the case.
(2) What is the significance of this decision?
(3) Do you agree with the decision? Why or why not? Do you see any limitations or problems with it?

Before entering into such discussions, teachers need to recognize that there is a delicate balance to be maintained between their personal freedom of speech and their duties to students and school boards. The court decision discussed above affirms the right of teachers, individually and as federations, to engage in issues of importance to education. Teachers as professionals have the right to discuss school, board, and provincial policies with students, and to express disagreement. They should not, however, abuse their position of trust and power in the classroom. This particular case focused on events that took place during the course of parent–teacher interviews. The court may have taken a very different view of the matter if the teachers had used their position of authority in the classroom to hand out federation materials or promote their own political agenda.

Here are five questions to consider:

(1) Am I properly informed about the issue? (Teachers as professionals can be disciplined for irresponsible statements.)
(2) Am I risking being insubordinate? (Teachers have a duty to support the principal in the implementation of approved policies.)
(3) Am I risking being unprofessional in my conduct? (See standards of practice.)
(4) Am I risking being abusive? (See case below.)

(5) Have I checked with my federation? (Get the best advice possible before taking action.)

Case Study: The Need to Avoid Threats
Toronto (City) Board of Education v. O.S.S.T.F., District 15 (1997)

Bhadauria applied for thirty-nine promotions in his school board and was turned down each time. He filed a complaint with the Ontario Human Rights Tribunal citing discriminatory promotion practices, but lost his case. In response, Bhadauria began writing abusive letters to his school board containing racist comments, defamatory comments, and threats against the director and other senior officials.

After a psychiatric report confirmed that Bhadauria was of sound mind, the board passed a resolution terminating his contract.

He filed a grievance with the board of arbitration, which ordered him reinstated. The Ontario Divisional Court disagreed and permitted the termination. The Ontario Court of Appeal sided with Bhadauria and his federation.

In the end, the Supreme Court of Canada ruled that the termination was warranted. At the heart of the Supreme Court's decision was the teacher's duty to act as a role model. The arguments of the court, which are featured earlier in this chapter, emphasize the duty of teachers under section 264(1)(c) of the *Education Act* to conduct themselves according to high moral principles.

Bhadauria faced a discipline panel at the Ontario College of Teachers, which found him guilty of professional misconduct—more specifically, that he issued documents that had false or misleading information; he failed to comply with the *Education Act*; he performed acts considered disgraceful, dishonourable, and unprofessional; and he engaged in conduct unbecoming of a member.

Bhadauria was ordered to receive a reprimand from the discipline panel, and his teaching certificate was suspended for eighteen months by the Ontario College of Teachers.

This case appears in *Professionally Speaking*, September 2004.

---

(1) Summarize the case.
(2) What is the significance of this decision?

(3) Do you agree with the decisions? Why or why not? Do you see any limitations or problems with the decision?

Case Study: What Teachers Say in Public Matters
Cromer v. British Columbia Teachers' Federation (1986)

After attending a meeting at her son's school, Mrs. Cromer, a member of the B.C. Teachers' Federation, made negative comments in public about a teacher at the school for her teaching of human sexuality. As a result, Mrs. Cromer was charged with breaching the Code of Ethics of the British Columbia Teachers' Federation on the grounds that she had publicly criticized a colleague and fellow member.

The case was appealed to the courts, since Mrs. Cromer believed that she should not be disciplined for expressing her views as a concerned parent.

Justice Lambert, writing for the majority of justices on the British Columbia Court of Appeal, concluded that teachers have to exercise discretion when speaking about other teachers and administrators:

> I don't think people are free to choose which hat they will wear on what occasion. Mrs. Cromer does not always speak as a teacher, nor does she always speak as a parent. But she will always speak as Mrs. Cromer. The perception of her by her audience will depend on their knowledge of her training, her skills, her experience, and her occupation, among other things. The impact of what she says will depend on the content of what she says and the occasion on which she says it.

(1) Summarize the case.
(2) What is the significance of this decision?
(3) Do you agree with the decisions? Why or why not? Do you see any limitations or problems with the decision?

Taken together, these three cases confirm the right of teachers as professionals to speak about educational issues, so long as other teaching professionals are not criticized and the comments are not abusive or discriminatory.

As professionals and role models, they need to ensure that they are always appropriate in their conduct and speech. The words of the Supreme Court of Canada in *Ross v. New Brunswick District No. 15* are worth bearing in mind at all times:

> Teachers are seen by the community to be the medium for the educational message and, because of the community position they occupy, they are not able to "choose which hat they wear on what occasion"... teachers do not necessarily check their teaching hats at the school yard gate and may be perceived to be wearing their teaching hats off duty.

TEACHERS' FREEDOM OF SPEECH IN THE PUBLIC DOMAIN

In chapter 4, the *Morin* case was used to delineate the academic freedom of teachers in the classroom. So long as teachers work within the parameters of the curriculum guidelines, they have the academic freedom to adapt curriculum to meet the learning needs of their students. The *Keegstra* case (1990), in which a teacher was found guilty of hate speech for denying the Holocaust and promoting antisemitism, makes it clear that hate speech is never acceptable in the classroom.

What happens when teachers respect these limits in their professional practice yet express opinions in public that may be regarded as hateful? Should such teachers still be allowed to teach?

Case Study: Understanding Discrimination
Ross v. New Brunswick School District No. 15 (1996)

Malcolm Ross was a mild-mannered teacher at Magnetic Hill School while on duty, yet a notorious anti-Semite off-duty. In his published writing and television appearances, Ross remarked that Christianity was being undermined by an international Jewish conspiracy.

The school board reprimanded Ross on more than one occasion, but he asserted his right to off-duty freedom of speech.

Ross was removed after the parent of a Jewish student brought forward a claim that the board's decision to allow Ross to teach constituted discrimination against her child by poisoning the educational environment. Because this case raised fundamental human rights questions, it ultimately wound its way to the Supreme Court of Canada. The court, in upholding Ross's removal from the classroom, wrote:

> The school is an arena for the exchange of ideas and must, therefore, be premised upon principles of tolerance and impartiality so that all persons within the school environment feel equally free to participate ... Teachers are inextricably linked to the integrity of the school system. Teachers occupy positions of trust and confidence, and exert considerable influence over their students as a result of their positions. The conduct of a teacher bears directly upon the community's perception of the ability of the teacher to fulfill such a position of trust and influence and upon the community's confidence in the public system as a whole.

Teachers could also face professional sanctions for publicly expressing views that may be offensive. This is illustrated by *Ontario College of Teachers v. PF (2012)*.

Case Study: The Limits of Freedom of Speech for Teachers
Ontario College of Teachers v. PF (2012)

PF was employed as a secondary school teacher with a school board from 1974 to 1997. In 1979, he co-founded an organization opposed to immigrants, refugees, and visible minorities. In 1981, he co-founded an organization against the principles of multiculturalism and tolerance. PF was seen participating in a white supremacist event with Heritage Front, a neo-Nazi organization. In 1991, he was seen attending a neo-Nazi event celebrating Hitler's birthday.

After many attempts at progressive discipline beginning in 1991, the school board fired PF in 1997, and referred his case to the Ontario College of Teachers.

PF's case was one of the first instances in which a College discipline panel examined a teacher's behaviour outside a school setting and determined that it could sufficiently influence the teacher's ability to teach effectively. The discipline panel referred to *Ross v. New Brunswick School District 15* (1996), in which the Supreme Court of Canada ruled that teachers are held to higher standard, both on and off duty.

Over the course of eleven days of hearings spanning a two-year period, PF remained steadfast in his defence that behaviour outside school was no business of the education system.

Ultimately, the discipline panel found PF guilty of professional misconduct—more specifically, that he failed to:

- strive at all times to achieve the highest professional competence;
- show consistent justice and consideration in all of his relations with pupils contrary to the *Teaching Profession Act*;
- concern himself with the welfare of his pupils;
- comply with section 264(1)(c) of the *Education Act*.

The discipline panel noted that, despite repeated warnings from his school board, and an investigation by the Ministry of Education, PF continued to participate in events and conversations deemed racist to non-Europeans, including Jewish, Indigenous, and Asian peoples. As PF's personal beliefs and activities had been widely covered by the media, it was impossible to ignore his discriminatory and racist behaviour.

This behaviour affected the teachers, staff, and students in his school, and created a "poisoned school environment." Even though PF never expressed his views while teaching, the discipline panel concluded that parents, students, and other teachers no longer had trust or confidence in his teaching ability.

On October 31, 2007, the discipline panel ordered the Registrar to immediately revoke PF's teaching certificate and that his name be published in *Professionally Speaking*, the College magazine, and under Disciplinary Decisions on the College's website.

PF did not appeal the decision.

This case appears in *Professionally Speaking*, March 2008.

Ross and PF voiced offensive opinions far from the boundaries of public acceptability. Speech in the public domain on a legitimate topic of debate, however, can also lead to professional sanction.

In the case of *Kempling v. British Columbia College of Teachers* (2005), the

British Columbia Court of Appeal upheld a decision made by the BCCT disciplining a public school teacher for an article and letters in a local newspaper that associated gays and lesbians with immorality, abnormality, perversion, and promiscuity. BCCT's disciplinary panel determined that the writings were discriminatory and that Mr. Kempling failed to accommodate core values of the education system. This off-duty conduct constituted professional misconduct, BCCT concluded, because it could contribute to a loss of public confidence in teachers and the public school system.

The Court of Appeal determined that BCCT had indeed infringed on Mr. Kempling's right to freedom of expression under the *Charter of Rights and Freedoms*. Despite this, the one-month suspension was upheld as reasonable and justified in a free and democratic society. This case serves as a warning to teachers to be respectful of all groups when expressing their views in the public arena.

CONCLUSION

Teachers need to be very careful when expressing their opinions in public. Many teachers are actively involved in public issues and in the political process. These teachers, through their engagement in public discourse, could be viewed as positive models of citizenship for students.

CHECKING YOUR UNDERSTANDING

- Teachers are expected to act as role models for students both in the classroom and in the community.

- Section 43 of the *Criminal Code* will protect a teacher who uses reasonable force to restrain or remove a child in appropriate circumstances. However, it is no longer considered reasonable for teachers to administer corporal punishment.

- As professionals, teachers must at all times respect the boundaries that exist between teachers and students.

- Failure to respect these boundaries or to meet the standards expected of them by the local community could lead to professional sanctions and board discipline or dismissal.

- *Sexual abuse* by a teacher of a student of any age is considered professional misconduct by the Ontario College of Teachers. "Sexual abuse" includes remarks of a sexual nature.

- *Sexual exploitation* by a teacher of a student who is sixteen or seventeen is a criminal offence, with a maximum penalty of ten years.

- *Sexual interference* or "invitation to sexual touching" by anyone with a person under the age of sixteen is a criminal offence, with a maximum penalty of ten years.

- Teachers have a legal and ongoing duty to report suspected child abuse directly to a children's aid society. For the purposes of the *Child and Family Services Act*, a child is defined as a person under the age of sixteen.

- Child abuse includes physical, sexual, and emotional abuse, as well as neglect.

- A teacher who reports another teacher for suspected sexual abuse of a student is not required to give the other teacher a copy of the report.

- The courts try to strike a delicate balance between teachers' human rights and the expectation that they act as role models.

- Lifestyle choices of teachers in public elementary and secondary schools are protected under the *Canadian Charter of Rights and Freedoms* and Ontario's *Human Rights Code*.

- Lifestyle choices of teachers in Roman Catholic separate schools could be a matter for discipline or dismissal, if the board is able to prove that the lifestyle is contrary to church doctrine.

- The courts have recognized the right of teachers to speak on political and educational issues, but teachers must avoid abusing their position of trust and power in the classroom.

- Despite the right to speak on political and educational issues, teachers could face professional sanctions for publicly expressing views generally considered hateful, offensive, or discriminatory.

- Teachers have a legal duty to report suspected abuse and neglect of students under the age of sixteen to the Children's Aid Society.

- Teachers have a professional duty to report bullying, cyber bullying, and homophobic bullying to their administration immediately.

APPLYING YOUR UNDERSTANDING

Sounding Off at the Diner

Raj and Al, recent B. Ed. graduates, were summer camp counsellors with the YMCA. While sipping sodas at the diner, Joe teased Raj about the dearth of South Asian players in baseball, and Raj yelled, "F____ off." Al responded with obscenities of his own and stormed out of the building.

Mrs. Wong, who was sitting in a booth with her eight-year-old daughter, was shocked at what she heard. Her daughter, who giggled as she witnessed this encounter between two of her counsellors, then told her mother that she heard Al swear as he fell on the baseball diamond and that Raj often said "oh shit" when he forgot something.

Mrs. Wong reported these incidents to Ms. Caputo, the manager of the summer camp. After a brief investigation, Ms. Caputo met with Raj and Al separately. They confirmed that they had sworn on these occasions, but minimized the significance of their off-duty use of obscenity.

Ms. Caputo reminded them that the Y's policy and procedures manual states that the "use of improper or inappropriate language in front of the children at any time" will result in dismissal. She then dismissed both Raj and Al for their behaviour.

Raj was very upset and decided to challenge his termination. He then met with Al, who agreed to join him in fighting the Y. Nothing like a common enemy to bring friends back together, Raj reflected.

(1) What was the basis of the dismissal of the two camp counsellors?

(2) What would be the basis of a challenge of their termination by Raj and Joe?

(3) How do you think the courts would rule on such a case?

(4) What do you think would happen if this incident had involved two classroom teachers?

(5) Do you think counsellors and teachers should be punished for off-duty use of obscenities?

PART C

ADDITIONAL RIGHTS AND RESPONSIBILITIES

CHAPTER 8

THE RIGHTS AND RESPONSIBILITIES OF STUDENTS AND PARENTS

After reading this chapter, you will have a keener appreciation of the legal rights and duties of students through consideration of school attendance, the right to learn, and freedom of expression and religion. You will become aware of the privacy of students and parents within the school system. You will begin to understand the rights (e.g., to religious accommodation and homeschooling) and responsibilities (e.g., health issues) of parents. Finally, you will be introduced to ways for educators to communicate with parents, through teacher–parent interactions and school councils.

Case Study: Students Have Rights
Constant-Daniels (Litigation Guardian of) v. Tournier (2014)

A student sued his vice-principal for damages for breach of privacy and negligence. The student was text messaging during class, and his teacher asked him to stop. The student ignored her requests. Instead, he turned his back to her and continued to text. The teacher then confiscated his cell phone and gave it to the vice-principal, informing him of the incident in class.

In the office, the vice-principal checked the student's phone in front of him and asked him about a text that referred to the theft of a car. The student stated he was not involved with the theft. Nevertheless, the vice-principal informed the police as part of his duty to report, but he did not notify the student's legal guardians that he had done so.

The police then asked the student to text one of the thieves for more information. This was a deviation in normal police procedure.

The student acknowledged that he should not have been texting in class and was aware that the school policy stated this was strictly prohibited. However, the student felt that his right to privacy was violated and that the vice-principal failed in his duty to care for him. For example, by reporting the incident to the police, the vice-principal had put the student in a dangerous situation.

The vice-principal justified checking the student's texts by saying he was concerned that the student would not stop texting despite being asked by a teacher. The vice-principal felt that, in order to ensure safety, it was his right as an administrator to check the student's cell phone. He also stressed his duty to report unsafe or illegal activity to the police as soon as possible.

The courts did not believe that the student's right to privacy had been violated, and they cited the Supreme Court ruling in *R. v. MRM* (1998), in which the court ruled that students have a diminished right to privacy in a public education setting. The student's case was dismissed.

> (1) Do you think an administrator has the right to check a student's cell phone?
> (2) What other steps could have been taken in this case?
> (3) Do you side with the courts that students have a diminished right to privacy in public schools?

Teachers draw on their professional expertise to serve the needs of students, parents, and the wider community. The concept of service recognizes the importance of working together with students and parents in an atmosphere of mutual respect.

Educators owe a duty of care to their students. Acting *in loco parentis*, teachers have a legal responsibility to protect their students from harm, while at the same time recognizing and respecting their rights and freedoms under the Canadian Constitution. Although there is a dynamic tension between these two imperatives, effective educators treat all students with dignity and respect. They also recognize the importance of helping students prepare for their role as adult citizens of Canada.

Effective educators understand and appreciate the critical role of parents in the lives of their children. Many engage parents as partners in student learning and are open to the perspectives parents have to offer. It is also increasingly recognized that engaging with parents of all backgrounds can have a significant impact on student learning. Epstein and Rodriguez-Jansorn (2004) write:

> Students who succeed in school are almost always supported by their families, while other students struggle without support from home. For a school to develop a partnership program involving all parents in ways that increase student success requires new ways of thinking about family and community involvement. All schools need a purposeful, planned partnership program creating a welcome environment and engaging families in activities that contribute to students' readiness for school, academic success, and positive attitudes and behaviors. (pp. 19–20)

This chapter discusses the legal rights and duties of students and parents. The rights of students include the right to attend school and the right to have their freedom of expression and freedom of conscience and religion respected. Both parents and students have the right to expect that a student's personal information will be kept safe from disclosure to others. Parents have a legal duty to ensure that their children are properly cared for and the right to make decisions about their children's schooling and medical care. They also have a duty to ensure that their children of school age attend school. Parents have the right to be involved in their child's schooling through the school council and through active engagement by teachers in student learning.

RIGHTS AND RESPONSIBILITIES OF STUDENTS

In 1959, the General Assembly of the United Nations proclaimed the *Declaration of the Rights of the Child.* This declaration, which was signed by

Canada, recognizes that the child, "by reason of his physical and mental immaturity, needs special safeguards and care, including appropriate legal protection." Key to this document are the statements that "the child is entitled to receive education, which shall be free and compulsory" and that "the best interests of the child shall be the guiding principle of those responsible for his education and guidance. The prolamation says that this responsibility "lies in the first place with his parents."

Canadian common law and education legislation recognized the vulnerability of children, and the duty of teachers to care for them, long before this declaration.

SAFE SCHOOLS

Students have a right to learn in a safe learning environment and are responsible for conducting themselves responsibly in their interactions with fellow students, teachers, and other members of the school community. Teachers, principals, and other school personnel have the duty to make the classrooms and schools safe for students.

SCHOOL ATTENDANCE

Compulsory Attendance

The *Education Act* stipulates that all persons of "compulsory school age" must attend school unless they are legally excused from attending. They are required to begin grade 1 in the September of the year they turn six years old, and, with the passage of the *Education Amendment Act (Learning to Age 18), 2006,* must remain in attendance until they attain the age of eighteen.

It is important to note that section 21 of the *Education Act* sets out a number of legal reasons for non-attendance, one of which is that the student has completed all the requirements for an Ontario Secondary School Diploma (OSSD).

A person is excused from attendance at school if,
   (a) the person is receiving satisfactory instruction at home or elsewhere;

(b) the person is unable to attend school by reason of sickness or other unavoidable cause;

(c) transportation is not provided by a board for the person and there is no school that he or she has a right to attend situated,

    (i) within 1.6 kilometres from the person's residence measured by the nearest road if he or she has not attained the age of seven years on or before the first school day in September in the year in question, or

    (ii) within 3.2 kilometres from the person's residence measured by the nearest road if he or she has attained the age of seven years but not the age of 10 years on or before the first school day in September in the year in question, or

    (iii) within 4.8 kilometres from the person's residence measured by the nearest road if he or she has attained the age of 10 years on or before the first school day in September in the year in question;

(d) the person has obtained a secondary school graduation diploma or has completed a course that gives equivalent standing;

(e) the person is absent from school for the purpose of receiving instruction in music and the period of absence does not exceed one-half day in any week;

(f) the person is suspended, expelled or excluded from attendance at school under any Act or under the regulations;

(g) the person is absent on a day regarded as a holy day by the church or religious denomination to which he or she belongs; or

(h) the person is absent or excused as authorized under this Act and the regulations.

Parents are legally required to ensure that their children of compulsory school age attend school, and the school principal is responsible for monitoring attendance on a daily basis and reporting to the school board the names of students of compulsory school age who are not attending. A school attendance counsellor, appointed by the school board, could take action if parents or guardians neglect or refuse to cause their children to attend school. As a further measure to ensure attendance, the act makes it an offence for employers to hire a person of compulsory school age during school hours.

Parents may determine that it is in the best interest of their children to attend private schools or be educated at home, in accordance with section 21(2)(a) of the *Education Act* (see above). In such cases, they must take steps to legally excuse the children by notifying school board officials of their intentions. A failure to provide satisfactory instruction can be the basis of prosecution by the courts.

The *Education Act*, section 21(2)(a) makes provision for children "unable to attend school by reason of sickness or other unavoidable cause." In cases where a child needs to be educated at home for medical reasons, the principal may arrange for "home instruction." Home instruction is provided by a school board teacher under *Regulation 298*, section 11(11). This is not to be confused with "homeschooling." (See Homeschooling under Rights and Responsibilities of Parents below.) Other students could be excluded if they lack proper immunization documentation; they, too, could be eligible for home instruction.

RIGHT TO ATTEND

Since education in Canada is a matter of provincial jurisdiction, in Ontario the right to an education is enshrined in the *Education Act*, which gives all persons the right to attend school, without payment of fee, in the jurisdiction of the school board in which they qualify to be a "resident pupil." The qualifications to be a resident pupil may be broadly divided into elementary and secondary.

To qualify as a resident pupil for elementary school purposes, a person must meet three criteria: age, residence, and tax support. The person must be between the ages of six and twenty-one and live in the district, and the person's parent or guardian must also live in the district and be a tax supporter of the board.

Society sees value in having children begin school even earlier than age six. This has led to the requirement that all school boards offer optional kindergarten classes. Children may enter kindergarten in the year they become five years old. Some boards now offer junior kindergarten a year earlier. If a board does offer junior kindergarten, the right to attend begins effectively at the age of four.

In 2009, the McGuinty government announced that Ontario would be rolling out a full-day kindergarten program across the province. Since then, many school boards in Ontario offer parents optional full-day kindergarten for their children. However, the program has been burdened with controversy around its costs and conflicting reports on its actual merits.

Secondary school qualifications are much more complex and depend on the age of the person. Up to the age of sixteen, there are essentially only two criteria: the person and the person's parent or guardian must live in the district and must be a tax supporter of the board. Even the tax support requirement can be waived, because there is "open access" between coterminous public and separate school boards for secondary school students. A parent could, then, be a separate school supporter, but their child would still qualify as a resident pupil of the coterminous public school board. Notice that, unlike the elementary qualifications, there is no lower or upper age limit specified. However, there is wording elsewhere indicating that a student who has been promoted from elementary school must be admitted to secondary school, and that after seven years of secondary schooling the board could charge a fee. These two statements have the practical effect of setting lower and upper limits.

There are various other clauses applying to persons over the age of sixteen who may have withdrawn from parental control and to persons over the age of eighteen. The overall effect of this further legislation is to enable all persons to complete their education. Even the children of parents unlawfully in Canada are entitled to attend school. The child's right to an education is seen as having primacy over other concerns.

Society presumes that "parents should make all significant choices affecting children, and has afforded them a general liberty to do as they choose" (*B. (R.) v. Children's Aid Society of Metropolitan Toronto* (1995)). This means parents can elect from French- or English-language public or Catholic schools, depending on their inclinations and whether or not their children qualify for admission.

Finally, the Ministry of Education offers adult education programs throughout the province for students who reach the age of eighteen and have not completed secondary school. Most school boards have a dedicated adult education program that separates secondary-school-aged students from those over the age of eighteen. Often these programs are held at night to accommodate students who work during the day. The Ministry of Education also offers courses online through their Independent Learning Centre.

RIGHT TO LEARN

Students have the right to learn and the responsibility to conduct themselves appropriately in the learning environment.

This has particular implications for exceptional students. Canadian courts have ruled that school boards must make *reasonable accommodations* with special education needs. In a landmark case, *Eaton v. Brant County Board of Education* (1997), the Supreme Court stated that "it is the failure to make reasonable accommodations to meet a child's needs which results in discrimination against disabled persons." This ruling has had significant implications for students identified as exceptional. School boards were required to make every reasonable effort to adapt the integrated classroom to meet the special needs of exceptional children. Only if "aspects of the integrated setting which cannot reasonably be changed interfere with meeting the child's special needs" will the principle of accommodation "require a special education placement" outside the regular classroom. This case made it clear that school boards have a *duty to accommodate* and that "certain adaptations to the classroom such as the provision of a special desk, physical assistance and extra supervision from educational assistants were reasonable." Previously, school boards could claim that these accommodations constituted *undue hardship*.

The Education Quality and Accountability Office (EQAO) is one instrument used by the Ministry of Education to monitor and improve education outcomes in Ontario. This independent body conducts standardized provincial tests, including literacy and numeracy tests that are taken by all grade 3 and 6 students and a grade 9 mathematics test and a grade 10 literacy test that must be taken by secondary school students. These tests are administered by board personnel. According to *Regulation 298*, section 20(j), teachers must "co-operate and assist in the administration of the test under the *Education Quality and Accountability Act, (1996)*." These tests are then publicly disseminated, with the results often publicized by local media.

Members of the public can easily access these data by going to school and school board websites. The results often prompt schools to create action plans to improve literacy and numeracy outcomes for their students. Lately the Ministry of Education has been helping schools with poor results by sending out teams of experts to help teachers improve their results. While EQAO has led to greater accountability and public discussion of literacy and numeracy, there are concerns that these tests are unnecessarily intrusive and often place undue stress on students, teachers, and schools in areas of low socio-economic status. This is particularly so with the grade 10 literacy test, successful completion of which is a requirement for a student to obtain a secondary school graduation diploma.

Human Rights

Citizens of Ontario, including students in schools, are guaranteed freedoms and rights. These are enshrined in the *Canadian Charter of Rights and Freedoms* and Ontario's *Human Rights Code*.

Students, by virtue of being under the supervision of teachers acting *in loco parentis*, have more limited rights than other people in society. Some of these limitations were explored in chapter 5, which focused on issues of good conduct and safety in schools. Nonetheless, students' human rights should be respected in the school setting.

As discussed in chapters 1 and 2, the *Charter of Rights and Freedoms* protects fundamental freedoms such as freedom of expression and freedom of conscience and religion. It also includes a wide range of legal rights, including the right to fair legal processes and security from unreasonable search and seizure. (See chapter 5.)

Ontario's *Human Rights Code*, enacted in 1962, protects people from discrimination in: employment; accommodation; contracts; goods, services, and facilities; and membership in vocational associations and trade unions. There are now fifteen possible proscribed grounds of discrimination, including race, ethnicity, religion, sex, sexual orientation, disability, and family status. The preamble to the document describes the purpose of the code as follows:

> ... its aim [is] the creation of a climate of understanding and mutual respect for the dignity and worth of each person so that each person feels

a part of the community and able to contribute fully to the development and well-being of the community and the Province ...

Persons who believe they have been discriminated against by any individual or organization in Ontario may bring a complaint to the Ontario Human Rights Commission, the overall function of which is to promote and advance human rights in the public interest. This includes reviewing statutes, regulations, and policies that may be inconsistent with the code (section 29, d) and conducting inquiries into "incidents of tension or conflict" involving human rights (section 29, e).

While most complaints are resolved through negotiation at the commission, applicants can apply to have their complaints heard by the Ontario Human Rights Tribunal. If discrimination is proven, the respondent will be required to make accommodations for the complainant, unless there is a *bona fide* reason for the discrimination or the accommodation would cause "undue hardship."

Right to Freedom of Expression
As discussed in Brown & Zuker, 2007, students have a right to freedom of expression and "may not be punished for expressing their personal opinion" (p. 261), whether in speech, on paper, or on clothing. At the same time, educators have "broad discretion in regulating student speech or writing that is part of the school curriculum" (p. 261). This discretion generally extends to other school activities, with the courts likely to uphold administrative control unless it is proven "unreasonable, arbitrary, or unrelated to legitimate educational goals" (p. 261).

Case Study: Advocate for Illegal Drugs or Free Speech?

Kieran King, a fifteen-year-old student at Wawota Parkland School in Saskatchewan, was sceptical about a classroom lesson on the dangers of marijuana. He researched the effects of alcohol and tobacco use and told classmates that he considered cannabis the least dangerous of the three. After being informed by a student, the school's principal, Susan Wilson, called Kieran's mother to express concern. She also indicated that she was going to call in the police.

Kieran believed his freedom of expression was being violated, and planned a school walk-out by students in support of free speech. Members of the Saskatchewan Marijuana Party, which he had contacted, were scheduled to attend.

When Kieran and several other students attempted to leave the school, school officials barred the doors, ordered a lockdown, and brought in the RCMP to conduct a threat-assessment against Kieran. A school superintendent was also videotaped stating that Kieran had been accused of selling drugs in school. According to his mother, Kieran had never been investigated or charged with possession or trafficking. Kieran was suspended for trying to leave the school and missed his final exams in June 2007.

---

(1) How would you defend King's right to speak on this issue?
(2) How would you defend the principal's right to curtail King's speech?
(3) Based on the information in this story, who do you think is right?

While this incident made headlines in Canada and attracted much attention on YouTube, it never went to court. In Canada, there is an absence of cases on the limits of student's freedom of expression. Thus, we must turn to the United States for cases to guide our understanding.

In *Tinker v. Des Moines Independent Community School District*, the Supreme Court of the United States stated that students "do not shed their constitutional rights at the school-house door." Thus, while free speech must be balanced with safety concerns, it was considered unreasonable to prohibit students from wearing black armbands to protest the Vietnam War.

On the other hand, American courts have supported schools in limiting speech on many other occasions. This includes the suppression of vulgar speech, sexual innuendo, and "T-shirts that promote violence, smoking, drugs, drinking or messages of a sexual nature" (Brown & Zuker, 2007, p. 261).

While nobody doubted that the school administration had the interests of the student population in mind, many wondered if the principal and the superintendent had overstepped their authority and violated Kieran King's rights. Illegal drug use is a major problem, but Kieran's intellectual stance was misinterpreted as dangerous speech, and he was falsely vilified by the superintendent as a troublemaker and even a drug dealer. The administration, alarmed about escalating drug problems, may have inflamed the situation and lost sight of the student's right to freedom of expression. At the same time, vigilance was warranted.

Right to Freedom of Conscience and Religion

The right to freedom of conscience and religion has often given rise to conflict in Canadian schools. For much of Canadian history, Christian values were infused into schools with little objection. As Canada become more diverse spiritually and religiously, the hegemony of Christianity has been challenged by atheists and by people other faiths.

Case Study: The Gideon Bible and the Atheist
RC (Next of Friend) v. District School Board of Niagara (2013)

It was common practice for schools in Niagara to permit Gideons International to distribute the New Testament in schools. Over the years, however, this practice occurred only with school council approval and parental consent.

RC and her parent, who objected to this practice, responded by requesting permission to distribute *Just Pretend: A Freethought Book for Children*. Distribution of this atheist tract was denied by the principal. The school board then adopted a policy requiring approval by the education director and principal "in consultation with the School Council and with pre-approved parental consent."

When RC's request was denied, she took her case to the Ontario Human Rights Commission. After hearing this case, the Tribunal ruled in favour of RC for several reasons, including that it was:

- incorrect to dismiss atheism as not being a religion;
- unfair to discriminate in favour of one religion;
- wrong to restrict material to "recognized sacred texts" not secondary material;
- inconsistent in that the Gideon Bible contains secondary texts.

The school board was ordered not to permit the distribution of religious materials until a new policy has been approved that is consistent with the Ontario *Human Rights Code*.

> (1) Why did the school board consider its policy fair?
> (2) Why did the Tribunal rule that the policy was discriminatory?
> (3) What are the implications for schools?

Accommodations for religious practices and attire have also become the norm in recent years. Tensions, however, have erupted over sports attire.

Case Study: Is Islam Compatible with Women's Soccer in Canada?

In February 2007, a girl was expelled from a soccer tournament in Quebec for wearing a hijab, a head covering worn by some Muslim women as a sign of modesty. Asmahan Mansour, age eleven, had played two games already when she was expelled by a Muslim referee in the third game. Her team forfeited its remaining games in protest.

The soccer association claimed that this was not a religious matter but one of banning headgear that could be unsafe to her and other players on the field. This ban was consistent with the FIFA International Football Association decision in 2007 to enforce bans on hijabs in soccer.

Controversy arose as public opinion in Quebec revealed underlying fears that society was making too many concessions to religious and cultural minorities. Even Premier Jean Charest defended the official decision as reasonable.

Islamic groups defended the hijab as religiously important and as perfectly safe when tucked into a shirt.

> (1) What are the facts of the situation?
> (2) What are the grounds for banning the hijab from soccer?
> (3) What are the grounds for permitting the hijab in soccer?

(4) Who do you think is right? Why?
(5) Are there any ways in which a "reasonable accommodation" can be reached between religious freedom and player safety?

In 2012, FIFA and the Quebec Soccer Federation lifted the ban on hijabs. This, along with accommodations for Islamic attire in the 2012 Olympics, reflected a trend toward making sports more accessible.

This incident, which has not been pursued in court, has many similarities to the case of *Multani v. Commission Scolaire Marguerite-Bourgeoys.* (See chapter 1.) At issue in that case was whether or not Gurbaj Multani should be allowed to wear a kirpan in school. Ultimately, the Supreme Court ruled that Gurbaj was so entitled, as long as it was sewn into his clothing in order to address safety considerations.

Multani, following the precedent of the *Eaton* case, discussed above, makes it clear that school boards must make every reasonable effort to accommodate students and teachers who may wish to observe their religious beliefs through their manner of dress or in other ways. As Mackay (2009) writes, "Diversity properly accommodated in the schools produces a sense of inclusion and belonging that is conducive to a safe and welcoming environment" (p. 58).

The case of *Islamic Schools Federation of Ontario v. Ottawa Board of Education* (1997), in which the school board was successful in defending its policies, illustrates suitable measures to put in place in order to reasonably accommodate students from religious minorities. In arriving at its decision, the Ontario Divisional Court considered the following steps taken by the board: (1) students were able to observe holy days; (2) examinations and other major events were not scheduled on holy days; (3) a multi-faith calendar had been distributed to all schools; (4) a document outlining religious observances and needs of students had also been distributed to all schools; (5) a board multiculturalism advisory committee was in place; (6) an anti-racism and race relations policy existed; and (7) space was provided for noon prayer meetings.

Urban school boards have already had to grapple with the challenge of reasonably accommodating diverse student populations. Their policies will serve as useful templates for other school boards across the province as their classrooms become more diverse.

Teachers are advised to develop differentiated learning activities and assessment tools in order to reasonably accommodate minority students in their classes. Rather than expecting all students to be the same, teachers should consider alternative ways to meet teaching and learning objectives.

Roman Catholic Schools and Freedom of Conscience and Religion

Catholic parents and students in Ontario have a constitutional right to attend Catholic schools and be taught a curriculum infused with Catholic values. (See chapter 2.) While Catholic school boards are constitutionally protected, there are also constraints on the degree to which Catholic schools can impose religious values on their students.

Case Study: Can Catholic Students Be Exempted from Religious Instruction?
Erazo v. Dufferin-Peel Catholic District School Board (2014)

An important part of Roman Catholic education in Ontario is religious observance in the form of the infusion of Catholic values in curriculum, religious education, liturgies, and spiritual retreats.

At the same time, the right of Catholic school districts to inculcate religious values is mitigated by its duties as operators of publicly funded schools. In Ontario, Section 43(13) of the *Education Act* states that "no person ... who attends a secondary school operated by a Roman Catholic board shall be required to take part in any program or course of study in religious education" upon written application from the parent or guardian. While many non-Catholics and non-observant Catholics choose to participate, the law makes clear that this is not required.

Erazo enrolled his son at Notre-Dame Catholic Secondary School not for its religious focus but for its proximity to home and its high academic reputation. When he sought to have his son exempted from religious studies courses in grade 10, the board initially refused. An exemption was granted only upon receipt of a letter from his lawyer noting Section 43.

Later, Erazo requested that his son be exempted from religious services and spiritual retreats. The board refused, arguing that these were required events for all students and essential to the Catholic nature of the school.

This case hinged on the interpretation of programs and courses of study. Erazo argued that liturgies and retreats constituted religious education. He also argued that requiring participation violated *Charter* protection of the right to freedom of conscience and religion. The board countered that these, along with prayers in class and school assemblies, were not part of religious education programming and, thus, were exempt from Section 43(13). The board argued that field trips, for example, were opportunities to build community, promote reflection, and build on important curricular and life skills themes.

While the court grappled with the problems posed by extending exemptions, it ultimately ruled that these events constituted programs in religious education based entirely on Section 43. Erazo's son was exempted from these religious activities.

---

(1) Why was the student granted an exemption even though his parents knowingly selected a Catholic school?

(2) What are the implications for the distinctiveness of Catholic education? Consider the case of Marc Hall (below) in your answer.

The right of Catholic schools in Ontario to infuse the curriculum with religious values was maintained in this decision. At the same time, recognizing that students and parents have the right to opt out of both religion classes and religious activities narrows their scope of action.

This tension between student freedom and the authority of Catholic schools became a public issue in the case of *Hall (Litigation Guardian of) v. Powers* (2002). Marc Hall, a gay student in the Durham Catholic District School Board, wanted to take his male partner to the school prom. The principal refused to allow this, citing Roman Catholic doctrine opposing homosexual acts. While the court granted the school board an injunction, preventing Hall from attending the prom until after the court case was heard, the judge claimed that "the role of a school is to enlighten and guide students—not to control their private thoughts or behaviour." He also added that a prom "is not part of the religious education component of the Board's activity" and is "not educational in nature." While this case was not pursued by Hall once the prom was over, the words of Justice McKinnon suggest that both public and Catholic schools are expected to respect students' right to freedom of expression.

This distinction between curricular and extracurricular activities was reinforced in Bill 13, *Accepting Schools Act* (2012). This legislation, among other things, requires publicly funded Catholic schools to permit student-initiated gay-straight alliances in schools. This is not an infringement on the right of these schools to promote Catholic doctrine in the curriculum, as extracurricular activities are outside the curriculum. While Catholic leaders protested against passage of this law, they recognized that they had no legal recourse.

RIGHT TO PRIVACY OF STUDENTS AND PARENTS

Information is power. While teachers and principals may not consciously think of themselves as having such power, they are often the guardians of important and sensitive information about students and their families. Teachers, therefore, must always be aware of students' and parents' right to privacy. They should not disclose information that may be regarded as private and confidential.

Ontario school boards must adhere to a range of laws concerning the collection and use of student information, including the *Education Act* and the *Municipal Freedom of Information and Protection of Privacy Act* (*MFIPPA*). The former gives school boards the authority to collect personal information about students when they register. By registering their children, parents are consenting to the potential use of the information in the interest of their child. Access to this information comes with a duty of care to ensure that it is properly stored and judiciously disseminated. Under *MFIPPA*, data such as name, address, ethnic background, blood type, and fingerprints are all considered personal information and subject to privacy provisions. This legislation also applies to information on employment, criminal history, financial dealings, and health records. This means the school board must treat teacher records with the same care as student records.

While these laws and their implications for professional practice are outlined below, there are two guiding principles for dealing with personal information:

- Do not divulge personal information without explicit consent.
- When in doubt, check with the school principal before divulging information.

In "Student Privacy and You," published in *Professionally Speaking* (March 2008), Graham F. Scott draws on recommendations by the Information and Privacy Commissioner of Ontario and the Access and Privacy Office of the Ontario government to recommend "seven virtues" of privacy protection:

(1) Collect only as much personal information as you need to do your job.

(2) Collect information directly from individuals, or for students under 18, directly from their parents or guardians—not from third parties.

(3) Explain why you need to collect the information and exactly how it will be used.

(4) Get consent from students, or for students under 18, from parents, for the collection, storage and use of personal information.

(5) Store personal information securely. Keep hard copies under lock and key, such as in a locked filing cabinet; keep electronic documents on a password-protected computer. A clean desk will help prevent sensitive information being misplaced or stolen.

(6) When in doubt, ask for advice from the school principal or the board staff member in charge of privacy. (Ontario law requires every board to have one such contact person.)

(7) When you no longer need the personal information to do your job, destroy it by shredding paper documents or securely erasing electronic ones.

ONTARIO STUDENT RECORD

The Ontario Student Record (OSR) is the single most common and sensitive document that is readily accessible to teachers and other school board employees. The OSR Folder includes:

- report cards;
- Ontario student transcript;
- office index card—which includes family contact information;
- documentation file;
- custody orders;
- verification of changes of surname;
- Identification, Placement, and Review Committee (IPRC) report;
- Individual Education Plans (IEPs);
- Violent Incident Reports;
- educational/psychological/health assessments.

Access to these confidential documents is restricted. They should be kept under lock and key in a secure office area, available only to those authorized by law. According to section 266 of the *Education Act*, the OSR is "privileged for the information and use of supervisory officers and the principal and teachers of the school for the improvement of instruction of the pupil." Teachers and principals often review OSRs to develop an understanding of a student's progress over time. Educational assessments are particularly useful for teachers working with students who have identified exceptionalities. Although section 266 of the act makes it clear that student records are for the use of all the teachers in the school, many schools have established protocols to help maintain confidentiality and ensure appropriate use of the files.

These documents are also available for review to students of any age, as well as to the parents and guardians of minors (under the age of eighteen). Both custodial and non-custodial parents have a legal right to "access" the OSR, but this right may be thought of as a read-only privilege. The principal of the school determines the contents of each student's OSR, in accordance with the provision of the *Education Act*, subject to the authority of the appropriate supervisory officer. Section 266 of the act sets out an appeal process for parents who disagree with the principal's decision. Parents also have the right to meet with teachers to discuss their child's progress and attend Identification, Placement and Review Committee meetings. If they request copies of the file, the school may charge five dollars plus photocopying fees. The local medical officer of health has limited access to a student's OSR. An adjudicator appointed by the Ministry of Education may also review an OSR if there is a dispute regarding its contents.

Disclosure may also be permitted if information is requested through a court order under the *Criminal Code*, in a civil suit, or under the *Child and Family Services Act*. In such cases, the principal is advised by the Ministry of Education to consult school board legal counsel before turning over any records.

Avoiding Inappropriate Disclosures

Teachers are often very accommodating and eager to help. These virtues can sometimes land them in trouble when it comes to the disclosure of confidential information. Following are a few examples that may serve as cautions.

Scenario 1

Two teachers talk about a student while in a coffee shop. One casually mentions that the student has an educational exceptionality, and the other wonders if this may have contributed to his failing grade. A relative of the student overhears the conversation and complains to the school principal.

Lesson: Do not casually disclose/share confidential information about students, especially in public places.

Scenario 2

John is socially awkward and many students are annoyed by his rude and insensitive conduct on the playground. In order to help John, a teacher explains to the other students that John has mild autism, which makes it difficult for him to read social situations. She urges them to be more forgiving and accommodating. John's mother later telephones the teacher to object to this unauthorized disclosure of personal information.

Lesson: Never disclose or divulge confidential information about a student to other students or parents without the prior written consent of the individual student's parents or adult student, as the case may be.

Scenario 3

A teacher is contacted by someone purporting to be a lawyer representing one of a child's parents. The lawyer asks about the student's IPRC and grades. The teacher states that she is busy and offers to call back once she has collected information. The principal then cautions her not to divulge this information without the written permission of the parent or a court order. Later, she calls the lawyer's office number (which verifies his legitimacy) and is careful not to knowingly reveal information from the OSR.

Lesson: It is wise to verify the identity of a person requesting confidential information and to check with the principal to ensure that you are protecting the student's privacy rights. The same principles apply when dealing with Family and Child Services or local medical officials.

Consequences of Breaching Privacy

While wilfully disclosing personal information can result in a fine of up to $5,000 under *MFIPPA*, this is rare because most privacy breaches are inadvertent or accidental. Parents could also sue the school board in civil court but this is unlikely given the cost of litigation and the need to prove harm. Breaches of privacy could also involve a complaint being filed with the College of Teachers, possibly leading to a finding of misconduct. While the penalty may be little more than a reprimand, it is a needless blemish on a teacher's career.

The penalties are relatively minor, yet these laws and the scenarios above serve as cautionary tales to ensure that teachers make every effort to be sensitive to the privacy rights of students and their parents.

Rights and Responsibilities of Parents

"The joys of parents are secret; and so are their griefs and fears," wrote the sixteenth-century philosopher Francis Bacon (1597; 1965, p. 15).

The word *parent* has multiple layers of meaning. Obviously it is understood to refer to maternity and paternity. More generally, it is a legal term referring to parents by birth or adoption. Finally, the term may include the legal guardians, stepparents, or someone standing in the place of the parent.

In this chapter, unless otherwise specified, the word is broadly defined to include parents and guardians as identified in law.

As society changes, our understanding of parents and families evolves. Teachers working in increasingly multicultural schools need to come to terms with very different conceptions of family and good parenting. They also need to recognize that changes to the legal definition of marriage and adoption laws mean that more children will grow up in non-traditional family units.

Teachers should always bear in mind that parents are the most important people in the lives of their children. Rich childhood experiences can contribute significantly to happiness and success in school and beyond. As Michael Howe (1990) writes in *The Origins of Exceptional Abilities*:

> Effective mothering in early childhood will usually give a child a good start in life. In most cases that will have beneficial long-term consequences, partly through a kind of snowballing effect. Other things being equal, a child who, as a result of the mother's effectiveness as a teacher, gains useful abilities that facilitate the acquisition of further useful skills will thereby have a definite advantage over less-favoured children. (p. 115)

Parents, like teachers, have a small number of rights and a large number of responsibilities. Instead of fundamental rights, they have conditional rights: rights connected with their obligation to provide for the rights and best interests of their children. The *Criminal Code* states that parents have a duty to give their children the "necessaries of life" until age sixteen. These include food, clothing, shelter, medical care, and education. Failure to supply these is punishable by up to two years in prison. The code also makes it illegal for a parent to abandon a child or expose a child under ten to danger. Ontario's *Child and Family Services Act* empowers the state to remove children from abusive parents. These legal responsibilities often pale in comparison with the moral and practical responsibilities that weigh heavily on parents.

Outside the home, schools are the most important institutions in most children's lives. The time they spend in school is critical to their intellectual and social development. Parents, as caregivers, have every right to take an interest in the education their children are receiving during this time. While teachers as professionals are empowered to make educational decisions for the students in their classrooms, they are also accountable to parents. Parents' requests and demands on the school system, which sometimes may seem unreasonable to teachers, stem from their secret joys, griefs, and fears.

Teachers and schools can be most effective in the education of children when they keep in close communication with the home and work together in an atmosphere of mutual respect and understanding.

EDUCATIONAL RIGHTS AND RESPONSIBILITIES

The Ontario Schools Code of Conduct (2012) states:

> Parents play an important role in the education of their children, and can support the efforts of school staff in maintaining a safe, inclusive, accepting, and respectful learning environment for all students.

According to the provincial *Code of Conduct*, parents fulfill their role when they:
- show an active interest in their child's school work and progress;
- communicate regularly with the school;
- help their child be neat, appropriately dressed, and prepared for school;
- ensure that their child attends school regularly and on time;
- promptly report to the school their child's absence or late arrival;
- show that they are familiar with the provincial *Code of Conduct*, the board's code of conduct, and school rules;
- encourage and assist their child in following the rules of behaviour;
- assist school staff in dealing with disciplinary issues involving their child.

Parents are understandably upset when their children are harassed, assaulted, or bullied by other students. In 2012, Bill 13, *Accepting Schools Act* set perimeters for parents with respect to communication with an administrator regarding bullying, including homophobic bullying and cyber bullying. Bill 13's "whole school approach" places the responsibility of maintaining a safe and caring school on everyone's shoulders, including teachers, support staff, parents, students, administrators, and the community. While parents have the right to be informed and consulted, there are limitations in sharing personal information about another student or about ongoing investigations.

RELIGIOUS ACCOMMODATION—CURRICULAR

One of the duties of teachers, according to Section 264(1)(c) of the *Education Act*, is "to inculcate by precept and example respect for religion and the principles of Judeo-Christian morality" and regard for virtues such as truth, benevolence, and industry. While the wording has not changed in decades, today this is read by the courts and society as a call for teachers to be good role models.

Public schools are largely secular in orientation. They are accepting and inclusive of all faiths, but do not abide by traditional religious beliefs, whether Judeo-Christian or other. This presents challenges when religious beliefs run counter to the public's wish for curriculum that is more responsive to social issues such as lesbian, gay, and transgender rights and sexual health. Whereas religious people once were successful in preventing these issues from being discussed, the majority of religious and non-religious citizens now support their inclusion in the curriculum.

This change in social norms has caused a significant and vocal minority of people of faith to feel uncomfortable about curriculum that is inconsistent with their religious values and cultural practices. These people include both Christians and members of other faith communities. For example, an update of the health and physical education curriculum implemented in 2015–2016 prompted protests in communities with large Muslim populations.

This raised the issue of religious accommodations for parents who do not wish to have their children exposed to elements of the curriculum that discuss sexuality. In their view, sex education should take place at home. Their cry was "my child, my choice."

In considering this issue, we draw on the Peel District School Board's *Administrator Religious Accommodation Resource Package* (2012). It notes obligations under the Ontario *Human Rights Code* to make respectful, good-faith processes for accommodating faith requirements on an individual basis. This includes accommodations for religious observances, prayer spaces, and clothing. The processes outlined here also provide for curricular accommodations.

Parents may request a religious accommodation to the curriculum for their children by describing their concern on a "Request for Religious Accommodation Form" and meeting with school administrators to discuss their request in relation to the curriculum. Accommodations are made on a case-by-case basis, as there are a wide range of religious observances within a single faith.

Efforts are made to employ inclusive pedagogical practices and curricular resources to make the curriculum culturally respectful. Also, students may be excused from class when the content does not conform to religious beliefs. A student could be excused from parts of sex education to work on a differentiated assignment.

In September 2015, the Director of the Peel District School Board indicated that removal from sex education would be but not allowed regarding sexuality education that includes topics such as LGBT families or homophobic bullying. The director stressed that all students need to be informed that LGBT rights are protected in Ontario under the *Human Rights Code* and in Canada under the *Charter*. He also said this was a question of student safety, and that LGBT students need to be treated with the same respect, care, and integrity as all other students in their public board.

Thus, it is likely that Peel and other school boards across Ontario will attempt to teach the new sex education curriculum as effectively as possible while making efforts to be inclusive and respectful of accommodations for religious and sexual minorities. However, these accommodations do have limits if they infringe on issues relating to the *Charter* or the Ontario *Human Rights Code*. In those circumstances, school boards, administrators, and teachers are obligated to teach the curriculum.

HOMESCHOOLING

As noted earlier, a child has a fundamental right to be educated, and parents have a legal responsibility to ensure that a child of mandatory school age attends school. Failure to do the latter can result in prosecution. It was also noted that parents have the right to make decisions regarding where and how their children are educated. This includes choosing publicly funded education from English-language or French-language boards and between public and Catholic education.

The *Education Act* also excuses a person from attendance at school if "the person is receiving satisfactory instruction at home or elsewhere" (section 21(2)(a)). This permits parents to enrol their children in private school or to opt for homeschooling. According to section 21(2) of the *Education Act*, parents may choose to have their children educated at home instead of at school so long as their children are receiving "satisfactory instruction" (which is not defined).

Over the years, the number of children schooled at home has risen as more families choose homeschooling for ideological or pedagogical reasons. It has also become more "possible and practical" (Van Pelt, 2015, p. iii) with new technologies and social networks. In 2011–2012, some 5,000 students in Ontario and 20,000 nationally were homeschooled, an increase of about 30% from 2006 to 2007 (Van Pelt, 2015, p. 23).

Homeschoolers are highly diverse. They include families that duplicate school at home, complete with textbooks, assignments, and report cards. They also include families that have a conception of learning involving children and adults living and learning together in a holistic manner. Some Christian homeschoolers select the homeschooling option because they are not comfortable with the values underlying publicly funded schooling in Ontario. Others, such as parents of students with special education needs, may believe that the school system cannot meet their children's unique learning needs. Students may be homeschooled for their entire education, or they may mix that form of schooling with periods of time in public or private schools.

Homeschooling involves a significant commitment by families. Parents must invest considerable time ensuring that their children learn. Many families make significant financial sacrifices to allow a parent to stay at home with the children. Many of these families enter into relationships with other homeschoolers in their communities. The Internet has also made it easier for parents to access quality educational resources at home, including lesson plans and assessment instruments.

The Ministry of Education, in Policy/Program Memorandum #131 (June 2002), requires parents who are homeschooling their children to provide their school board annually with a letter of intent. This letter is to include names, ages, and gender of the school-age children and an indication that the parents understand their responsibility to provide for the education of their children as indicated in section (21)2 of the *Education Act*. The memorandum also directs school boards to excuse children of compulsory school age from attendance at school once the board has received this notification from the family. School boards are no longer required to investigate the adequacy of homeschool instruction, unless they are given reason to do so. Indeed, "the board should accept the written notification of the parents each year as evidence that the parents are providing satisfactory instruction at home" and provide educational resources to support homeschooled children. These changes reflect the success of the homeschool movement in articulating its case to policy-makers and in presenting clear evidence that homeschooling does not diminish educational outcomes (Van Pelt, 2015).

IMMUNIZATION OF STUDENTS

Schools, as public places in which large numbers of children congregate, are particularly susceptible to outbreaks of disease. The *Immunization of School Pupils Act* was enacted to ensure that students are immunized against designated diseases. Parents are now required to have their children immunized in order to be admitted to school. A standard letter goes out once a year to parents stating that children will be suspended from school until proof of immunization or a notarized letter stating refusal of immunization is provided.

The local medical officer of health may order a school to suspend students who have not been immunized to avoid an outbreak or in the event of an outbreak. Principals are also required to refuse admission to persons whom they believe are infected with or have been exposed to communicable diseases.

HEALTH AND MEDICAL INFORMATION IN SCHOOLS

Parents are responsible for the health and well-being of their children. They bear the responsibility to inform the school of any medical or health information that the school may need in order to respond to medical emergencies, allergic reactions, or other health situations that may arise. They then have the right to assume that the school acting *in loco parentis* will take reasonable steps to use this information to ensure the safety of their children. Indeed, one of the duties of the school principal, according to section 265(j) of the *Education Act*, is to "give assiduous attention to the health and comfort of the pupils." In order to assist the school, parents are required to provide updated medical and health information on their children. Teachers, as appropriate, are then informed of health risks and how to prevent or respond to situations that may arise.

Medication in Schools

In the past, principals and teachers have sometimes been reluctant to administer medication to students, and have sought to have the parents themselves administer the medication at home or at school. Students have the right to take medication in school, and parents in our day and age cannot reasonably be expected to be available during the school day. As a result, schools now have a duty to administer medication when necessary. This duty is balanced with parental obligations.

The *"Medication" Procedure (PR 536 SCH)* of the Toronto District School Board (TDSB) illustrates the obligations of schools and parents in ensuring children's right to good health. It states that designated staff members are authorized to administer essential medication, but only when it is:

- prescribed by a physician;
- essential to the student's attendance at school;
- required to be taken during school hours;
- unable to be self-administered;
- not reasonably able to be administered by the parents at school.

The TDSB also stipulates parental obligations. A parent and a physician are required to complete *Form 536A, The Administration of Prescribed*

Medication before medication can be administered. This form requires the following:

- a set of clear instructions;
- one week of medication, clearly labelled;
- encouragement of the student to wear medical alert bracelet/pendant;
- dissemination of information by principal to staff/volunteers;
- Waiver of Liability (which does not cover negligence).

Sabrina's Law, 2005

Sabrina Shannon, a thirteen-year-old from Pembroke with a dairy allergy, died at school in 2003 after eating French fries containing traces of cheese. Two years later, a private member's bill passed in the Ontario legislature requiring all Ontario school boards to have protection plans in place by January 2006.

Sabrina's Law states that school boards shall establish and maintain policies to deal with the health needs of students with anaphylactic allergies. These policies are designed to reduce risk of exposure to causative agents by disseminating information on life-threatening allergies (e.g., eggs, peanuts, milk, and shellfish), and providing regular training for all employees and others in direct contact with students on a regular basis.

Principals are required to develop an individual plan for each pupil with an anaphylactic allergy. These plans should include:

- sharing detailed information with all employees;
- asking all parents/pupils about allergies at registration;
- keeping a current file of treatment information, instructions from physician/nurse, and emergency list.

CONSENT FOR HEALTH CARE

If an individual has the capacity to provide consent under the *Health Care Consent Act*, teachers and principals need to receive consent before beginning treatment. This consent is for the *administration* of medication and in no way implies that the school board employee is responsible for the treatment itself (e.g., determining the appropriateness of the medication or the dosage).

The law offers no specific age of consent, but common law suggests the following general guidelines. If the student is over sixteen, s/he is capable of giving informed consent. If the student is under twelve years of age, s/he cannot give informed consent. Educators are advised, when dealing with the intermediate range, ages twelve to sixteen, to obtain consent from both parents and students.

With regard to emergency situations, Sabrina's Law authorizes school employees to administer epinephrine or other prescribed medication without preauthorization. They are also immune from civil court action for damages if they acted in good faith, unless they are found guilty of gross negligence.

DEFAMATION AND PARENTAL HARASSMENT

Concerns about the educational process can often lead to strong emotions in students, teachers, and parents. While the vast majority of people discuss issues and concerns thoughtfully and respectfully, some cross the line and behave unacceptably.

Defamation, in the educational context, refers to intentional, false statements about a student, teacher, or parent, damaging to his or her reputation. While defamation can involve any of these parties, it is parents who are most likely to be charged with defamation. The courts recognize that parents have a qualified privilege to file complaints against educators, but court rulings in cases such as *McKerron v. Marshall* (1999) demonstrate that there is little sympathy for malicious public statements.

Teachers and administrators have sometimes been accused of defamation for the comments they make on student report cards or teacher performance appraisals. Brown and Zuker (2002) write in *Education Law* that judgments made by school personnel "are not defamation, assuming that they are statements of fact or *bona fide* professional observations" (p. 122).

There is a growing recognition among educators of parental harassment, and educators are increasingly taking stands against aggressive parents. In 2005, the three largest teacher federations in Ontario, OSSTF,

ETFO, and OECTA, conducted a provincial study on parental harassment. The study reported that 30% of all teachers in Ontario have been bullied or harassed by a parent or guardian. The study also revealed that elementary teachers were more likely to be bullied than secondary teachers, and female teacher more likely than their male counterparts. These statistics were troubling and the federations lobbied to have more supports put in place for educators.

Both the *Ontario Human Rights Code* and the *Occupational Health and Safety Act* (1990) provide further protection for educators. The latter act specifically addresses workplace violence and harassment. Section III .0.1 states that an employer must have a policy on workplace harassment and that it must be made public.

Educators who think they are being harassed should document all incidents and consult the principal for direction, which may include consulting board guidelines for responding to harassment. Options in serious cases may also include contacting the police to investigate possible criminal harassment charges, and pursuing civil action such as defamation suits or restraining orders. In most cases, the principal's power to exclude the parent from the school premises is sufficient to address the issue.

School boards are beginning to develop parent harassment protocols in order to prevent, and, when necessary, respond to harassment. These protocols are included in parent handbooks. Lawyer R.G. Keel (2001) writes:

> Boards should consider any case of harassment to be the responsibility of the board and not the individual employee. Otherwise, the failure to act can create morale issues or could result in friction with a union or association representing the employee. (p. 64)

Rather than wait until harassment becomes a problem, a teacher should take steps to develop effective lines of communication with parents. Teachers who provide parents with regular newsletters and telephone calls are more likely to enjoy positive relations with parents. Regardless of the level of communication, intimidation and harassment are never acceptable behaviours and thus should be reported to the principal with documentation.

Tips for Effective Parent–Teacher Collaboration

Presume Good Intentions
- Parents and teachers want what is best for the child but may differ in how to achieve it.
- Each brings knowledge (e.g., observations on behaviour and past actions) and expertise that are crucial to enhancing learning.
- Overworked teachers should be sensitive to the stresses facing parents today.
- Exhausted parents need to respect the challenges of teaching diverse students in today's classrooms.
- Each child is special and deserves consideration of his/her unique learning needs.
- Parents and teachers who presume good intentions and work as allies are effective in helping the child grow.

Strategies for Teachers Working in Collaboration with Parents
1. Avoid Conflict by Acting/Appearing Professional
- Provide detailed information.
- Record multiple assessments and observations.
- Save samples of student work.
- Present materials in a polished manner.
- Encourage and praise the student's strengths while you provide direction for areas of improvement.
- Offer some strategies that other parents have found useful.
- Be careful not to explicitly or implicitly criticize their parenting.

2. Set the Stage for Success
- Arrange ample time to talk.
- Greet parents warmly, and acknowledge their commitment, knowledge, and expertise.
- Commit to working together to help their child learn.

- Share information about the student's performance in school, past and present.
- Ask for information about the child at home and in other contexts.
- Ask about family experiences that may help you better understand the child.

3. Develop and Implement an Education Plan
- Teacher and parents together prioritize needs.
- Teacher develops a plan of action for student learning at school.
- Parents develop strategies to support the education plan.
- Ongoing communication—e.g., e-mailing list of upcoming assignments, occasional notes or telephone calls—about good and bad news.
- Review progress and adapt expectations accordingly.
- Recognize that learning involves change, and that trial and error is part of the process.
- Support one another in the challenges you are facing together.
- As you address the educational challenges, always think of the student as a worthwhile person to be nurtured.

SCHOOL COUNCILS

There is a growing trend toward greater parental involvement in education. Since 2000, school boards in Ontario have been required to establish school councils for each school in their jurisdiction (*Education Act*, section 170). These councils must meet at least four times a year, and meetings are open to the public. According to *Regulation 612/00*, their purpose is, through the active participation of parents, to improve pupil achievement and to enhance the accountability of the education system to parents. The primary means by which school councils achieve their purpose is making recommendations to the principal and school board on educational matters. The operative word here is *recommendations*, because the school council is not a decision-making body with authority over the principal or school board. Nevertheless, the principal or school board is required to advise the council of the action taken in response to a recommendation.

Regulation 612/00 outlines a number of areas where the school board and principal must consult the council. School councils may *make recommendations* to the principal on such matters as:

- school year calendars;
- codes of student behaviour;
- curriculum priorities;
- programs and strategies to improve school performance on provincial and school boards tests;
- safe arrival programs (elementary schools);
- communications to parents and communications to the community;
- community use of the school, and community programs and services provided at the school through school-community partnerships;
- school board policies that will affect the school;
- selection of principals.

However, it would not be appropriate for the council to discuss individual teachers or students.

Parents must form a majority of the school council members. The principal is a member, though s/he is not eligible to vote. Other members include: a teacher (elected by peers); another employee of school (elected by secretaries, custodians, educational assistants, etc.); a student representative (selected by student council in secondary schools); at least one community member appointed by school council; and, where appropriate, a representative appointed by the home and school association. There are guidelines in place concerning the announcement and reporting of school council activities.

Many school councils are not very active and do not attract many parents or teachers to their meetings. This is unfortunate, for two reasons.

First, such councils can be co-opted by disgruntled parents with specific agendas or grievances. Second, they have the potential to bring teachers and parents together to support one another's work. Although the school council, as noted above, has no authority over the principal, a wise principal will try to work with the council as much as possible. In many schools, the school council is active in raising supplementary funds for school activities. Also, school council meetings can serve as a place for principals to vet potentially controversial issues with parents. For example, a new sex education unit or anti-bullying initiative may be presented to parents for feedback.

Some visionary principals strive to attract large gatherings by promoting these meetings and inviting interesting guest speakers. These principals understand that the school council can be an enormous force for good in a school. The members of the council are often the school's strongest supporters and can help the school develop as a learning community that promotes excellence for all students.

Regulation 612/00 also permits school councils to engage in fundraising activities, provided that the activities are conducted in accordance with board policy and the purpose of the fundraising is also authorized by the board. Although fund-raising is not one of the stated purposes of school councils, many councils do spend considerable time and energy on various fund-raising projects throughout the year, providing supplementary resources for the school.

FILING WITH THE ONTARIO COLLEGE OF TEACHERS

If students or parents think that their rights have been violated by a teacher, they can file a written complaint with the Ontario College of Teachers. The mandate of the College is to investigate complaints against members in order to ensure that the students, parents, and the general public have confidence in the education system. If a teacher's or principal's behaviour toward students or parents is deemed to constitute professional misconduct, the member may be disciplined by the College.

CHECKING YOUR UNDERSTANDING

- Both the right to an education and the obligation to attend school are enshrined in Ontario's *Education Act*.

- All persons between the age of six and eighteen must attend school, unless legally excused. Legal excuses include homeschooling, attendance at a private school, illness or other unavoidable cause, and achievement of a secondary school diploma.

- All persons have the right to attend school, without payment of fee, in the jurisdiction of the school board in which they qualify to be a resident pupil.

- Schools are required to make every reasonable accommodation to meet the educational needs of individual students.

- Schools must try to balance the rights of the individual with the safety of everyone.

- Every student has an Ontario Student Record, including report cards, documentation file, office index card, and transcript (in secondary schools).

- The OSR is for the use of supervisory officers and the principal and teachers of the school "for the improvement of instruction" of the student.

- "Students of any age and parents of students who are minors are entitled to examine the OSR," according to section 266(3) of the *Education Act*.

- The contents of the OSR are confidential and must not be disclosed to a third party without the written consent of either the parents of a student who is a minor or the student who is an adult.

- Parents who homeschool their children have to provide the school board with an annual letter of intent. The school board is not required to monitor homeschooling unless there is reason to do so.

- Students who are not immunized against certain diseases may be excluded from school.

- Schools are expected to administer necessary medication to students within board guidelines.

- Sabrina's Law requires all school boards to have policies and procedures in place to deal with anaphylactic allergies. School personnel may administer prescribed medication without prior authorization in emergencies.

- Parents and teachers are most effective when they work together as partners in the education of children. Teachers who are subject to defamation or harassment by parents should consult their principal and federation representative.

- Every school in Ontario is required to have a school council, consisting of a majority of parents. The council's role is to make recommendations to the principal/board in an effort to improve the effectiveness of the school. The principal/board must advise the council of action taken in response to a recommendation.

- Although the council may make recommendations on any matter, it would not be appropriate for the council to discuss individual teachers or students.

- When the rights of parents and students are not being met, a complaint could be lodged with the Ontario College of Teachers.

APPLYING YOUR UNDERSTANDING

Accommodating Religious Diversity

June Callwood Public School is a diverse school in a suburb of a large city. Immigration in recent years has caused a dramatic increase in the number of students from Sikh households. The school has made efforts to accommodate students of different religious backgrounds by informing staff of Sikh customs and holidays, not scheduling major assignments on Sikh holidays, providing a prayer room for Muslim students, and permitting days off for religious observance. At the school council meeting, a group of parents demanded that the school and school board schedule Sikh holy days into the school year calendar. They said they intended to pursue their right to religious accommodation in the courts if their demands were not met.

(1) What are the human rights issues? How might Ontario's *Human Rights Code* and the *Canadian Charter of Rights and Freedoms* apply in this case?

(2) Has the school made reasonable accommodations? Explain.

(3) Do you think the parents would be successful if they pursued this case before the courts? Explain.

CHAPTER 9

SPECIAL EDUCATION LAW: MEETING THE NEEDS OF STUDENTS WITH EXCEPTIONALITIES

After reading this chapter, you will be familiar with the legislative framework for special education in Ontario, including the processes involved in identification, placement, and review. Decisions by the courts and the Ontario College of Teachers will be used to illustrate the rights of students with exceptionalities and the responsibilities of the educators who serve them.

Case Study: Taking Care of Vulnerable Students
Ontario College of Teachers v. LSF (2015)

LSF was a special education teacher who was accused by his colleagues of yelling at mentally disabled students, being physically aggressive with disabled students, making inappropriate comments about the students in the presence of others, and not seeking medical attention for a disabled student with a very high temperature.

LSF yanked a student by the hair, grabbed another student by the back of the neck, pushed another student by the back of his head despite the student's serious medical condition, and physically forced a student to unclench his/her hand even though they had a serious medical condition. LSF's conduct was brought to the attention of the administration, and he was placed on disciplinary unpaid leave.

Children's Aid was notified and conducted an investigation into LSF's conduct and concluded that the students were "in need of protection."

During a contested trial at the Ontario College of Teachers, three witnesses gave testimony regarding LSF's conduct and attitude toward physically and mentally disabled students in the classroom. All of the students had severe physical disabilities, and many of them could not talk. Witnesses also stated that LSF did not work well with his team of educational assistants, and many felt bullied, dismissed, or verbally abused by him.

One witness described LSF forcefully turning the head of a student who had a severe medical disability.

The discipline panel found LSF guilty of professional misconduct—more specifically, that he failed to maintain the standards of the profession; abused students physically, verbally, emotionally, and psychologically; failed to comply with the *Education Act*; committed acts seen as dishonourable, disgraceful, and unprofessional; and engaged in conduct unbecoming of a member.

Counsel for the College requested that LSF appear before the discipline panel to receive a reprimand, that his teaching certificate be suspended for thirty days, and that he take a course on classroom management with special needs students and a course on workplace relations, at his own expense.

However, the discipline panel rejected the penalty and directed the Registrar to immediately revoke LSF's certificate. The discipline panel wrote in its decision: "The Member, on numerous occasions, verbally, physically, and psychologically or emotionally abused several extremely vulnerable students with [XXX], whose parents trusted that their children would be taken care of at school only to have that trust violated in the most reprehensible way."

This case appears in *Professionally Speaking*, December 2015.

---

(1) Why do you think the discipline panel delivered a harsher penalty? Do you agree with their decision?

(2) What would you do if you witnessed a colleague being physically aggressive with a disabled student?

(3) Are there policies on how to physically handle disabled students? How can you find them?

(4) What are some ways that you can make your classroom safe, inclusive, and respectful to all students?

The case above is extremely disturbing considering that the students were completely relying on a teacher who was abusing them on many levels. The students could not disclose the abuse to their parents or other teachers.

Teachers have a legal, moral, ethical, and professional responsibility to protect students, especially those considered the most vulnerable.

The right to an education is a fundamental tenet of liberal democracy. This right is enshrined in the *Declaration of the Rights of the Child* (United Nations, 1959) and implicit in Canada's *Charter of Rights and Freedoms* of 1982. In Ontario it is made explicit in the *Education Act*, where every person who qualifies has the right to attend a school free of charge (section 32(1)). The educational needs of students who are "exceptional," however, were often neglected prior to the 1980s. Even today, in an era when special education programs and placements exist across Ontario, the education of students with exceptionalities remains an issue of contention in schools and in the courts.

Special education in Ontario supports students who have been identified as "exceptional." This refers to students who have been labelled as having:

- a learning disability;
- an intellectual disability;
- a physical disability, including chronic illness;
- an emotional disability that affects the student's ability to learn;
- a mental disability that affects the student's ability to learn.

Two pieces of legislation have played a critical role in ensuring that special education is provided to meet the needs of exceptional learners in Ontario: the *Canadian Charter of Rights and Freedoms* and the *Education Amendment Act*, generally known as Bill 82.

The *Charter* guarantees every Canadian "the right to life, liberty, and security of the person" (section 7). This right has been interpreted by courts to include the right to an education (*R. v. Kind* (1984)). The court ruling on *Andrews v. Law Society of British Columbia* (1989) further clarified *Charter* rights by stating that the "accommodation of difference ... is the true essence of equality." This decision has led to provisions such as wheelchair ramps in buildings and permission for alternative testing for persons with learning exceptionalities. Canadian courts now expect that school districts will make reasonable efforts to accommodate students with identified special needs. Section 15 of the *Charter*, which guarantees equality before the law, has been used by parents to challenge schools boards in cases involving a student's right to reasonable accommodations.

Bill 82 (*Education Amendment Act*) amended the *Education Act* in 1980 to include provisions for special education in Ontario schools. Whereas school boards previously had the option of providing special education services, the principle of universality underlying Bill 82 means that all public school boards are now obliged to offer programs and services to all students with identified exceptionalities. Due process and the right to review identification and placements were also enshrined in the legislation. The process for identifying and placing students with exceptionalities today has changed little from what was outlined in this landmark piece of legislation, which reflected a shift from ignorance—ignoring, marginalizing, and institutionalizing exceptional learners—to an awareness that all learners benefit from being full participants in diverse learning environments.

Special education has evolved a great deal in the Ontario education system and it is fully integrated in all schools. The identification, placement, and review processes can involve parents, teachers, and principals in considerable debate, paperwork and, at times, litigation. It is important that all educators have a broad understanding of the rights of learners with exceptionalities, special education law in Ontario, and the administrative processes involved.

SERVING THE NEEDS OF STUDENTS WITH EXCEPTIONALITIES: PAST AND PRESENT

Until recent times, people with special needs were generally ignored. The Greek philosopher Aristotle believed that people who were deaf were incapable of reason. In medieval times, intellectual or behavioural disabilities were often regarded as signs of demonic possession. Carnival freak shows in the nineteenth century often exhibited physically disabled people such as John Merrick (the Elephant Man). By the early twentieth century, institutions were established to meet the needs of some people with disabilities. In particular, segregated settings provided services for children with physical exceptionalities: for example, sign language for those with hearing impairments, Braille for those with visual impairments, and wheelchairs for those who could not walk. On the other hand, people with intellectual or behavioural exceptionalities were often harshly treated in asylums and reformatories. As Bennett & Dworet (2013) write:

> Framed as a concern for the public good and a seemingly well-intentioned concern for the less able, supporters of eugenics were successful in effecting a policy that not only segregated people with special needs, but also, in practical terms, isolated them. (p. 5)

In the 1960s and 1970s, advocacy by parents and educators dissatisfied with unsatisfactory educational opportunities for students with exceptionalities led to increased awareness. These efforts culminated in the *Individuals with Disabilities Education Act* (1977) in the United States and Bill 82 in Ontario (1980).

Programming, placements, and curriculum for students with exceptionalities have changed considerably since the 1970s. Instead of focusing on "presumed underlying cognitive processes that caused disabilities ... teachers shifted toward providing remedial academic instruction at each student's level of functioning" (Gersten, Baker, Pugach, Scanlon & Chard, 2001). Many excellent special education programs have been developed to meet the needs of special education students generally as well as the specific needs of students with particular exceptionalities.

There is also a general understanding that persons with disabilities have fundamental rights. This is reflected in Canada's decision to ratify the *United Nations Convention on the Rights of Persons with Disabilities* in 2010. By becoming a signatory to this agreement, the federal government committed Canada to:

- change laws that discriminate against individuals with disabilities;
- eliminate barriers to accessibility in schools, hospitals, parks, and new housing;

- ensure that people with disabilities are treated equally in the justice system;
- accommodate students with disabilities in elementary and secondary schools in their community;
- foster respect for the rights and dignity of people with disabilities.

This treaty could lead to an increased commitment to special education in Canada and to a greater role for the courts in affirming and promoting education rights for learners with exceptionalities.

Currently, in Ontario and around the world, there is a movement to inclusionary schooling as the primary means of addressing exceptional learning needs. Segregation in special classrooms is increasingly viewed as a violation of human rights, because it denies access to the larger learning environment (McPhail & Freeman, 2005). Bunch & Valeo (2004) call on classroom teachers to take responsibility for all learners in the class. Attention has shifted to "the creation of forms of teaching that can reach out to all learners within a class and ... the establishment of school conditions that will encourage such conditions" (Ainscow, 2008, p. 244). In 2009, 94,364 elementary students and 98,166 secondary students were identified as exceptional in Ontario's publicly funded school system and receiving special education services. Another 114,490 students were not formally identified but still received services (Ministry of Education, as cited in Bennett, Dworet & Weber, 2013). Both ethical and economical concerns therefore suggest the need for greater inclusivity.

Inclusion has become the norm in Ontario since the Supreme Court ruled in the case of *Eaton v. Brant County Board of Education* (1997). While advocates for learners with exceptionalities were disappointed that the court rejected the parents' insistence that their child be placed in a regular classroom rather than a special class, they were pleased by the court's affirmation that consideration must first be given to placement in regular classroom with appropriate special education supports. In response to the public debate concerning this issue, the Ontario Ministry of Education strengthened its resolve to favour inclusion, as is evident from the *Special Education Transformation* report (Bennett & Wynne, 2006). This report clearly states that, in cases in which special education classes are the only option, these "placements would be duration-specific, intervention-focused, and subject to regular reviews" (Bennett & Wynne, 2006, p. 8).

For inclusion to be successful, regular classroom teachers will need extensive professional development. Their thinking and teaching methods need to be shifted so they can support the 15 percent of students who require some form of special education services. There is evidence to suggest that initial teacher education and ongoing professional development go a long way in engendering in teachers and principals the attitudes and skills needed to effectively address the learning of all students (e.g., Praisner, 2002).

However, in Ontario a gap was identified in teacher education programs, and many new teachers did not feel prepared to work with exceptional students in their classroom. Additional Qualification Special Education Part 1 has consistently been the most popular course taken by teachers, according to the Ontario College of Teachers.

As of 2015, all faculties of education must offer an extended Bachelor of Education Program. *Regulation 283/13: Accreditation of Teacher Education Programs* states:

Schedule 1
Curriculum Knowledge
1. The program provides a student of a program of professional education with knowledge and understanding of the current Ontario curriculum and provincial policy documents that are relevant to the student's areas of study and curriculum, including planning and design, special education, equity and diversity, and learning assessment and evaluation.
2. The program prepares the student of a program of professional education to use current research in teaching and learning.

Pedagogical and Instructional Strategies Knowledge
The program includes the following elements:

1. How to use educational research and data analysis.
2. How to use technology as a teaching tool.
3. How to use inquiry-based research, data and assessment and the selection and use of current instructional strategies to address student learning styles.
4. How to use learning and teaching theories and methods and differentiated instruction.
5. A focus on the development of classroom management and organization skills.
6. Child and adolescent development and student transitions to age 21 and through kindergarten to grade 12.
7. How to use current strategies relating to student observation, assessment and evaluation.
8. How to teach students whose first language is not the language of instruction, whether English or French.
9. Pedagogy and the assessment and evaluation of learning in the relevant areas of study in relation to specific curriculum subjects.
10. The policies, assessments and practices involved in responding to the needs and strengths of all students, including students identified as requiring special education supports.

Three of the most significant changes in the regulation were the inclusion of special education, education law, and technology education. This will better prepare new teachers to work with exceptional students, understand their rights and responsibilities, and utilize technology in the classroom to its best potential.

THE EDUCATION ACT
ON SPECIAL EDUCATION

Special education provisions were incorporated into the *Education Act* when the *Education Amendment Act* of 1980 (Bill 82) received royal assent. While the broad provisions of Bill 82 remain, the last thirty years have seen many amendments to the legislation. The key provisions regarding special education in the current *Education Act* are identified below. Section 170(1)(7) states that it is the responsibility of school boards to "provide or enter into an agreement with another board to provide in accordance with the regulations special education programs and special education services for its exceptional pupils." Section 1(1) states: "Special education program ... means, in respect of an exceptional pupil, an educational program that is based on and modified by the results of continuous assessment and evaluation and that includes a plan containing specific objectives and an outline of educational services that meets the needs of the exceptional pupil." An "exceptional pupil" is defined in section 1(1) as "a pupil whose behavioural, communicational, intellectual, physical or multiple exceptionalities are such that he or she is considered to need placement in a special education program." The responsibility of the Minister of Education, according to section 8, subsection 3, is to "ensure that all exceptional children in Ontario have available to them, in accordance with this Act and the regulations, appropriate special education programs and special education services without payment of fees by parents or guardians." This section also indicates that the minister shall "provide for the parents or guardians to appeal the appropriateness of the special education placement" and that, to this end, the minister shall:

(a) require school boards to implement procedures for early and ongoing identification of the learning abilities and needs of pupils, and shall prescribe standards in accordance with which such procedures be implemented; and

(b) in respect of special education programs and services, define exceptionalities of pupils, and prescribe classes, groups or categories of exceptional pupils, and require boards to employ such definitions or use such prescriptions as established under this clause.

The *Education Act* also provides for the establishment of an Ontario Special Education Tribunal to provide final and binding arbitration in disagreements between a parent and school board concerning the identification or placement of an exceptional pupil.

SPECIAL EDUCATION REGULATIONS IN ONTARIO

The provisions in the *Education Act* are supplemented by a number of regulations made under the authority of the act. These include:

- *Regulation 181/98: Identification and Placement of Exceptional Pupils*, which governs: the identification and placement of exceptional pupils; IPRC reviews; appeal procedures; and the role of parent(s)/guardian(s) in these processes.

- *Regulation 464/97: Special Education Advisory Committees*
  This act outlines the role, requirements, and scope of Special Education Advisory Committees (SEACs) at the school board level. A SEAC, which is composed of representatives of parent advocate groups and school board trustees, is charged with the responsibility of making recommendations "in respect of any matter affecting the establishment, development and delivery of special education programs and services for exceptional students of the board" (*Regulation 464/97*, section 11(1)). This group also plays a significant role in the review of SEP and the budget for special education services.

Other legislation relevant to special education is included in *Regulation 298: Operation of Schools–General* and *Regulation 296: Ontario Schools for the Blind and Deaf*.

Special Education Policy Documents

While the overarching legal requirements governing special education are outlined in the *Education Act* and its accompanying regulations, teachers are guided in their professional practice by many policy and planning documents issued by the Ministry of Education.

For example, *Individual Education Plans: Standards for Development, Program Planning and Implementation* (2000) outlines in considerable detail the standards teachers and principals need to apply in developing, implementing, and monitoring Individual Education Plans (IEPs).

Special Education: A Guide for Educators (2001) is a good general guide to the topic. In addition, many of the elementary and secondary program and curriculum policy documents also include guidance for teachers working with students with exceptionalities.

Caring and Safe Schools in Ontario: Supporting Students with Special Needs Through Progressive Discipline, Kindergarten to Grade 12 (2010) is an important document that helps teachers understand some of the complexities when trying to discipline exceptional students. For example, some students who are autistic may become violent if noises or lights trigger them. Their aggressive behaviour is not related to mal-intent but rather is a response to over-stimulation.

Learning for All: A Guide to Effective Assessment and Instruction for All Students, Kindergarten to Grade 12 (2011) replaced *Education for All* (2005), which referenced only elementary students. The resource informs teachers about evidence-based and research-based effective teaching methods such as universal design, differentiated instruction, and the tiered approach.

THE IDENTIFICATION, PLACEMENT, AND REVIEW PROCESS

While the regular school curriculum and program meets the needs of most students, some students require modifications—or even significant accommodations—to the program in order to have the opportunity to learn.

The process typically begins when a teacher or parent identifies a student whose learning needs merit discussion. The first intervention may involve the teacher and resource teacher adjusting the instructional practice or the program to meet specific needs. Alternatively, or subsequently, the student may be referred to the "in-school team"—which generally consists of the principal (who leads the team), a special education resource teacher, one or two classroom teachers and possibly, other personnel—who may be called on to recommend other interventions and develop an Individual Education Plan for the student.

The "response to interventions" is then assessed by the team. If the team determines that problems still persist despite the steps taken so far, it may recommend that the principal initiate the formal referral process for identification and placement.

The principal of the school may then decide to refer the student, with written notification to the parents, to an Identification, Placement, and Review Committee (IPRC). An IRPC consists of at least three members, one of whom must be a principal or superintendent of the board.

Note that although the process outlined above is typical of many schools, the legal responsibility for referring a student to an IPRC rests with the principal, who could initiate the referral process at any time. The principal must also refer a student to an IPRC at the written request of the parents.

Parents of the student (and students who are sixteen years of age or older) are entitled to be present and participate in all IPRC discussions about the student. They are also entitled to be present when the committee's decisions are made, although they are not entitled to be part of the final decision making. Experts such as educational psychologists may be called on to administer a battery of educational tests and provide an overall assessment of the student's level of exceptionality. Once students are identified as exceptional, they are placed in a classroom setting appropriate to their needs and an Individual Education Plan is developed. The regulation governing the identification and placement of exceptional pupils directs the IPRC to consider the integration of exceptional pupils into regular classes before considering a placement in a special education class, provided that this meets the pupil's needs and is consistent with parental preferences. There are also processes for reviewing the student's situation each year and parents have opportunities to appeal school board decisions if they believe their children's needs are not being served.

The schema below, which was developed by Sheila Bennett and Don Dworet for *Special Education in Ontario Schools* (2008), outlines the main features of *Ontario Regulation 181/98*.

Figure 9-1

Identification and Placement of Exceptional Pupils

Step One

Every school board is required to appoint one or more IPRCs.

Student is formally referred to an IPRC by the school's principal.

Principal may initiate referral (notifies parent*). Must initiate referral if asked by parent in writing.

IPRC has minimum of three members. One must be a principal or supervisory officer of the board (or designate).

Step Two

IPRC obtains and considers educational assesment. May interview student with permission of parent.* Receives information put forward by school and parent. Shares all written information with parent.

Medical and/or psychological data may be requested, subject to *Health Care Consent Act* (1996).

School board must publish a detailed Parents' Guide.

Teacher interview and/ or input not required by regulation, but most school boards will include these.

* *Parent* here includes *parent(s) and guardian(s)*. Wherever *parent* appears, note that students 16 years and older may be part of the process along with parent.

Step Three

IPRC must consider all information and proposals for special education programs and services.

Parent may present proposals in addition to those from school board.

Parent entitled to have a representative of choice present.

Parent and representative may participate in all discussions except decision making.

Step Four

IPRC decides student is not exceptional.

or

IPRC identifies student as exceptional, and decides on a placement. May make recommendations (but not decisions) regarding programs and services.

Process ends, unless parent appeals, or requests follow-up meeting.

Written decision of IPRC goes to parent, referring principal, and school board.

Decision statement must list placement, category(s) and definition(s) of exceptionality, and student's strengths/ needs.

Parent may request IPRC meet again to reconsider.

Placement to be regular class if it meets needs, and if parent wishes. IPRC must give reasons if special class is chosen.

Within 30 school days principal of school where student is placed must see to development of IEP
and
for 14 year olds and older, a Transition Plan.

Step Five

Student is placed according to IPRC decision. IEP is developed and implementation begun.

If parent signs consent
or
if consent is not signed, but parent does not appeal.

Rights and requirements as in Step One to Five.

- - - - - - ▶ Step Five stayed if parent appeals.

Review

Student's situation to be reviewed at least once every school year by an IPRC. Parent may request review after three months.

Reviews confirm existing situation, or may make changes. Principal to review and update IEP.

Identification and Placement
How the IPRC works
A recommendation in the fall of 2006 from the then Deputy Minister outlined what for some school boards across Canada would be a shift in practice with regard to IPRC. The memorandum suggested that school boards re-examine their procedures around IPRC and consider dispensing with a formal IPRC process in those cases where the board and parent were in agreement that the student's placement be in the regular classroom.

In Cases of Appeal
Step One (A)

Parent may appeal identification as exceptional, or placement, or both.

Parent and/or representative entitled to participate in all discussions except decision making.

School board convenes a three member Appeal Board to review the IPRC material and decisions.

One member chosen by board; one by parent; the two select a third as chair (in case of disagreement, chair is chosen by MoE).

Step Two (A)

Written recommendation to parent, principal, school board and chair of IPRC.

Appeal Board agrees with IPRC and recommends its decisions be implemented,

or

disagrees with IPRC and makes recommendation to school board about identification or placement or both.

May interview anyone whom Appeal Board chair feels has information to contribute.

Written reasons must accompany written statement of recommendation.

Step Three (A)

School board considers recommendation and decides what action to take.

School board is not limited to recommendation of Appeal Board.

Written decision of school board goes to all parties.

Step Four (A)

If parent signs consent

or

if consent not signed but parent does not appeal.

School board decision is implemented.

Step Four (A) stayed if parent appeals.

Final appeal stage is to Special Education Tribunal.

IDENTIFYING STUDENTS WITH EXCEPTIONALITIES

In the *Education Act*, section 1(1), under the definition of "exceptional pupil," five broad categories of exceptionality are recognized: (1) behavioural; (2) communicational; (3) intellectual; (4) physical; and (5) multiple. The categories and definitions of exceptionalities are outlined in *Standards for School Boards' Special Education Plans* (Ontario Ministry of Education, 2000, pp. 32–34), as follows:

Behaviour

A learning disorder characterized by specific behaviour problems over such a period of time, and to such a marked degree, and of such a nature, as to adversely affect educational performance, and that may be accompanied by one or more of the following:

a) an inability to build or to maintain interpersonal relationships;

b) excessive fears or anxieties;

c) a tendency to compulsive reaction;

d) an inability to learn that cannot be traced to intellectual, sensory, or other health factors, or any combination thereof.

Communication

Autism

A severe learning disorder that is characterized by:

a) disturbances in:

   – rate of educational development;

   – ability to relate to the environment;

   – mobility;

   – perception, speech, and language;

b) lack of the representational symbolic behaviour that precedes language.

Deaf and Hard-of-Hearing

An impairment characterized by deficits in language and speech development because of a diminished or non-existent auditory response to sound.

Language Impairment

A learning disorder characterized by impairment in comprehension and/or the use of verbal communication or the written or other symbol system of communication, which may be associated with neurological, psychological, physical, or sensory factors, and which may:

a) involve one or more of the form, content, and function of language in communication; and

b) include one or more of the following:
- language delay;
- dysfluency;
- voice and articulation development, which may or may not be organically or functionally based.

Speech Impairment

A disorder in language formulation that may be associated with neurological, psychological, physical, or sensory factors; that involves perceptual motor aspects of transmitting oral messages; and that may be characterized by impairment in articulation, rhythm, and stress.

Learning Disability

A learning disorder evident in both academic and social situations that involves one or more of the processes necessary for the proper use of spoken language or the symbols of communication, and that is characterized by a condition that:

a) is not primarily the result of:
- impairment of vision;
- impairment of hearing;
- physical disability;
- developmental disability;
- primary emotional disturbance;
- cultural difference; and

b) results in a significant discrepancy between academic achievement and assessed intellectual ability, with deficits in one or more of the following:

> – receptive language (listening, reading);
> – language processing (thinking, conceptualizing, integrating);
> – expressive language (talking, spelling, writing);
> – mathematical computations;
> c) may be associated with one or more conditions diagnosed as:
>> – a perceptual handicap;
>> – a brain injury;
>> – minimal brain dysfunction;
>> – dyslexia;
>> – developmental aphasia.

Intellectual

Giftedness

An unusually advanced degree of general intellectual ability that requires differentiated learning experiences of a depth and breadth beyond those normally provided in the regular school program to satisfy the level of educational potential indicated.

Mild Intellectual Disability

A learning disorder characterized by:
> a) an ability to profit educationally within a regular class with the aid of considerable curriculum modification and supportive service;
> b) an inability to profit educationally within a regular class because of slow intellectual development;
> c) a potential for academic learning, independent social adjustment, and economic self-support.

Developmental Disability

A severe learning disorder characterized by:
> a) an inability to profit from a special education program for students with mild intellectual disabilities because of slow intellectual development;
> b) an ability to profit from a special education program that is designed to accommodate slow intellectual development;

c) a limited potential for academic learning, independent social adjustment, and economic self-support.

Physical
Physical Disability

A condition of such severe physical limitation or deficiency as to require special assistance in learning situations to provide the opportunity for educational achievement equivalent to that of pupils without exceptionalities who are of the same age or developmental level.

Blind and Low Vision

A condition of partial or total impairment of sight or vision that even with correction affects educational performance adversely.

Multiple
Multiple Exceptionalities

A combination of learning or other disorders, impairments, or physical disabilities, that is of such nature as to require, for educational achievement, the services of one or more teachers holding qualifications in special education and the provision of support services appropriate for such disorders, impairments, or disabilities.

Special Education in Ontario Schools, seventh edition (2013)
by Sheila Bennett and Don Dworet with Ken Weber

This book, written for new and practicing teachers, provides an overview of special education in Ontario, including government policies, administrative procedures, and classroom practices.

It also includes chapters on particular exceptionalities. These chapters, accompanied by short case studies, begin by identifying misconceptions, defining the exceptionality, and listing characteristics. They include information about how these students are served in Ontario schools. Each chapter concludes with a list of strategies for teachers.

THE PLACEMENT OF STUDENTS WITH EXCEPTIONALITIES

Once a student has been identified as exceptional through a written decision of the IPRC, the next step is to identify an appropriate placement in the school system. If a student's needs cannot be met in the regular classroom, a range of placement options is available. These include:

- *A regular class with indirect support* where the student is placed in a regular class for the entire day and the teacher receives specialized consultative services.
- *A regular class with resource assistance* where the student is placed in a regular class for most or all of the day and receives specialized instruction, individually or in a small group, within the regular classroom from a qualified special education teacher.
- *A regular class with withdrawal assistance* where the student is placed in a regular class and receives instruction outside the classroom, for less than 50 percent of the school day, from a qualified special education teacher.
- *A special education class with partial integration* where the student is placed by the IPRC in a special education class in which the student–teacher ratio conforms to *Regulation 298*, section 31, for at least 50 percent of the school day, but is integrated with a regular class for at least one instructional period daily.
- *A full-time special education class* where the student–teacher ratio conforms to *Regulation 298*, section 31, for the entire school day.

Another option is for the IPRC to refer a student to a provincial committee for consideration of eligibility for admission to one of the provincial schools for blind, deaf, or deaf-blind students, or to one of the Provincial Demonstration Schools for students with severe learning disabilities.

Although a parental preference for a regular classroom setting must be taken into account, the committee may decide that a special education setting is more appropriate to the student's needs. A parent who agrees with the identification and placement made by the IPRC is required to consent in writing to the statement of decision. A parent who does not agree may request a meeting with the committee to discuss revising the decision. If these discussions do not result in an amended statement of decision, the parent has the right to appeal the decision to a special education appeal board convened at the local level. A parent who is still dissatisfied with the decision of the appeal board may appeal to a provincially appointed Special Education Tribunal. Its decision is final and binding.

As the decision in *Eaton v. Brant County Board of Education* affirmed, while parents have the right to express a preference for regular rather than special classes, it is nevertheless up to the IPRC, appeal board, or, ultimately, provincial tribunal to determine what is in the best educational interests of the child. The role and legal rights of parents will be explored in more detail later in this chapter.

INDIVIDUAL EDUCATION PLAN

Good educators, recognizing that the starting points for lesson planning are the students not the textbook or curriculum document, adapt their teaching to the learning needs and preferences of their students (Ontario Ministry of Education, 2007). One way of meeting these needs and preferences is to develop individual student learning profiles. Such profiles, which are beneficial to any students who need extra attention, are legally required for students who have been formally identified as exceptional and are receiving accommodations or modifications to their programs.

An Individual Education Plan (IEP) is a written plan that describes the special education program and/or services to be provided for a particular student. According to *Individual Education Plans* (2000), an IEP

> identifies learning expectations that are modified from or alternative to the expectations given in the curriculum policy document for the appropriate grade and subject or course, and/or any accommodations and special education services needed to assist the student in achieving his or her learning expectations. (p. 3)

Accommodations are the teaching strategies, supports, and/or services that provide students with access to the curriculum and enable them to demonstrate learning. Modifications are changes made to the grade-level curriculum expectations for a subject or course to meet the needs of the student.

As noted above in the discussion of the IPRC process, IEPs are often created for students with special education needs, even if they have not been formally identified. However, *Regulation 181/98* requires educators, once a student has been formally identified as exceptional and placed in a suitable classroom environment, to develop an IEP. Standards for developing such plans are outlined in *Individual Education Plans* (2000) by the Ontario Ministry of Education. As with the identification and placement, parents have thirty days to appeal the contents of the IEP.

While the IEP outlines all the necessary accommodations and modifications, teachers are expected to use their professional judgment in how they incorporate these provisions into their daily lesson planning. Many lesson plan templates include space for teachers to identify curriculum and instruction modifications for exceptional learners.

One of the main benefits of an IEP is that it helps teachers and parents monitor and discuss a student's progress and, as appropriate, periodically update the record to reflect student progress over time. Continuous assessment and evaluation of student achievement culminates in an annual review of goals and learning expectations. While regular and special education teachers are primarily responsible for the implementation of the IEP, the principal and the school board are responsible for ensuring that IEP requirements are met.

REVIEW OF IDENTIFICATION AND PLACEMENT

A review of the identification and placement must be performed at least annually, unless the parent dispenses with the review in writing to the principal. The principal of the school may refer a student to an IPRC for review at any time. Note that a parental request for review may be made only *after* the placement has been in effect for three months. From then on, such a request may be made only once in every three-month period. The guidelines for the review process are set out in *Regulation 181/98: Identification and Placement of Exceptional Pupils*, section 21. Most of the time, the focus will be the refinement of the IEP to better meet the needs of the child or to revise expectations and strategies in response to changing developmental and learning needs. Of particular concern may be the student's transition from elementary to secondary school or transition out of schooling. The review process may also be an opportunity for educators or parents to challenge the identification or placement, except in the cases of students who are identified as gifted.

FUNDING FOR SPECIAL EDUCATION

Special education is primarily provided at the local level. The Ontario Ministry of Education allocates funding to each school board using a formula that is based on student enrolment and the unique needs of students in each board. Most of the funding comes in the form of a Foundation Grant providing a basic level of funding for each student. This is supplemented by a Special Education Grant (SEG), which provides additional funding for students who need special programs, services, and equipment; this funding is enveloped so it can be used only for the students who have been funded through this grant.

Most of the SEG comes in the form of a Special Education Per-Pupil Amount (SEPPA) allocated to boards on the basis of total enrolment. SEPPA recognizes the cost of providing additional assistance to the majority of students with special education needs. This is supplemented by the High Needs Amount and Special Equipment Amount to address the additional costs of supporting students who require supports well beyond that required by most students with exceptionalities.

RESOLVING IDENTIFICATION OR PLACEMENT ISSUES

The identification, placement, and review process works well for most of Ontario's students who receive special education programs and services. Through consultation and discussion, parents, administrators, teachers, and support professionals are generally able to agree on the needs of the student and on the programs and services that will best meet those needs.

Appealing an IPRC Decision

There are times when parents and the school board cannot agree on special education programs and services. Parents who are not satisfied have several options under special education legislation. The first step is to request a follow-up meeting with the IRPC. If the two sides are still not in agreement, the parent has thirty days to appeal the decision in writing to the school board's Special Education Appeal Board. The final administrative body to which a parent may appeal is the *Ontario Special Education Tribunal* (*Education Act*, section 57). This body, which has statutory powers of decision making, is required to hold a hearing if asked to do so, and both parties have the right to be represented by lawyers, call witnesses, and cross examine witnesses. The decision of this body is final and binding on both parties, though either side can request that its decision be reviewed by a court.

The courts have played a useful role in clarifying sensitive special education issues. The *Eaton* case provides clarification concerning a school board's right to determine that a special education placement may be preferable to an integrated placement. An appeal could be made to the Divisional Court, where a three-judge panel would hear arguments from lawyers for both sides. The first category of judicial review concerns procedural fairness. The appellant would need to prove that the Special Education Tribunal failed to meet the standards of procedural fairness outlined in the *Statutory Powers Procedures Act* or rules of procedural fairness in common law. A challenge could also be made concerning the tribunal's decision. The courts "exercise a considerable degree of deference to administrative tribunals when reviewing the substance of their decisions" (Bowlby, Peters & Mackinnon, 2001, p. 160).

This was evident in the Supreme Court's ruling in favour of the school board in the *Eaton* case. The court acknowledged that special education is a necessary adaptation for students with exceptionalities. It also gave legal recognition to the benefits of social integration. While the court placed a high burden on school boards to justify limiting access to programs and services, it made clear that the right of access is not an absolute right. While reasonable accommodations should be made, they are subject to "reasonable limits," such as not imposing "undue hardships" on the system. This ruling was reinforced by the Supreme Court's decision in *Auton v. British Columbia (Attorney General)* (2004). The court declined to order the government to fund Applied Behaviour Analysis (ABA) for children with autism, arguing that it was a non-core medical service.

The court's deference to education authorities is also evident in a land-mark Ontario case involving students with autism spectrum disorders. The rights of autistic children has been an area of recent litigation as the diagnosis of autism has dramatically increased and as effective yet expensive treatments have emerged. Can parents compel school boards to provide and pay for highly expensive ABA?

Case Study: Wynberg v. Ontario (2006)

The government of Ontario began providing funding for a form of Applied Behaviour Analysis, an intensive early intervention program, for children up to five years old with autism spectrum disorders. This one-to-one therapy, generally recommended for very young children, typically ranged from twenty to forty hours a week for one to two years. Because of high demand, and a lack of qualified service providers, many children were unable to access this service before the age cut-off. The parents in this case sought to require the government or school boards to extend similar assistance to school age children with autism.

In the initial trial, the judge agreed with the parents that exclusion from the program and the failure of schools to provide ABA constituted discrimination on the basis of age and disability, thus violating equality guarantees in the *Charter of Rights and Freedoms.*

The Ontario Court of Appeal subsequently overturned the decision of the trial judge on the grounds that equality rights had not been infringed. The court ruled that the program had been targeted at the two-to-five age group since its inception and that this was generally viewed to be most effective with children in that age group.

Furthermore, the appeals court concluded that the Ministry of Education was not obliged to provide a particular program of special education. It has the option of offering other appropriate programs or services to that group. The judges found that "the existing jurisprudence does not permit us to interpret section 7 of the *Charter* as imposing a constitutional obligation on the appellant to ensure that every school-age autistic child has access to specific educational services." Schools had the option of offering other appropriate programs or services to that group, including ones that were not as costly as ABA.

(1) Why did the Ontario Court of Appeal overturn the decision of the trial judge?
(2) Do you agree with this decision? Consider the implications for parents and educators.

Legal scholar Wayne Mackay (2009) argues that while the equality provisions in section 15 of the *Charter* have not led to significant changes in special education legislation,

> the greater impact of s. 15 on special education has been to provide a vehicle through which parents can challenge school board and government decisions on the programs and services to be provided to exceptional students. (p. 83)

Mediation

As the legal process is slow, cumbersome, and costly, the Ministry of Education has been actively promoting mediation as an alternative means of resolving special education issues. The *Special Education Transformation* report (Bennett & Wynne, 2006) promotes this mediation as preferable to appeal boards and tribunals. Also, given that the courts have consistently respected the judgment of school boards, parents are more likely to have an impact in this forum.

Mediation is a voluntary and consensual dispute resolution process. The mediator, an experienced and neutral third party, works with the two parties to resolve the issues under dispute. Both parties typically agree that the matters discussed in mediation are protected from disclosure in court should mediation not be successful.

As Bowlby, Peters & Mackinnon (2001) observe:

> Mediation is also an extremely flexible method of dispute resolution. Mediation provides parties the opportunity to be creative in finding a

resolution to their dispute. The parameters of the resolution are not limited by the possible outcomes of litigation but only by the imagination of the parties. (p. 98)

Once an agreement is reached, a mediation agreement is drawn up and signed by the mediator, the school board, and the parents.

Shared Solutions: A Guide to Preventing and Resolving Conflicts Regarding Programs and Services for Students with Special Education Needs (Ontario Ministry of Education, 2007)

The best way to prevent, minimize and/or resolve conflicts concerning special education is for educators and parents to treat one another with respect and work together through transparent decision-making processes. This document by the Ontario Ministry of Education offers strategies that can help prevent and resolve problems.

For example, it indicates that a "culture of collaboration" can help parents and educators work constructively together to address concerns related to programs and services before they become sources of conflict. To create such a culture, boards and schools need to promote a positive school climate and establish effective lines of communication among parents, students, and educators (p. 19).

The document has the following to say about a shared perspective between parents and educators:

> Disagreements may arise and strong emotions may surface when people discuss complex issues such as programs and services for students with special education needs. Knowing how to prevent conflicts from escalating and/or resolve them cooperatively helps maintain a climate where all students thrive. Where the parties already have a good relationship, they can air their concerns in a constructive way, exploring options and seeking creative, student-focused solutions to problems.

> While both educators and parents are seeking solutions to address complex problems, it is important for all parties to balance strong advocacy of their own views with a commitment to inquiry— a willingness to ask and respond to questions to clarify all parties' understanding of the issues and positions under discussion. Inquiry and exploration enable participants to discover or disclose their own and others' reasoning and assumptions and enhance each party's awareness and appreciation of other points of view. The use of an inquiry approach allows participants to avoid over-commitment to unrealistic positions, to build on one another's insights, and to work together to arrive at a shared solution (pp. 20–21).

SPECIAL EDUCATION IN THE TWENTY-FIRST CENTURY: THE MENTAL HEALTH NEEDS OF STUDENTS

While it is evident that exceptional students in Ontario receive substantial support, students with mental health issues often fell through the cracks. Mental health issues received major attention only in 2013 and were not part of teacher education until 2015. Additional Qualification courses in Special Education and in Guidance did little, if at all, to address mental health, and in schools, students with mental health issues may or may not be identified.

Special education teachers primarily work with exceptional students, and guidance counsellors focus on timetable issues and graduation requirements. It seemed no one was attending to mental health, and students were engaging in a greater amount of high-risk behaviour. High-profile suicides in Canada brought this issue to a head, and the Ontario Ministry of Education has responded.

The Ministry announced that, beginning in 2013, it would be providing funding to have a Mental Health professional in each district school board.

It also produced *Supporting Minds: An Educator's Guide to Promoting Students' Health and Well Being* (OME, 2013). There had been a wide division between the mental health system and the education system for many years in Ontario. *Supporting Minds* was written for teachers in a classroom who in the past had failed to recognize signs of depression, stress, anxiety, and addiction. It was simply not considered part of a teacher's job, which primarily was to teach.

An excerpt from *Supporting Minds* (p. 6) states:

1. 1 in 5 students will experience a serious mental illness.
2. Teachers have always done a great deal to support student well-being and positive mental health. The new emphasis on mental health is meant to provide information and resources to help support the range of students.
3. Teachers are not mental health professionals. Your role is to provide a supportive and engaging classroom environment for all students, to identify when a student is struggling, and to help the student to and from specialized support.
4. Teachers are not alone in this work. We are part of a system of care in schools, boards, and communities.

SPECIAL EDUCATION AND THE COLLEGE OF TEACHERS

According to the Ontario College of Teachers' standards of conduct, teachers have a professional responsibility to attend to the learning needs of their students. Specific responsibilities related to special education include:

- following board policies and procedures for special education;
- working with parents and special education staff to develop and review IEPs for students with exceptionalities;
- implementing the IEP in the classroom;
- communicating progress to parents.

Teachers who work with exceptional learners have a particular obligation to be sensitive to the heightened vulnerability of their students and to their specific learning needs. In the OCT case quoted below, it is likely that the vulnerability of the exceptional student was a factor in the decision to reprimand the teacher and instruct him to take a course in classroom management.

Case Study: Improper Physical Intervention with Students
Ontario College of Teachers v. IG (2014)

IG intervened in a physical altercation between a student and an educational assistant. The student was spitting, kicking, and hitting the assistant. IG slapped the student across the face, causing him to bang his head. The student cried out loud and wanted a hug from the assistant. IG made a comment to the student along the lines of, "How does it feel?" CAS investigated the incident, and the board suspended him for five days without pay.

IG appeared before a discipline panel at the Ontario College of Teachers and pleaded guilty to professional misconduct—more specifically, to physical abuse of a student. The panel was concerned that IG had extensive qualifications in special education and that the student was young and vulnerable. His lack of judgment and use of physical force was not professional and not acceptable.

IG was given a reprimand and instructed to take a course in classroom management; in addition, his name was published in *Professionally Speaking*.

This case appears in *Professionally Speaking*, March 2015.

---

(1) What evidence is there that the teacher's conduct was unprofessional?

(2) Why might this conduct be particularly harmful to a learner with an exceptionality?

(3) Do you think that the penalty imposed by the discipline panel was appropriate?

School boards and the Ontario College of Teachers are clear in their decisions that it is never acceptable to hit a student. Teachers need to keep calm, especially when students become violent and there is a potential for harm. Many school boards offer non-physical intervention training and de-escalation courses free to their teachers.

The case below is much more complex than the case above. It demonstrates that all educators can be disciplined for failing to protect exceptional and vulnerable students.

Case Study: A Failure to Protect Vulnerable Students
Ontario College of Teachers v. JRJP (2013)

A former principal, JRJP, had his certificate of qualification revoked by a discipline panel of the Ontario College of Teachers for failing to report to the police and CAS the sexual abuse by another staff member of several intellectually and physically vulnerable students. This abuse occurred repeatedly over a period of years, and JRJP had seen a film of the staff member abusing students.

JRJP also lied to another staff member and stated that he reported the abuse when he had not. Despite repeated concerns and complaints from teachers, bus drivers, and educational assistants about the sexual and inappropriate behaviour of one staff member, JRJP refused to take action. He repeatedly threatened and lied to staff about the allegations of sexual abuse of several students.

During a disciplinary hearing at the Ontario College of Teachers, twelve witnesses gave testimony of many examples of ways physically and mentally challenged students were abused. JRJP was also accused of failure to perform many of his duties as a principal, including criminal record checks, proper hiring procedures, misuse of school funds, improper reporting and communication with parents and staff, and failure to keep the school clean and safe.

The discipline panel was deeply troubled by the fact that a principal knowingly let a teaching assistant sexually abuse a student for many years, and covered it up in order to protect their relationship.

The discipline panel both revoked JRJP's licence and, given the severity of the case, ordered that he not be allowed to have his certificate reinstated for a period of five years . His name was published in *Professionally Speaking*.

This case appears in *Professionally Speaking*, March 2014.

(1) What do you think you could have done if you were a teacher in this school?

(2) What sort of protocols are in place in schools to protect vulnerable students?

(3) If you were a member of this discipline panel, what sort of sanctions would you have placed on the member?

CONCLUSION

In today's "inclusive classroom" there is little separation between a regular classroom teacher and a special education teacher. It is common for all teachers to have students in their class with IEPs, and it is the responsibility of teachers to understand them and follow them properly. It is their responsibility as well to know the signs of mental health problems and to seek immediate help for students who show them.

Beyond knowing and following the legislation, teachers need to treat exceptional students with care and compassion. Teachers who attend to the special learning needs of these students can have a very positive impact on their success in school and life.

CHECKING YOUR UNDERSTANDING

- Bill 82 (*Education Amendment Act*) amended the *Education Act* to include provisions for special education in Ontario schools.

- The *Canadian Charter of Rights and Freedoms* has been interpreted by the courts to mean that school boards should make reasonable efforts to accommodate students with identified special needs.

- The *Education Act* requires school boards to provide special education programs and services, including early and ongoing procedures for identifying students with special needs and abilities.

- The school board is also required to establish a Special Education Advisory Committee (SEAC), which may make recommendations about any aspect of the board's special education program and services.

- The *Education Act* identifies five broad categories of exceptionality: (1) behavioural; (2) communicational; (3) intellectual; (4) physical; and (5) multiple.

- The principal of the school may, with written notice to the parents, refer a student to an Identification, Placement, and Review Committee established by the board, one of whose members must be a superintendent or principal of the board.

- The principal must refer a student to an IPRC at the written request of the parents.

- Although the parents (and students over sixteen) may participate in the IPRC deliberations, they are not part of the final decision making.

- The IPRC is required to consider the integration of exceptional pupils into regular classes before considering a placement in a special education class.

- Classroom teachers must follow the accommodations and modifications of students' Individual Education Plans.

- Students with an IEP are also accommodated on EQAO testing.

- Student mental health has become a growing concern in schools. Classroom teachers must be vigilant in recognizing the signs of mental health problems for students.

APPLYING YOUR UNDERSTANDING

Special Gifts, Special Classrooms

Raheem Singh is identified as intellectually gifted in an IPRC meeting. The committee develops a series of enrichment recommendations for his teacher to implement.

Raheem's parents are sceptical that his gifts, particularly his prodigious mathematical abilities, can be nurtured in a regular classroom setting. They have observed Raheem becoming increasingly bored, distracted, and socially isolated at school. Also, they have observed that his academic motivation has declined significantly and worry that he will not be able to reach his potential unless he leaves the mainstream classroom. They are convinced that the best placement for their son is a classroom with other gifted learners.

The school board does not have any "congregated" gifted classrooms and, instead, relies on classroom teachers to differentiate the program in order to serve high ability students.

The Singhs refuse to sign the report of the Identification, Placement, and Review Committee.

(1) What are the next steps in the process?
(2) What can the IPRC do to allay the concerns of Raheem's parents?
(3) What options are available to the Singhs?
(4) What are some possible outcomes of this case?

CHAPTER 10

TEACHERS IN THE WORKPLACE: BRINGING IT ALL TOGETHER

> *After reading this chapter, you will have a greater understanding of employment law issues, the teacher appraisal process, and several operational issues that affect the daily lives of teachers.*

Case Study: Terminating a Probationary Teacher
Ontario English Catholic Teachers' Association v. Dufferin Peel
Catholic District School Board (2014)

A first-year teacher was evaluated by his principal under the procedures outlined in the New Teacher Induction Program in 2006. The principal determined that the teacher failed to meet the minimum standards for six of the eight competencies assessed. A second evaluation, after an Enhancement Plan, resulted in no improvement. As a result of the second unsatisfactory review, the teacher was formally identified as needing to participate in developing an Improvement Plan.

After moving to a new school in 2007, the teacher underwent a third appraisal under NTIP. The principal founded him incompetent in seven of eight competencies. Following NTIP protocol, the principal recommended termination.

OECTA, acting on the teacher's behalf, challenged the fairness of the final evaluation through the arbitration process. The union suggested that the "just cause" standard was not met and the results were discriminatory, arbitrary, or in bad faith. The teacher argued that the first two appraisals were not accurate and the second principal failed to help him meet the competency standards.

The arbitrator rejected these arguments, noting that the teacher (a) did not adopt most of the Improvement Plan, (b) did not share it with his principal, (c) ignored emails from the principal about his performance (which he characterized as harassment). On the other hand, the principal was seen as properly trained in assessment and the assessment was deemed reasonable. As a result, the decision to terminate the teacher was upheld. The Ontario College of Teachers was notified of the result.

---

(1) Review this case in relation to the Performance Appraisal of New Teachers Flow Chart (Figure 10-1, below). Was the process properly observed?

(2) What are the implications for the appraisal of new teachers? Experienced teachers?

This case was selected to illustrate the teacher appraisal process in action. It also was intended to illustrate that the appraisal process, while providing teachers with many opportunities to improve, could lead to the termination of educators deemed to be incompetent. The story of this teacher, however, gets more complicated.

Case Study: Vindicating a Probationary Teacher
Ontario College of Teachers v. The Teacher (2015)

Although OECTA was unsuccessful in overturning his termination at arbitration, the teacher launched a vigorous defence when he was brought before a discipline panel of the College for incompetence and professional misconduct.

According to the panel, it was presented with two general theories of the case: either "the Member was the author of his own demise" or was "put in an extremely difficult position as a new teacher at School 1" and the appraisal in School 2 was unjustified.

The panel, after hearing extensive testimony and cross-examination, accepted the teacher's theory of the case. It found his evidence credible and cast doubt on the credibility of the second principal's testimony and criticized the board's preparation of principals for a provincial appraisal process that was initiated the year the teacher began teaching.

The panel noted that it was not surprising that the teacher struggled at his first school, as he "was assigned to a very challenging class ... was not informed of the NTIP appraisal process in a timely manner, and ... was not provided with the required mentorship in a timely manner." Evidence of competence and valid explanations for his shortcomings, combined with doubts about the validity of the second principal's appraisal, led the panel to conclude that the teacher was not incompetent and not guilty of professional misconduct.

(1) Review the case in relation to the Performance Appraisal of New Teachers Flow Chart (Figure 10-1, below). Was the process properly observed?

(2) What are the implications for the appraisal of new teachers? Experienced teachers?

(3) In considering the two cases together, how have your views changed or become more complicated?

(4) What does this case reveal about discipline panels as quasi-judiciary bodies?

This book has put great emphasis on teaching as a professional activity grounded in a legislative framework and an ethic of caring. It is important to remember that teachers are also employees of school boards. As such, they have the same rights, duties, and responsibilities to their employer as any other person employed in a workplace setting.

THE TEACHER AS AN EMPLOYEE OF THE SCHOOL BOARD

Teachers' professional lives are governed by many laws. As you have seen in earlier chapters, the professional rights, responsibilities, and duties of teachers are outlined in common law, school acts, and similar legislation governing publicly funded schools, and in codes of professional conduct.

The *Education Act* empowers school boards to hire and fire teachers. It also establishes a framework for collective agreements between school boards and teacher federations. These collective agreements, which have become increasingly complex, govern issues ranging from salaries to hours of instruction to procedures for dealing with grievances by school boards or employees.

PERSONAL CRIMINAL HISTORY

Under *Regulation 521/01*, school boards are required to collect a "personal criminal history" of everyone who is either an employee of the board or a service provider at one or more school sites. As employees, teachers are required to submit a criminal background check before they begin employment with the board and an offence declaration before September 1 during each subsequent year of employment.

LINES OF AUTHORITY

Although a teacher may be interviewed and hired by the school principal or a specially convened hiring committee, legally the local school board is the teacher's employer and the individual contract of employment is between the school board and the teacher.

The school board has the overall responsibility at the local level for running the school system, but individual trustees have no executive authority. School boards have authority only insofar as they act as a corporation to formulate and approve board policy. Under the *Education Act*, the director of education appointed by the school board acts as chief executive and chief education officer with ultimate administrative and executive authority, working within the frameworks of board policy and provincial legislation.

The superintendents appointed by the board to assist the director in carrying out the various administrative functions generally are assigned responsibility for a family of schools within the board. Each family may consist of one or two high schools along with their elementary feeder schools. These area superintendents often may be seen in schools, meeting with the principal or individual teachers and representing the senior administration at ceremonial occasions, such as graduation and awards assemblies.

Classroom teachers are under the direct authority of the school principal. Under the *Education Act*, the board is required to appoint a principal for each school in its jurisdiction, and, as has already been noted, the principal has overall authority for the organization and administration of the school, subject to the authority of the appropriate superintendent. As mentioned earlier in this book, principals may properly be considered, from a professional point of view, as the principal teacher of their school, because principals are also bound by many of the same legal duties as teachers.

However, in labour relations terms, the principal, as the board's agent, is the manager of the school and therefore the immediate supervisor of teachers in the school. Principals often experience tension between their role as principal teacher and as manager. This tension was inevitably heightened by the removal of principals and vice-principals from the Ontario Teachers' Federation in 1997. As a result, teachers often view principals and vice-principals as having little in common with the daily concerns and practice of the classroom teacher. Wise principals tread a very careful line between these two roles. They understand the difference between management and leadership, and the truth of the adage that one can lead only with the consent of the led.

The role of vice-principal is not defined precisely in the *Education Act*. A board is not required to appoint a vice-principal for a school, although most secondary schools and large elementary schools have at least one or two full or part-time vice-principals. The vice-principal is required to perform duties as assigned by the principal of the school and, in the absence of the principal, to be in charge of the school and perform the duties of the principal. In hierarchical terms, the vice-principal may be thought of the second in command, who shares the authority of the principal in the daily operation of the school.

TEACHERS IN CHARGE OF ORGANIZATIONAL UNITS

The *Education Act* does not clearly define the place of department heads in the chain of command in a secondary school or of division leaders in an elementary school. Boards are not required to appoint people to these roles, although most secondary schools and some large elementary schools do have teachers in

Getting Along with Your Principal
- Be committed to your classroom and your students.
- Be modest and appreciative.
- Know school procedures, as outlined in handbooks and memos.
- If you're not sure, don't be afraid to ask, but "bundle" your questions.
- Keep a file or binder of memos from the office.
- Obey the rules.
- Share with your principal the interesting things you are doing in the classroom.

various positions of responsibility. The number of such positions and the nature of the units for which they are responsible are usually negotiated between the board and the local federation affiliate. For example, while many boards have maintained traditional subject discipline departments in secondary schools, some have chosen to amalgamate these departments into larger groupings, each overseen by an area chair. Section 14(3) of *Regulation 298* sets out the terms of reference for such teachers:

A board may appoint for each organizational unit of an elementary or secondary school a teacher to direct and supervise, subject to the authority of the principal of the school, such organizational unit.

While the words *in charge of* and *direct and supervise* indicate the leadership role of the department head or division leader, the lack of any explicit statutory powers or duties makes it difficult to determine the precise nature of their authority. For example, these heads or leaders play no direct role in the performance appraisal of teachers but may be asked to assist a teacher who is perceived by the principal as needing improvement. Board policy, of course, could elaborate the expectations for positions of responsibility, provided that the expectations remain within the terms of reference of the *Education Act*. Even though the place in the chain of command of teachers in positions of responsibility is not well defined, classroom teachers do have a legal duty to cooperate with them, as well as with consultants and coordinators. This duty is established in *Regulation 298*, section 20(c):

> Where the board has appointed teachers under section 14 or 17, [a teacher shall] co-operate fully with such teachers and with the principal in all matters related to the instruction of pupils.

At the very least, teachers in the organizational unit should be willing to attend department/team meetings convened by the teacher in charge, collaborate in developing third-generation curriculum documents at the school level, and cooperate fully in ensuring consistency across sections of the same course in secondary schools and among classes at the same grade level in elementary schools.

TEACHING ASSIGNMENTS

Because it is the duty of a teacher "to teach diligently and faithfully the classes or subjects assigned to the teacher by the principal" (*Education Act*, section 264(1)(a)), a teacher has a legal duty to teach the classes or subjects assigned by the principal.

While teachers may express preferences, it is ultimately the principal, as the person in charge of the organization and management of the school, who has the authority to assign classes and duties to teachers. In secondary schools, department heads, in consultation with members of their department, may be given the responsibility for drafting a proposed allocation of classes and courses, but these are just recommendations to the principal, who makes the final determination.

The legal authority of the principal to assign classes is limited by further wording in *Regulation 298*, which limits the nature of the classes that teachers can be assigned. Section 19 essentially states that teachers can be assigned or appointed to teach *only* those classes or subjects that they are qualified to teach according to their certificate of qualification issued by the Ontario College of Teachers. The principal, therefore, cannot insist that a teacher teach a class for which the teacher does not hold appropriate qualifications, if the teacher is unwilling to do so.

There are two subsections elsewhere in section 19 that provide some flexibility in the match between qualifications and classes assigned, provided that the teacher and principal are in agreement. To understand these subsections, it is important to understand the distinction made in the legislation between "general studies" and "technological education." For convenience, general studies may be thought of as any subject or course that is not listed in the technological education guidelines.

The first subsection providing some flexibility states that a teacher whose certificate indicates qualifications in the primary division, junior division, intermediate division in general studies, or senior division in general studies, by mutual agreement of the teacher and the principal (and with the approval of the appropriate supervisory officer), may be assigned or appointed to teach in a division or a subject in general studies for which no qualification is recorded. For example, a teacher in an elementary school who is qualified in the primary/junior divisions by mutual agreement could teach in grade 7 or 8. A secondary school teacher qualified to teach geography and physical education in the intermediate/senior divisions could teach mathematics, if the teacher is willing to do so and is deemed to have an appropriate background.

There are other provisos and exceptions in section 19 of *Regulation 298*, but the above summary gives a general outline of the way in which the principal's right to assign teachers to classes and subjects is limited by legislation. *Regulation 298* says nothing about the number of classes or courses that the principal may assign; this matter is for school boards and federations to negotiate.

TEACHER PERFORMANCE APPRAISAL

All workers, including professionals such as teachers, benefit from meaningful performance appraisals. The challenge is to develop a system of appraisal that is rigorous and fair and provides teachers with plenty of opportunities to grow professionally.

Teacher performance appraisals have been a politically sensitive issue in Ontario since the late 1990s. The teachers' federations resisted the efforts of the Progressive Conservative government during that time to reform the education system. Among the reforms resisted was one that established a mandatory teacher appraisal process.

The subsequent Liberal government has continued the previous government's provincial teacher appraisal system but has worked to develop processes that are acceptable to teachers, principals, and members of the public. This includes the development of the New Teacher Induction Program (NTIP), which is a requirement for all teachers who are new to Ontario's publicly funded schools system and who are hired as permanent teachers, either full-time or part-time. Under certain circumstances, new teachers who are hired on long-term occasional contracts are also required to participate in some elements of the program. In addition, the Teacher Performance Appraisal (TPA) system, mandatory for experienced teachers, was modified in 2007 to build on the NTIP performance appraisal process. This growth-focused appraisal process is designed for teachers as they move through the various stages of their careers.

New Teacher Induction Program (NTIP)

New teachers often find it difficult to make the transition from pre-service teacher education programs to the everyday reality of classroom teaching. For many, the journey from survival in the first years to successful classroom practice to instructional expertise is not an easy path (Berliner, 1994).

It is increasingly recognized that teachers in their first years of practice benefit from systemic support. In the United States, which has been facing high attrition rates among education graduates (Guarino, Santibanez & Daley, 2006), a great deal of effort has been put into developing teacher induction programs and training mentors for new teachers.

The Ministry of Education in Ontario describes the purpose of the NTIP in the following way:

> The New Teacher Induction Program (NTIP) has been designed to support the growth and professional development of new teachers. It is the second step in a continuum of professional development for teachers to support effective teaching, learning, and assessment practices, building on and complementing the first step: pre-service education programs. It

provides another full year of professional support so that new teachers can develop the requisite skills and knowledge that will enable them to achieve success as experienced teachers in Ontario. (Retrieved in September 2015 from http://www.edu.gov.on.ca/eng/teacher/induction.html.)

For the purposes of the program, new teachers are defined as all new teachers certified by the Ontario College of Teachers who have been hired into permanent positions or, in certain circumstances, have been hired on long-term occasional contracts.

Beginning in 2006–2007, publicly funded school boards were required to systematically address the diverse learning needs of large numbers of new teachers. This institutional undertaking offers opportunities to maximize the potential of a large pool of highly qualified new teachers. Several school boards have already developed interesting and effective projects in response to this challenge.

All school board programs consist of three interrelated elements:

- orientation for all new teachers to the school and the school board;
- mentoring for new teachers by experienced teachers;
- professional development and training appropriate for new teachers.

School boards are encouraged to develop relationships among these components and situate the induction of new teachers into the larger continuum of building excellence in the profession.

The role of the principal is critical to the effective induction of new teachers. This role includes ensuring that the induction components are responsive to the needs of the new teacher. Principals can make a difference by providing effective school orientations, identifying effective mentors, and providing guidance in the selection of professional development sessions.

The principal is also the appraiser who determines whether a new teacher has been successfully inducted into the profession. Successful completion of the program is evidenced by two satisfactory performance appraisals conducted by the principal (or vice-principal). The Ontario College of Teachers then places a notation on the Certificate of Qualification of the teacher who has successfully completed the program.

Participation in the Program

All new teachers, regardless of experience, must receive an orientation. Teachers who have never taught before in permanent positions must participate in all three elements of the program. Teachers who have taught before but who were certified elsewhere in Canada or internationally are required to participate in the elements of the program that complement their particular teaching experience and help orient them to the Ontario curriculum and educational context. The principal is responsible for working with the new teacher and the teacher's mentor to determine the precise content and delivery mode of each element of the program.

Beginning teachers who are hired on a long-term occasional contract of at least ninety-seven days for the same teacher must also be included in the induction elements of the NTIP. Other non-permanent first-year teachers, such as those hired on short-term occasional contracts, are not required to participate in the NTIP, but school boards may offer them the opportunity to do so. Neither of these two groups of teachers is eligible for the notation of successful completion on their certificate, but if they subsequently enter into a permanent contract, the principal may take their previous participation into account when determining which elements of the program they still need to complete.

Performance Appraisal Process

According to the Ministry of Education's *New Teacher Induction Program: Manual for Performance Appraisal of New Teachers* (OME, 2009), the performance appraisal process is part of a growth-oriented effort to promote excellence in teaching and learning:

> In conjunction with the orientation, mentoring, professional development and training elements of the New Teacher Induction Program, the performance appraisal process for new teachers has been designed

to support and promote the continued growth and development of new teachers. In the larger context of school improvement, the performance appraisal system provides principals and teachers with processes and procedures that can bring about improvements in teacher and student learning. The appraisal can also foster the collaboration and relationship building that are essential to creating and sustaining a professional learning community in schools. It is especially important to see the appraisal process as a supportive and effective way of helping new teachers develop into confident and proficient Ontario teachers. (p. 9)

There are four components of the performance appraisal framework for new teachers:

- **Competency statements** based on the Ontario College of Teachers' Standards of Practice for the Teaching Profession. The sixteen competency statements were developed with all teachers, new and experienced, in mind. For this reason, the appraisal process for new teachers is based on a subset of *eight* competency statements that focus on the immediate needs of teachers new to Ontario's classrooms. (See Figure 10-1.)
- **Appraisal meetings.** The principal must arrange a pre-observation meeting with the teacher in preparation for the classroom observation, and a post-observation meeting. These processes are outlined in detail in the manual.
- **A summative report** that formally documents the appraisal process. The form is a standardized Ministry of Education document.
- **A rating scale and rubric** to assess overall performance and provide feedback about strengths and weaknesses. The scale for new teachers is *Satisfactory* or *Development Needed.* The scale in subsequent appraisals for a teacher who receives a *Development Needed* is *Satisfactory* or *Unsatisfactory.* The manual also outlines an extensive process for providing additional support to new teachers who struggle to meet the satisfactory level necessary for induction into the teaching profession.

Figure 10-1

The Sixteen Competency Statements with Eight Competencies Highlighted for New Teachers

DOMAIN	COMPETENCY
Commitment to Pupils* and Pupil Learning	• Teachers demonstrate commitment to the well-being and development of all pupils. • Teachers are dedicated in their efforts to teach and support pupil learning and achievement. • Teachers treat all pupils equitably and with respect. • Teachers provide an environment for learning that encourages pupils to be problem solvers, decision makers, lifelong learners, and contributing members of a changing society.
Professional Knowledge	• Teachers know their subject matter, the Ontario curriculum, and education-related legislation. • Teachers know a variety of effective teaching and assesment practices. • Teachers know a variety of effective classroom management strategies. • Teachers know how pupils learn and factors that influence pupil learning and achievement.
Professional Practice	• Teachers use their professional knowledge and understanding of pupils, curriculum, legislation, teaching practices, and classroom management strategies to promote the learning and achievement of their pupils. • Teachers communicate effectively with pupils, parents, and colleagues. • Teachers conduct ongoing assessment of pupils' progress, evaluate their achievement, and report results to the pupil and parents regularly. • Teachers adapt and refine their teaching practices through continuous learning and reflection, using a variety of sources and resources. • Teachers use appropriate technology in their teaching practices and related professional responsibilities.
Leadership in Learning Communities	• Teachers collaborate with other teachers and school colleagues to create and sustain learning communities in their classrooms and in their schools. • Teachers work with professionals, parents, and members of the community to enhance pupil learning, pupil achievement, and school programs.
Ongoing Professional Learning	• Teachers engage in ongoing professional learning and apply it to improve their teaching practices.

Note: Principal must provide a comment for each of the eight highlighted competencies as a minimum requirement in the Summative Report Form for New Teachers.

*In the *Education Act*, students are referred to as "pupils."   Ontario Ministry of Education

As Figure 10-1 illustrates, the program provides new teachers with multiple opportunities to develop their skills in order to meet the standards expected of a satisfactory teacher.

The *New Teacher Induction Program: Manual for Performance Appraisal of New Teachers* states:

> The appraisal process for new teachers is designed to strengthen schools as learning communities in which new teachers are provided with plentiful opportunities to engage in professional exchange and collective inquiry that lead to continuous growth and development. It provides a framework to encourage improvement efforts aimed at ensuring student success. Essential in this process is the engagement of new teachers in professional dialogue that deepens their understanding of what it means to be a teacher as described in the Ontario College of Teachers' *Standards of Practice for the Teaching Profession.* (p. 6)

If this initiative is successful, the benefits could be great for new teachers, their students, and the quality of public education in Ontario.

PERFORMANCE APPRAISAL SYSTEM FOR EXPERIENCED TEACHERS

Experienced teachers in Ontario are also required to be part of a teacher performance appraisal process. In response to concerns about the original Teacher Performance Appraisal process, the Ministry of Education consulted with the Education Partnership Table of educational stakeholders, including teacher federations, for advice on how to improve the system. A revised process was implemented in September 2007 that is more streamlined and teacher-friendly than the previous appraisal process.

The Ministry of Education describes the system in the following way:

> Professional dialogue and collaboration are a critical part of the appraisal process and an essential part of a healthy school culture. The performance appraisal process for experienced teachers provides a framework to assess experienced teachers' practices in a manner that reflects their needs for

growth and development, and in which both the teacher and the principal take an active role. This includes the engagement of teachers in a professional dialogue that deepens their understanding of what it means to be a teacher as described in the Ontario College of Teachers' *Standards of Practice for the Teaching Profession. (Performance Appraisal of Experienced Teachers: Technical Requirements Manual,* 2009, p. 5)

Once teachers successfully complete the NTIP, they are placed on the experienced teachers' performance appraisal schedule. This schedule requires that a teacher must have an evaluation year in every five-year period. During the evaluation year, a teacher must receive at least one performance appraisal. Teachers may request appraisals in years other than their evaluation year, and principals may choose to conduct appraisals in other years. The first year in which an experienced teacher is employed by a board is also considered an evaluation year.

Following are the six key components of the appraisal process.

- **Competency Statements**, designed to focus the appraisal on the knowledge, skills, and attitudes that reflect the standards described in the Ontario College of Teachers' Standards of Practice for the Teaching Profession. The sixteen competency statements outline the standards expected of an experienced teacher in Ontario.

- **Annual Learning Plan (ALP)**, intended to help teachers identify strategies for professional growth during their teaching career. According to legislation in the *Education Act*, teachers are required to complete an ALP in consultation with the principal every year. During their evaluation year, the ALP becomes part of the appraisal process. Although boards are no longer required to survey parents and senior students as part of the teacher appraisal process, teachers are encouraged to consider how they might gather parental and student input when developing their ALP.

- **Appraisal meetings**, which promote professional dialogue between the teacher and the principal, consisting of a pre-observation meeting to prepare for the classroom observation and a post-observation meeting. The meetings are intended to foster the teacher's professional growth and improvement. Note that classroom observation is only one component of the appraisal process. For some competencies, the principal will gather evidence in other ways.

- **Summative report**, which formally documents the appraisal process in Ministry-approved format. This report includes: the principal's comments about those competencies identified by the teacher and principal as the focus of the appraisal (the principal may also comment on other competencies); recommendations for professional growth goals and strategies for the teacher to consider when developing his or her ALP; and an overall rating based on all sixteen competencies. Teachers may also add their own comments to the summative report. Teachers must sign the final version of their TPA. If they do not agree with the comments on the TPA, they should contact their federation representative. Once the TPA is signed, a teacher is expected to follow through with any suggestions made in the TPA. Failure to do so could result in termination and in disciplinary sanctions by the Ontario College of Teachers.
- **Rating scale** to assess the teacher's overall performance. The rating scale for experienced teachers is *Satisfactory* or *Unsatisfactory.*
- **Process for Providing Additional Support**, depending on the outcome of the appraisal. (See Performance Appraisal Process (Overview) below, which is Appendix G of *Performance Appraisal of Experienced Teachers: Technical Requirements Manual* (2009).)

Boards may also identify additional requirements for the performance appraisal of its experienced teachers, such as additional competencies or other material that must be taken into account in the appraisal process, provided that these requirements do not conflict with those set out in the *Education Act.* Teacher federations have also developed resources to help teachers negotiate the performance appraisal process.

ANNUAL LEARNING PLAN

One recommendation of the Education Partnership Table was to adapt the Annual Learning Plan (ALP) to "provide a more meaningful vehicle for the teacher's professional learning in the intervening years between appraisals" (Ontario Ministry of Education, 2006). This led to *Regulation 98/02*, which came into effect on September 1, 2007. It makes the following changes to the Annual Learning Plans:

- Every experienced teacher shall have a learning plan each year that includes the teacher's professional growth objectives, proposed action plan, and timelines for achieving those objectives.
- Each year after the first year that a teacher has a learning plan, the teacher and the principal shall consult to review and update the plan.
- Both the teacher and principal shall sign and retain copies of the teacher's learning plan for the year.

In this process, teachers direct and author their own professional growth in consultation with the principal. The process is also a streamlined one that allows the individual teacher to focus on as few as one professional growth objective. That said, teachers are invited to consider linking their personal objectives to school board expectations. This appraisal process also provides continuity by allowing the extension of professional development plans across more than one year. Extracurricular activities and community involvement, according to the federations, should not be part of the ALP because they are not among the duties of teachers indicated in the *Education Act* and regulations.

DISCIPLINE AND DISMISSAL OF TEACHERS

The discipline of teachers by school boards is governed by education legislation and school board policies. Disciplinary action could range from minor admonishment (such as an oral reprimand) to severe actions (such as suspension without pay or dismissal). Later, it could lead to disciplinary action by the Ontario College of Teachers.

Figure 10-2

PERFORMANCE APPRAISAL OF NEW TEACHERS FLOW CHART

NTIP YEAR ONE (two appraisals are required in the first 12 months after the teacher begins teaching)

1st Appraisal

Process to be completed in 1st appraisal and subsequent appraisals:

- pre-observation meeting
- classroom observation
- post-observation meeting as soon as possible following the observation
- completed summative report, including assignment of overall rating

1st Satisfactory

Development Needed
(Inform teacher within 15 school days)

Enrichment Plan developed and implemented

2nd Appraisal
within first 12 months of teaching

2nd Appraisal
within first 12 months of teaching

2nd Satisfactory

Development Needed
(Inform teacher within 15 school days)

1st Satisfactory

1st Unsatisfactory
(Inform teacher within 15 school days)

Successful Completion of NTIP
Notification by board to OCT* within 60 calendar days

Enrichment Plan developed and implemented

Teacher is on review status. Improvement Plan developed and implemented.

Notification of Successful Completion of NTIP on publuc register within 60 calendar days of board notice to OCT*

Participation in Year Two of NTIP

Participation in Year Two of NTIP

3rd Appraisal required within 120 school days from time teacher is notified of review status

Outcomes from Year One

*Ontario College of Teachers

Ontario Ministry of Education

NTIP YEAR TWO–IF REQUIRED (must be completed within the teacher's first 24 months of teaching)

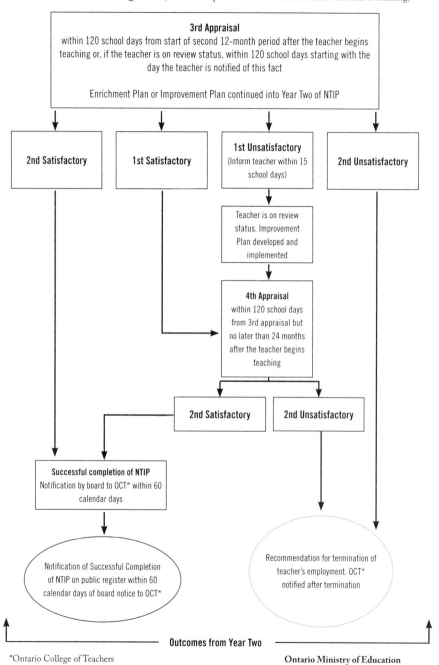

3rd Appraisal
within 120 school days from start of second 12-month period after the teacher begins teaching or, if the teacher is on review status, within 120 school days starting with the day the teacher is notified of this fact

Enrichment Plan or Improvement Plan continued into Year Two of NTIP

2nd Satisfactory

1st Satisfactory

1st Unsatisfactory
(Inform teacher within 15 school days)

2nd Unsatisfactory

Teacher is on review status. Improvement Plan developed and implemented

4th Appraisal
within 120 school days from 3rd appraisal but no later than 24 months after the teacher begins teaching

2nd Satisfactory

2nd Unsatisfactory

Successful completion of NTIP
Notification by board to OCT* within 60 calendar days

Notification of Successful Completion of NTIP on public register within 60 calendar days of board notice to OCT*

Recommendation for termination of teacher's employment. OCT* notified after termination

Outcomes from Year Two

*Ontario College of Teachers

Ontario Ministry of Education

There are three broad grounds for discipline or dismissal: professional misconduct, insubordination, and incompetence.

In all cases, the principal and other school officials must ensure substantive due process (fundamental fairness) and procedural due process (adherence to formal process). This includes giving teachers notice of specific charges and sufficient time to defend themselves and, where appropriate, improve. Discipline should also adhere to the principle of progressive discipline: for example, the first or second failure to arrive at school fifteen minutes before classes begin may result in an oral warning only; the third or fourth time in a formal written reprimand. At this latter stage, the superintendent may meet with the teacher to emphasize the seriousness of the situation and warn of possible suspension. If the teacher continues to ignore the principal's direction, the teacher may be suspended for a period of time.

Note that it is not always necessary or appropriate for the principal to use the progressive discipline steps sequentially. Some instances of misconduct are so egregious that they may call for an immediate formal written reprimand, suspension, or dismissal. For example, if a teacher is charged and found guilty of assault or sexual assault of a minor, the school board has the right to dismiss the teacher once found guilty.

A copy of the record of an oral warning or a written reprimand will normally be placed in a teacher's personnel file. Depending on board policy, these files will be kept either in the teacher's school or at the board office, or duplicates may be kept in both places. Under the *Municipal Freedom of Information and Protection of Privacy Act*, teachers have the right to look at the information contained in their file and ask for something to be corrected. If the principal or board declines to make the requested change, the teacher can request that a statement of disagreement be attached to the information.

Teachers should consult their union representatives to ensure that their interests and rights are protected.

PROFESSIONAL MISCONDUCT

Teacher misconduct was covered in detail in chapters 1 and 3. The main points to remember are that, as a teacher, you are held to a higher standard than the rest of the community. Your conduct in your classroom, school, and even at home, needs to be ethical at all times.

Insubordination

Insubordination may be thought of as the refusal to carry out an order given by someone with the proper authority to give that order. In the school workplace, the person with proper authority is clearly the principal or vice-principal. A classroom teacher, then, must carry out a direction given by the principal or vice-principal.

Failure to comply with such a direction constitutes insubordination in most circumstances. If a principal disciplines a teacher for insubordination, the discipline will be upheld if it is proven that the conduct violated an order, the order was reasonable or valid, the violation was willful, and the discipline is proportionate to the offence.

Given the complexities of collective agreements, education statutes, and common law, teachers are advised to obey the principal, especially if the request is timely in nature. They should do so even if they think the task at hand is not something the teacher would normally be asked to perform, or contravenes the teacher's understanding of the terms of the local contract made between the branch of the federation affiliate and the district school board. They can then consult their teachers' federation representatives at a later time and, if appropriate, file a grievance against their principals.

There are three circumstances in which it is legitimate to refuse to carry out an order given by the principal or vice-principal: first, if the teacher genuinely believes that doing so would endanger his or her own health and safety; second, if the teacher is being asked to perform an illegal act; and third, if carrying out the order would expose the teacher to potential liability. The range of tasks assigned to teachers on a daily basis does not tend to include any that fit these criteria, because principals are experienced educators, chosen largely for their integrity and professionalism.

At all costs, avoid insubordination or even the impression of insubordination, because these could lead to complex disciplinary procedures and even dismissal.

INCOMPETENCE

Incompetence is generally defined as inadequate work performance. In education, this usually involves inadequate teaching or supervision, failure to maintain classroom discipline, and willful neglect of duty. The Teacher Performance Appraisal process must be followed before a teacher with a permanent contract can be dismissed for incompetence. New teachers go through a similar performance appraisal process before they are offered permanent contracts; failure to meet the competency standards could lead to non-renewal of a contract. Both teacher performance processes involve many stages and provide teachers with multiple opportunities to improve their practice. If a teacher repeatedly fails a Teacher Performance Appraisal or refuses to make changes documented in the Appraisal, the board refers the case to the Ontario College of Teachers for further discipline.

OPERATIONAL ISSUES IN SCHOOLS

Teachers are not responsible for the organization of the school day or the school year. Nonetheless, it is important for them to understand how their classroom teaching situation is shaped by provincial legislation and school board policies.

SCHOOL DAY

According to *Regulation 298*, section 3, the length of the instructional program for pupils of compulsory school age must be not less than five hours, excluding a lunch period, recesses, and travel time between classes. For example, in secondary schools on a semester system, most students are assigned four classes per day of seventy-five minutes each, for a total of three hundred minutes (five hours). The length of the instructional program for kindergarten and junior kindergarten is established by the local school board. Note that the five-hour minimum requirement applies only to students. Teacher workloads, including the number of classes taught and supervisory duties assigned, are a matter of negotiation between local teacher affiliates and school boards. Teachers may be required to assume additional supervisory or administrative duties under the *Education Act* and *Regulation 298*. (See chapter 4.)

Without special permission of the Minister of Education, the local school board must schedule the instructional program in each of its schools between 8 a.m. and 5 p.m.

When classes actually begin and end, frequently known as "bell times," is a matter for the local school board—or, failing that, the school principal—to decide. There is a trend in some school boards toward starting and ending secondary school classes earlier so buses can then collect elementary school students for their school day, which begins later. This also means that more daylight time is available at the end of the secondary school day for co-instructional activities.

Co-instructional activities, however, may take place outside the official 8 a.m. to 5 p.m. school day. Sports teams, school bands, and other groups often meet early, before classes begin, or in the late afternoon and early evening; many school events, such as graduation, concerts, plays, and fashion shows, take place in the evening.

Before and After Class

The *Education Act* requires teachers to ensure that their classroom or teaching area is ready to receive pupils at least fifteen minutes before classes begin in the morning and, where applicable, five minutes before they begin in the afternoon. Apart from this, there is nothing in the act that speaks to the time a teacher is expected to arrive in the morning and leave at the end of the day, or come and go during the day. As professionals, teachers are not paid by the hour or even by the day.

The presence of teachers in classrooms and hallways plays an important role in establishing the tone of a school and building relationships with students and colleagues. Teachers have a professional obligation to their students to arrive in the morning early enough to attend to any necessary business or respond to changes of plan before classes begin. They should also consider staying long enough at the end of the day to allow students and colleagues to meet with them informally.

Teachers also have a professional and legal obligation to attend meetings called before or after classes, and a legal obligation to attend parent–teacher meetings, which may be scheduled in the evening. Protocols with regard to whether teachers can leave the school during the school day when they have no assigned classes or duties are usually a matter of school culture. Some schools require teachers to sign out and in at the main office, while others require the teacher to see the principal personally. Teachers should know the expectations and procedures in their schools. (See chapter 4 for administrative duties under education legislation.)

Lunch

Teachers and students are required to have a scheduled lunch break of at least forty consecutive minutes. In many schools, lunch periods are longer than this. Some elementary schools have longer lunches to allow students to return home for lunch. In secondary schools, this may be because there is more than one lunch block, with lunch often being the same length as an instructional period. Schools with large numbers of bused students may schedule two lunch periods, with half of the student body scheduled for lunch break while the other half is still in class.

It may be necessary to assign teachers to supervision duties during lunch periods. When this happens, the teacher will have a scheduled lunch break at a different time of day, to ensure that they still receive the required forty consecutive minutes. Local contracts may sometimes limit the times within which a teacher's lunch break may be scheduled without the mutual consent of principal and teacher. Although it sometimes may be necessary to schedule an emergency meeting during the lunch break, a wise principal is sensitive to the time constraints placed on teachers and the importance for them of having some time during the day to rest and recuperate and to meet and socialize with colleagues, not to mention to make any last-minute preparations.

Opening or Closing Exercises

Changes to the opening or closing exercises provisions in the *Education Act* illustrate the *ad hoc* way in which the act has been amended over the years in response to the changing nature of Ontario society.

In 1988 the Ontario Court of Appeal struck down section 28(1) of *Regulation 262*, which dealt with religious exercises in public elementary schools. (This subsection did not apply to schools operated by separate school boards.) The court determined that no religion may be given primacy of place in public schools, and that the content of any opening or closing exercises should reflect the multicultural nature of Ontario society. In the wake of the court's decision, the Ministry of Education in 1993 amended the regulation (now renumbered as *Regulation 298*) and published Policy/Program Memorandum 108 in 1993 outlining the new expectations for the exercises:

> The purposes of opening or closing exercises are patriotic and educational. Such exercises are intended to nurture allegiance to Canada and to contribute to the social, moral, and spiritual development of the pupils.
>
> Contributing to the social, moral, and spiritual development of pupils includes reinforcing the positive societal values that, in general, Canadians hold and regard as essential to the well-being of our society. These values transcend cultures and faiths, reinforce democratic rights and responsibilities, and are based on a fundamental belief in the worth of all persons.

Section 4 of *Regulation 298* was amended again, in 2000, to nurture allegiance to Canada. As a result of these changes:

All public and separate schools in Ontario *must* hold opening or closing exercises.

These exercises *shall* include the singing of *O Canada*. (Before the revisions of the late 1990s, the requirement was simply that the exercises include *O Canada*.)

Parents or adult students may request an exemption from the exercises. No reason need be given.

Regulation 435/00 states, in addition:

> The principal *may* decide to include a pledge of citizenship. This decision must be consistent with board policy, taken in consultation with the school council, and reviewed annually.

This option to include the pledge was another revision made in the late 1990s.

Section 4 of *Regulation 298* also provides further guidance for public schools, as opposed to separate schools, that may wish to extend opening or closing exercises. The exercises *may* include:

- the singing of *God Save the Queen*;
- a period of silence, intended for personal reflection or silent prayer;
- scriptural writings, including prayers;
- secular writings.

Since the social, moral, and spiritual development of Canadians has roots in many religious and philosophical traditions, readings must be drawn from a variety of scriptural and secular sources representative of our multicultural society. Prayers, including the Lord's Prayer, may be included, but only as readings. The courts have ruled that the collective recitation of a specific reading from a particular religious tradition is inconsistent with the *Canadian Charter of Rights and Freedoms*.

It is clear from the above discussion that the question of opening and closing exercises in schools has been the topic of much debate and legislation over the past twenty years. The intensity of debate reflects the seriousness with which society views activities that have patriotic and religious associations. Schools, then, need to give due weight and consideration to their opening or closing exercises.

One of the key factors in ensuring that students treat opening exercises with the solemnity they deserve is insisting that they arrive in good time, rather than rushing through the school corridors during the singing of *O Canada*. Many schools have pre-recorded programs to encourage students to get to class on time in the morning before the opening exercises begin (including "get to class music" and time checks).

Teachers bear a special responsibility to model the solemnity the exercises deserve and to ensure that their students conduct themselves appropriately. If students elect not to sing *O Canada*, they should at least stand in an attentive manner. Whether students stand or sit during any other components of the exercises is a matter of school culture. Whatever the cultural expectations of the school may be, the classroom teacher should insist that students remain attentive and respectful of the school's expectations.

Where students have been exempted by the principal from participating in the opening or closing exercises (often for religious reasons), the school should make special arrangements so they are not singled out in class.

SCHOOL YEAR

The local school board has the annual responsibility of drawing up a school year calendar to be submitted to the Minister of Education and eventually published for parents and students. In drafting the calendar, the school board must follow the requirements prescribed in *Regulation 304*. This regulation provides an overall framework by stating that the school year must begin on or after September 1 and end on or before June 30, and that between those two dates boards must ensure that a minimum of 194 school days are scheduled. Boards that wish to alter this framework or any of the other requirements in the regulation must have the approval of the minister.

Of the 194 school days, the board must designate *two* professional activity days, and *may* designate an *additional four* such days. "Professional activity" is described in *Regulation 304* as including "evaluation of the progress of pupils, consultation with parents, the counselling of pupils, curriculum and program evaluation and development, professional development of teachers and attendance at educational conferences." It does not include preparation by teachers for classes or instruction.

If the board chooses to designate one or more additional professional activity days, it must ensure that some of the activities relate to curriculum development, implementation, and review. When submitting its calendar to the Ministry, the board is required to provide a general outline of the activities that will take place on all professional activity days identified on the calendar. The board must also prepare an agenda for each professional activity day and make it available to teachers and parents at least ten days in advance of the day. Principals are responsible for informing parents of professional development days in advance and these notices can be found on a school website, in the school calendar and agenda, through a letter sent home, and often through an automated phone call home. Teachers have a legal duty as well as a professional responsibility to attend professional activity days.

Boards may also designate up to ten examination days during the school year. How these days are allocated is left to the discretion of the individual board. A typical configuration in schools on a semester system is to allocate five days at the end of each semester. The regulation also requires teachers to be in school during regular school hours and available to students, unless the board directs otherwise. In many jurisdictions, teachers are permitted to work at home during examination days if they are not supervising an examination, attending meetings, or carrying out other assigned duties. If this is the case in your school, bear in mind that the flexibility to fulfill your school-related obligations elsewhere is a privilege, not a right. Choices should be exercised with professional responsibility. Parents and students are not likely to look favourably on teachers who golf or shop during an examination day.

Regulation 304 also identifies days in the school year that are school holidays, including every Saturday and Sunday, Thanksgiving, the Easter weekend, and Victoria Day. Ten days are designated for a Christmas vacation and five days in March. Remembrance Day is no longer a school holiday, but schools are required to hold a Remembrance Day service on November 11, or on the preceding Friday if November 11 falls on a weekend.

Teachers' professional responsibilities do not begin and end with the school day, nor are they limited by the definition of the school year in *Regulation 304*. Most teachers have tasks directly associated with their classroom teaching, such as lesson preparation and student assessment, that require them to work evenings and weekends. Similarly, as outlined in chapter 4, teachers have a legal obligation under *Regulation 298* to attend graduation ceremonies, even if they occur in the evening.

Most teachers also commit themselves to professional development or to helping with co-instructional activities outside the instructional day. Many teachers attend professional workshops or take additional qualification courses during evenings, weekends, or summers to upgrade their professional qualifications. Many also devote considerable time to coaching sports, directing arts performances, chaperoning students, or supervising other co-instructional activities. These activities often take place after school in the evening, on the weekend, and sometimes even during school holidays.

Involvement in co-instructional activities can be very rewarding to both students and teachers. These voluntary contributions are integral to school life. Indeed, there is evidence to suggest that students who participate in such programs tend to be more successful in the instructional program. Teachers, however, should be careful to maintain their focus on their central role as classroom teacher.

ATTENDANCE REQUIREMENTS FOR STUDENTS

The legislation concerning a person's right to attend school and the requirements concerning compulsory attendance at school were discussed in chapter 8. But what are the obligations of a person already registered at school?

According to section 23 of *Regulation 298*, all students, whatever their age, have a legal duty to attend classes regularly and punctually. Only the principal has the legal authority to excuse a student from attendance at school.

In the case of students under the age of eighteen, the parents are required to give the reason for a student's absence to the principal. They have the obligation to request in writing that the student be excused. Since the *Education Amendment Act (Learning to Age 18)* in 2006, all students under the age of eighteen are also bound by the requirements of section 21 of the *Education Act*, which sets out the legal reasons for non-attendance. For a person under the age of eighteen already registered as a student in a school, who has not attained an Ontario Secondary School Diploma and has not been suspended or expelled, these reasons effectively come down to sickness or "other unavoidable cause," religious holy days, and a half day a week for music instruction. Parents must have the principal's prior authorization for a student's absence for reasons beyond these.

Adult students are not bound by the compulsory attendance provisions of section 21 of the *Education Act*, but they are still bound by the Requirements for Pupils set out in section 23 of *Regulation 298*. When students register in a school, it is as if they have entered into an unwritten contract with the principal to comply with the *Education Act* and regulations, as well as the school's code of conduct. As adults, these students may write their own request to be excused from attendance. Should persistent lateness and poor attendance patterns develop, the principal may well decide not to accept a reason for absence or grant a request to be excused. If the adult student is unwilling to comply with the principal's expectations, the principal could make it a disciplinary matter.

Although it is the principal who has the legal duty to monitor students' attendance, classroom teachers have an important role to play. The teacher usually has the task of taking attendance at the beginning of the day and reporting the names of absent students to the principal. Where students move from class to class with different teachers, each teacher is usually responsible for checking attendance and reporting the names of students whose absence is unexplained. The teacher may also be responsible to collect information from students after an absence. Schools have different protocols for handling attendance and contacting parents of students whose absence is unexplained, but the reliability of the whole system is primarily based on the meticulousness of the classroom teacher. Unexplained or frequent absences by younger students should raise overriding concerns about the student's safety and welfare. Teachers who respond early to poor attendance patterns, even with older students, can make the difference between a student's success and failure in school.

COPYRIGHT ISSUES

Effective teachers draw on a wide variety of print, audio-visual, and web-based resources to engage students and enhance learning. A teacher might download a funny video clip as an ice-breaker activity, photocopy a newspaper story on a refugee crisis, or reproduce part of a chapter on a scientific discovery.

While this approach may be educationally enriching, does it infringe on the rights of copyright holders? Is it "fair dealing" under the *Copyright Act*?

According to that act, teachers may reproduce short excerpts from copyright-protected works for the purpose of education. Under the Fair Dealing Guidelines, the excerpts should be properly attributed to the source and authors/creators. A single copy of a short excerpt—such as a chapter, single article in a magazine, a poem, or song score—could be included in a class handout, a posting on a learning-management system, or a course pack. Teachers may also play a sound recording, or turn on a radio or TV, with relative impunity. They may also show a purchased or rented DVD or video (not an infringing copy) or YouTube video, but not a copy made at home.

Copyright issues can be complex, and complications arise with emerging technologies. You are advised to check with experienced colleagues, abide by school board policies, and refer to *Copyright Matters!* (Noel & Snel, 2012).

CHECKING YOUR UNDERSTANDING

- The principal is the teacher's immediate supervisor in the workplace.
- Teachers have a duty to cooperate with department heads or division leaders in all matters related to classroom instruction.
- Teachers have a duty to teach the classes or subjects assigned by the principal but can be assigned only the classes that they are qualified to teach according to their certificate of qualification.
- Within certain limits, teachers may teach classes for which they do not hold qualifications, provided that both the principal and teacher are in agreement.
- The local affiliates of OTF negotiate collective agreements with individual school boards on behalf of their members and provide teachers with advice and support.
- Discipline of teachers must be substantively and procedurally fair, and should be progressive in nature.
- In most situations, teachers should carry out an order given to them by the principal or vice-principal in the school. Insubordination could lead to dismissal.
- All new teachers hired into permanent contracts are required to participate in the New Teacher Induction Program. Successful completion of the program is evidenced by two satisfactory performance appraisals by the principal.

- Beginning teachers hired on a long-term occasional contract of at least ninety-seven days for the same teacher are required to participate in the induction elements of the NTIP.
- On successful completion of the NTIP, a teacher is placed on the experienced teachers' performance appraisal schedule, in which every fifth year is an evaluation year.
- Experienced teachers are required to develop an Annual Learning Plan each year.
- The instructional program for students of compulsory school age must not be less than five hours, and must be scheduled between 8 a.m. and 5 p.m.
- Teachers have a legal and professional obligation to participate in meetings scheduled outside the limits of the school day.
- Both teachers and students must have a lunch break of forty consecutive minutes.
- All schools are required to hold opening or closing exercises. The exercises must include the singing of *O Canada*, and may include a pledge of citizenship, the singing of *God Save the Queen*, a period of silence, and appropriate readings.
- The school year must contain at least 194 school days, and must begin no earlier than September 1 and finish no later than June 30.
- Every school board must designate two professional activity days, and may designate an additional four. Teachers have a legal duty to attend professional development days.
- A school board may designate up to a maximum of ten examination days per year.
- All students of any age have a duty to attend classes regularly and punctually. Only the principal may excuse a student from attendance at school.
- According to the *Copyright Act*, teachers may reproduce short excerpts from copyright-protected works for the purpose of education.

Applying Your Understanding

Case Study: The Argumentative Teacher

A cloud hung over Mr. Rubens. He had received a written reprimand for insubordination the previous year. In February, Mr. Rubens had been suspended for four days for insubordination. Although he had a short temper, and still felt contempt for his ineffectual principal, he was determined to stay out of trouble.

When helping to chaperone the school dance on Friday, May 13, Mr. Rubens noticed two girls going off with men from outside the school. While he told the girls that he would not tell their parents, he did inform the principal on Monday morning. The principal informed the parents, who reproved the girls that evening.

The next day, immediately after hearing from the girls, Mr. Rubens encountered the principal in the busy front foyer. An argument ensued. Mr. Rubens then shouted, "Leave them alone! You have done enough damage already!"

The next day, Mr. Rubens was dismissed for insubordination. The school board noted his acts of insubordination in its letter of dismissal.

Mr. Rubens and his federation legal counsel appealed the dismissal to an arbitration panel. Mr. Rubens argued that the principal had acted inappropriately. His lawyer also argued that the punishment was excessive and not consistent with principles of progressive discipline.

(1) Did Mr. Rubens's conduct fulfill his legal and professional duties as a teacher under the *Education Act*, *Regulation 298*, and the *Foundations of Professional Practice*? Explain.

(2) Was Mr. Rubens insubordinate? Were there mitigating factors?

(3) Was dismissal warranted, or should there have been another penalty?

(4) How do you think the arbitration panel would rule in this case?

Offering Advice

At the end of the school day, a colleague steps into your classroom.

"Got a minute?" she asks.

Closing the door and sitting down, she informs you that she received an unsatisfactory report.

"Actually, it is my second unsatisfactory evaluation," she adds.

You are not entirely surprised by the news. She has seemed overwhelmed by classroom management issues this year.

"I am worried that I could lose my job," she says, suppressing a sob.

Then she asks for your advice.

---

(1) What advice would you give her if she is a new teacher (under NTIP)?

(2) What advice would you give her if she is an experienced teacher (under TPA)?

(3) In your answer, consider how to enhance her professional growth and protect her employment rights.

References

Note: References do not include legal codes, legal decisions, provincial education documents, and teacher federation or Ontario College of Teachers materials. These are all readily available electronically.

Ainscow, M. (2008). Teaching for diversity: The next big challenge. In Connelly, F., He, M. & Phillion, J. (eds.). *The Sage handbook of curriculum and instruction* (pp. 240–58). Thousand Oaks, CA: Sage Publications.

Bacon, F. (1597; 1965). Of parents and children. *Bacon's essays.* London: Macmillan.

Bateman, D. (2015). High school teacher fired after investigation into 'racist' tweets. *Toronto Star.* September 9, 2015 http://www.thestar.com/yourtoronto/education/2015/09/09/high-school-teacher-fired-after-investigation-into-racist-tweets.html.

Bennett, S. & Dworet, D. with Weber, K. (2013). *Special education in Ontario schools*, seventh edition. St. Davids, ON: Highland Press.

Bennett, S. & Wynne, K. (2006). *Special education transformation: The report of the co-chairs of the working table on special education.* Toronto: Ontario Ministry of Education.

Bowlby, B., Peters, C. & Mackinnon, M. (2001). *An educator's guide to special education law.* Aurora, ON: Canada Law Books.

Brown, A. (2004). *Legal handbook for educators*, fifth edition. Toronto: ThomsonCarswell.

Brown, A. & Zuker, M. (2002). *Education law*, third edition. Toronto: ThomsonCarswell.

Brown, A. & Zuker, M. (2007). *Education law*, fourth edition. Toronto: ThomsonCarswell.

Browne, L. (2007). 84 per cent of teachers have been cyberbullied. *Professionally Speaking*, September 2007, p. 51.

Bunch, G. & Valeo, N. (2004). Student attitudes towards peers with disabilities in inclusive and special education schools. *Disability and Society* 1(1), 61–78.

Campbell, E. (2003). *The ethical teacher.* Maidenhead, UK: Open University Press.

Cook, K. & Truscott, D. (2007). *Ethics and law for teachers.* Toronto: Thomson Nelson.

Dewey, J. (1938). *Experience and education.* New York: Collier.

Dickinson, G. (2009). School searches and student rights under the Charter: Old wine in new skins. In Manley-Casimir, M. & Manley-Casimir, K. (eds.). *The courts, the Charter, and the schools: The impact of the Charter of Rights and Freedoms on educational policy and practice, 1982–2007* (pp. 155–80). Toronto: University of Toronto Press.

Epstein, J. & Rodriguez-Jansorn, N. (2004). School, family, and community partnerships link the plan. *Educational Digest* 69(6).

Freeman, R.E. (1984). *Strategic management: A stakeholder approach.* Cambridge, UK: Cambridge University Press.

Gersten, R., Baker S., Pugach, M., Scanlon, D. & Chard, D. (2001). Research on teaching in special education, in Richardson, V. (ed.). *The handbook of research on teaching,* fourth edition. Washington: American Educational Research Association.

Glegg, A. (2013). The British Columbia College of Teachers: An obituary. *Historical Studies in Education* 25 (2), 45–64.

Guarino, C., Santibanez, L. & Daley, G. (2006). Teacher recruitment and retention: A review of the recent empirical literature. *Review of Educational Research* 76(2), 173–208.

Hansen, D. (2001). Teaching as a moral activity. In Richardson, V. (ed.). *Handbook of research on teaching,* fourth edition (pp. 826–57). Washington, DC: American Educational Research Association.

Howe, M. (1990). *The origins of exceptional abilities.* Oxford: Basil Blackwell.

Keel, R.G. (2001). The spectre of parental and intruder harassment. *Orbit* 32(2), 64.

Kindred, K. (2006). The teacher in dissent: Freedom of expression and the classroom. *Education Law Journal* 15(3), 207–32.

Kitchen, J. & Bellini, C. (2013). Making schools safe and inclusive: Gay-straight alliances and school climate in Ontario. *Canadian Journal of Educational Administration* 146, 1–37.

McBrien, M.S. (2015). *Teacher perspectives on safety policy and procedures in Ontario public schools.* Unpublished Master of Education thesis, North Bay, ON: Nipissing University.

McIntyre, E. & Bloom, D. (2002). *An educator's guide to the Ontario College of Teachers.* Aurora, ON: Aurora Professional Press.

Mackay, W. (2009). The lighthouse of equality: A guide to "inclusive" schooling. In Manley-Casimir, M. & Manley-Casimir, K. (eds.). *The courts, the Charter, and the schools: The impact of the Charter of Rights and Freedoms on educational policy and practice, 1982–2007* (pp. 39–63). Toronto: University of Toronto Press.

McPhail, J. & Freeman, J. (2005). Beyond prejudice: Thinking toward genuine inclusion. *Learning Disabilities Research and Practice* 20(4), 254–67.

Medway, J. (2014). *Equitable and inclusive education for all? Public funding for denominational schools in Ontario.* Cologne, Germany: LAP Lambert.

Milner, M., Jr. (2004). *Freaks, geeks and cool kids: American teenagers, schools and the culture of consumption.* New York: Routledge.

National Academy of Education (2005). *A good teacher in every classroom: Preparing the highly qualified teachers our children deserve.* San Francisco: Jossey-Bass.

Noddings, N. (2001). The caring teacher. In Richardson, V. (ed.). *Handbook of research on teaching,* fourth edition (pp. 99–105). Washington, DC: American Educational Research Association.

Noel, W. & Snel, J. (2012). *Copyright matters! Some key questions and answers for teachers,* third edition. Toronto: Council of Ministers of Education, Canada. Retrieved from http://cmec.ca/publications/lists/publications/attachments/291/copyright_matters.pdf.

Ontario College of Teachers (2006). *Foundations of professional practice.* Toronto: Ontario College of Teachers.

Ontario Ministry of Education (2000). *Standards for school boards' Special Education Plans.* Toronto: Queen's Printer.

Ontario Ministry of Education (2001). *Special education: A guide for educators.* Toronto: Queen's Printer.

Ontario Ministry of Education (2004). *The individual education plan (IEP): A resources guide.* Toronto: Queen's Printer.

Ontario Ministry of Education (2005). *Ontario First Nation, Métis, and Inuit education policy framework.* Toronto: Queen's Printer.

Ontario Ministry of Education (2005). *Education for all: The report of the expert panel on literacy and numeracy instruction for students with special education needs, Kindergarten to Grade 6.* Toronto: Queen's Printer.

Ontario Ministry of Education. (2006). *Report to the Partnership Table on a Revised Teacher Performance Appraisal System for Experienced Teachers: Recommendations of the Working Table on Teacher Development, October 23, 2006.*

Ontario Ministry of Education (2007). *Shared solutions: A guide to preventing and resolving conflicts regarding programs and services for students with special education needs.* Toronto: Queen's Printer.

Ontario Ministry of Education (2009). *New teacher induction program: Manual for performance appraisal of new teachers.* Toronto: Queen's Printer.

Ontario Ministry of Education (2009). *Performance appraisal of experienced teachers: technical requirements manual.* Toronto: Queen's Printer.

Ontario Ministry of Education (2013). *Supporting minds: An educator's guide to promoting students' health and well being.* Toronto: Queen's Printer.

Ontario Ministry of Education (2015). *Provincial model for a local police/school board protocol.* Toronto: Queen's Printer.

Ontario Secondary School Teachers' Federation (2014). *Teacher's pocket guide.* Toronto: OSSTF District 19.

Ontario Secondary School Teachers' Federation (2015). *Your duty to report under the education act.* Retrieved from http://www.osstf.on.ca/resource-centre/member-protection/duty-to-report.aspx.

Ontario Secondary School Teachers' Federation (2015). Advice on your annual learning plan. Retrieved from http://www.osstf.on.ca/~/media/Provincial/Documents/About%20Us/OSSTF-FEESO%20Issues/Teacher%20Performance%20Appraisal/Teacher%20Performance%20Appraisal%20for%20Experienced%20Teachers/alp-advice.ashx?sc_lang=en-CA.

Ontario Secondary School Teachers' Federation (n.d.) Grievance types. Retrieved from https://osstf.on.ca/adx/aspx/adxGetMedia.aspx?DocID=880e6c75-3ce8-4ffe-a224-74feb6e36742&MediaID=380d9f55-0fd4-48e8-aa0e-a42ed2cb6142&Filename=grievance-types.pdf&l=English.

Piddocke, S., Magsino, R. & Manley-Casimir, M. (1997). *Teachers in trouble: An exploration of the normative character of teaching.* Toronto: University of Toronto Press.

Praisner, C. (2003). Attitudes of elementary school principals toward the inclusion of students with disabilities. *Exceptional Children* 69(2), 135–45.

Richter, B. (2006a, October). It's elementary: A brief history of Ontario's public elementary teachers and their federations: Part I. *ETFO Voice.* Retrieved from http://www.etfo.ca/Resources/ForTeachers/Documents/It's%20Elementary%20%E2%80%93%20A%20Brief%20History%20of%20Ontario's%20Public%20Elementary%20Teachers%20and%20their%20Federations%20-%20Part%201.pdf

Richter, B. (2006b, December). It's elementary: A brief history of Ontario's public elementary teachers and their federations: Part II. *ETFO Voice*. Retrieved from http://www.etfo.ca/Resources/ForTeachers/Documents/It's%20Elementary%20%E2%80%93%20A%20Brief%20History%20of%20Ontario's%20Public%20Elementary%20Teachers%20and%20their%20Federations%20-%20Part%202.pdf

Richter, B. (2007, February). It's elementary: A brief history of Ontario's public elementary teachers and their federations: Part III. *ETFO Voice*. Retrieved from http://www.etfo.ca/Resources/ForTeachers/Documents/It's%20Elementary%20%E2%80%93%20A%20Brief%20History%20of%20Ontario's%20Public%20Elementary%20Teachers%20and%20their%20Federations%20-%20Part%203.pdf

Robbins, S. (2000). *Protecting our children: A review to identify and prevent sexual misconduct in Ontario schools*. Toronto: Queen's Printer of Ontario.

Roher, E.M. (1997). *An educator's guide to violence in schools*. Aurora, ON: Aurora Professional Press.

Rouleau, P.S. (2006). *Education in transition: A delicate balance*. Paper presented at LawWorks, Toronto, August 2006.

Royal Commission on Learning (1994). *For the love of learning*. Toronto: Queen's Printer of Ontario.

School Community Safety Advisory Panel (2008). *The road to health: A final report on school safety*. Toronto: Toronto District School Board.

Scott, G.F. (2008). Student privacy and you. *Professionally Speaking*, March 2008, 43–47.

Strike, K. & Ternansky, L. (eds.) (1993). *Ethics for educational professionals: The place of ethics in their preparation and practice*. New York: Teachers College Press.

Taylor, C., & Peter, T. (2011). *Every class in every school: The final report on the first national climate survey on homophobia, biphobia, and transphobia in Canadian schools*. Toronto: EGALE Canada Human Rights Trust. Retrieved from www.egale.ca.

Tom, A.(1997). *Redesigning teacher education*. Albany, NY: SUNY Press.

Van Pelt, D.N. (2015). *Home schooling in Canada: The current picture—2015 edition*. Toronto: Fraser Institute. Retrieved from www.fraserinstitute.ca.

Zuker, M.A., Hammond, R. & Flynn, R. (2005). *Children's law handbook*. Toronto: Thomson Carswell.

Zuker, M.A., Redmond, K., & Gannon, R. (2013). *An educator's guide to the law and the Ontario College of Teachers*. Toronto: Canada Law Book.

INDEX OF LEGAL CASES

INDEX